# Re-Tayloring Management

# Re-Tayloring Management

## Scientific Management a Century On

EDITED BY

**CHRISTINA EVANS**
*Roehampton University Business School*

**LEONARD HOLMES**
*Roehampton University Business School*

Routledge
Taylor & Francis Group

LONDON AND NEW YORK

First published 2013 by Gower Publishing

2 Park Square, Milton Park, Abingdon, Oxfordshire OX14 4RN
52 Vanderbilt Avenue, New York, NY 10017

*Routledge is an imprint of the Taylor & Francis Group, an informa business*

First issued in paperback 2020

**Gower Applied Business Research**
Our programme provides leaders, practitioners, scholars and researchers with thought provoking, cutting edge books that combine conceptual insights, interdisciplinary rigour and practical relevance in key areas of business and management.

**British Library Cataloguing in Publication Data**
Re-Tayloring management : scientific management a century on.
    1. Industrial management.  2. Industrial engineering.
    3. Taylor, Frederick Winslow, 1856-1915--Influence.
    I. Evans, Christina, 1955- editor of compilation.
    II. Holmes, Leonard editor of compilation.
    658'.001-dc23

**Library of Congress Cataloging-in-Publication Data**
Re-Tayloring management : scientific management a century on / [edited] by Christina Evans and Leonard Holmes.
    p. cm.
    Includes bibliographical references and index.
    ISBN 978-1-4094-5075-7 (hbk. : alk. paper) -- ISBN 978-1-4094-5076-4 (ebook) -- ISBN 978-1-4724-0165-6 (epub)
    1. Taylor, Frederick Winslow, 1856-1915. Principles of scientific management.
  2. Industrial management.  3. Industrial engineering.  4. Management science.
  I. Evans, Christina, 1955-.  II. Holmes, Leonard.
  T55.9.T377R48 2013
  658.5--dc23

                                        2012040318

ISBN 13: 978-1-4094-5075-7 (hbk)
ISBN 13: 978-0-367-60547-6 (pbk)

# Contents

# List of Figures and Tables

## Figures

## Tables

# About the Editors

**Dr Christina Evans** is a Principal Lecturer in the University of Roehampton London Business School, where she teaches human resource management/ development and organizational behaviour at undergraduate and postgraduate level. Christina's research interests fall into two key areas. She has a strong interest in individual career development and the strategies that individuals adopt to build and maintain a successful 'subjective' career. Her other area of interest is in organizational approaches aimed at building a diverse workforce, with a particular focus on gender diversity within the ICT and related sectors. She has published several academic papers and practitioner-focused reports on this topic. She is the author of *Managing for Knowledge: HR's Strategic Role*, published in 2003.

**Dr Leonard Holmes** is Reader in Management in the University of Roehampton London Business School. He has previously held academic roles at the University of Bedfordshire and London Metropolitan University, following an earlier career in human resource management and development. He is a member of the British Academy of Management, where he is the Chair of Knowledge and Learning Special Interest Group. Leonard is the author of several publications, particularly in the areas of learning, skills and competence in relation to employment. He co-edited, with Dian Marie Hosking and Margaret Grieco, *Organising in the Information Age: Distributed Technology, Distributed Leadership, Distributed Identity, Distributed Discourse*, published by Ashgate in 2002. His most recent book, *The Dominance of Management: A Participatory Critique*, was published by Ashgate in 2010.

# Notes on Contributors

**Christopher Bond** is Head of Postgraduate Programmes and MBA Programme Director at Roehampton University London Business School. He teaches organizational behaviour and cross-cultural management across the management programmes in the School. He is a UK National Teaching Fellow and has published articles and chapters and delivered international conference papers on personal and organizational development.

**Professor Tony Cutler** is Honorary Senior Research Fellow at Roehampton University. Until his retirement from university teaching in 2008, he was Professor of Public Sector Management at Royal Holloway, University of London. His principal research interests are the history of management techniques in the public sector and contemporary debates regarding the 'reform' of public sector pensions. Recent publications (2011) include *In Defence of Public Sector Pensions: A Critique of the Independent Public Service Pensions Commission* (with Barbara Waine) (at www.cresc.ac.uk) and articles on the history of public sector management in *Public Policy and Administration* and *Contemporary British History*.

**Professor Yiannis Gabriel** is Professor of Organizational Theory at Bath University. He is known for his work into organizational storytelling and narratives, leadership, management learning, psychoanalytic studies of work, and the culture and politics of contemporary consumption. He has used stories as a way of studying numerous social and organizational phenomena including leader–follower relations, group dynamics and fantasies, nostalgia, insults and apologies. More recently, Yiannis has carried out research on leadership and patient care in the hospital sector and on the experiences of sacked leaders and senior professionals. He is the author of ten books and has been editor of *Management Learning* and associate editor of *Human Relations*. His enduring fascination as a researcher lies in what he describes as the unmanageable qualities of life in and out of organizations.

**Professor Judith Glover** is Emeritus Professor of Employment Studies at the University of Roehampton Business School. She has published numerous books and academic papers in the field of women's employment, with particular emphasis on science, engineering and technology. Her latest book, *Women, Employment and Organizations* (with Gill Kirton), was published in 2006.

**Professor Yvonne Guerrier** is Professor of Organization Studies in the Business School at the University of Roehampton. She has wide interests but these are linked by a focus on work: on the way individuals experience it, how it fits with broader lives, on the way in which aspects of identity (for example, gender) affect and are affected by work. Yvonne is particularly known for her work on employees in the hospitality and tourism industry. A particular focus is on customer service employees and the interactions between them and customers. Although Yvonne adopts a critical perspective, she is interested in conducting research which is useful to organizations. Her work has been widely published in academic journals, including *Human Relations, International Journal of Hospitality Management, Personnel Review* and *Work, Employment and Society*.

**Professor Colin Hales** is a Senior Honorary Research Fellow at the University of Roehampton Business School's Centre for Organizational Research. Prior to that he had been Professor of Management at the University of Westminster and, latterly, Professor of Organizational Behaviour at the University of Surrey School of Management, from which he took retirement following that institution's evangelical embrace of Taylorist methods in general and the Babbage Principle in particular. He is author of numerous articles on managerial work and forms of work organization and has recently completed a major NIHR/SDO-funded project on continuity and change in the role of first-line managers in healthcare.

**Professor Huw Morris** is Pro-Vice Chancellor (Academic and External) at the University of Salford. His academic and professional background is in human resource management. He has worked in seven university business schools in the UK over the last twenty-five years: Putteridge Bury Management Centre, Kingston, Surrey, Bristol, Kingston, Manchester Metropolitan and Salford. These experiences have fuelled his interest in the history of business and management education in the UK and USA. It also prompted the research which forms the basis for his chapter in this book.

**Dr Darren O'Byrne** is Principal Lecturer in Sociology and Human Rights in the Department of Social Sciences, University of Roehampton London. He is the author of *Human Rights: An Introduction* (2002), *The Dimensions of Global*

*Citizenship* (2003), *Theorizing Global Studies* (2011, with Alexander Hensby), and *Introducing Sociological Theory* (2011), plus many articles and chapters on such areas as human rights, globalization, sociological theory and political sociology. He was founding Chair of the Global Studies Association, and convenes the undergraduate and postgraduate programmes in human rights at the University of Roehampton.

**Dr Shuchi Sinha** is an Assistant Professor in the area of Human Resource Management and Organization Studies at the Indian Institute of Technology, Delhi. She has taught and researched in the areas of identity work, leadership, contemporary workplace controls, employee resistance and other aspects of organization studies at University of London, University of Bath and University of Roehampton in the United Kingdom. Recently, Shuchi has carried out research on the nature of power-sharing between clinicians and managers and the future of leadership development in the National Health Service in the UK. She has previously worked as a consultant and trainer in the areas of change management, leadership development and talent assessment across different industry verticals.

# Acknowledgements

The editors would like to express their thanks to all of the co-contributors to this collection. It has been a great pleasure working with them all. We hope that our readers find the perspectives on management that each has shared will stimulate them to think about management in a more reflexive way.

# 1

# Introduction

*Christina Evans and Leonard Holmes*

A centenary on from the publication of Taylor's *Principles of Scientific Management*, there is continuing debate as to whether 'scientific management', although much maligned, has yet become an historical artefact (Cooper and Taylor 2000, Adler 2007, Brown et al. 2011).

In this edited collection we take a critical look at Taylor's philosophy on management, contrasting this with other perspectives on management that have emerged over the past century in response to the changing landscape of global business and thus changing organizational structural forms. We present a number of case examples to illustrate how the 'ghost of Taylor' is still very much alive in 'high value' (so high skill) knowledge and service sector organizations, highlighting how contemporary knowledge workers are just as constrained by Taylor's principles of scientific management as the industrial workers that Taylor studied in the early twentieth century. This is despite the business imperative of attracting skilful and talented individuals so engaged with what they do that they unquestionably go the 'extra mile' to satisfy the ever-demanding needs of customers and management; hence the 'grand managerial discourse' of empowering workers (Mabey 2009) and building an engaged workforce (Macleod and Clarke 2009).

Thus, in contrast to the low-involvement employment relationship in Taylor's era, high-commitment human resource management has been a prominent feature of many organizations (particularly in Western economies) in the latter part of the twentieth century. In Taylor's era, the only commitment that workers needed to demonstrate was the discipline of keeping themselves physically fit for work. But as Yvonne Guerrier points out later in this volume (see Chapter 9), there are some remarkable similarities between the expectations of workers in Taylor's era and those of contemporary professional workers, particularly those employed in the newer professions such as management consultancy.

Perhaps these similarities are understandable given the continuing debates on the extent to which developed economies have transitioned from de-industrialization (long-term decline of manufacturing) to post-industrial, knowledge-based economies (see Gamble et al. 2004, and Sinha and Gabriel later in this volume): this is perhaps understandable, given that the different definitions and interpretations of the scope of the knowledge economy make it difficult to build a definitive picture. International knowledge industry definitions for example encompass three broad areas: high-tech manufacturing (pharmaceuticals, aerospace, electronics); medium high-tech manufacturing (chemicals, motors, other transport equipment); and knowledge services (telecommunications, business services, finance, education and health) (see Brinkley 2008: 26).

Despite these difficulties with definitions and measurement within the UK, as with other OECD economies, there has been a reported rise in the number of people employed in knowledge-intensive businesses, as opposed to in manufacturing. However, what remains of the manufacturing sector appears to have been through significant transformation in response to global competition. Thus the boundaries between traditional manufacturing and contemporary knowledge and service work have become somewhat blurred: 'firms do not consider themselves to be in "services" or "manufacturing" but providing solutions for customers that involve a combination of products and services' (BERR 2008: 26).

So although the number of people employed in the manufacturing sector has been falling, the skills expectations have been changing, with a reported shift towards higher-skilled occupations (BERR 2008, Brinkley 2008). The contemporary workforce then, unlike in Taylor's era, appears to be valued (in theory at least) for their brains, not brawn. Drawing on *The Employment in Britain (EIB) Survey*, Tomlinson (1999: 25) points out that the transformation of the manufacturing sector has had consequences for management; thus 'knowledge embodied in people in manufacturing dispersed throughout the rest of the economy during the 1980s. A substantial proportion of these managers actually became professional … This implies that the management skills that these people possessed became augmented with skills normally associated with professionals.' Furthermore, there is some evidence of the adoption of high-trust, high-commitment HRM practices within manufacturing environments within newly industrialized economies, similar to those adopted in knowledge-intensive firms (Gamble et al. 2004).

Given this changing economic and employment landscape we might assume that the managerial imperative – of systematically extracting and codifying knowledge, so that the issue of worker initiative no longer presents a problem to management (Taylor's Principle One), as highlighted in this exert from Taylor's original work – has no place in the contemporary workplace:

> *The managers assume, for instance, the burden of gathering together all of the traditional knowledge which in the past has been possessed by the workmen and then of classifying, tabulating and reducing this knowledge to rules, laws and formulae which are immensely helpful to the workmen in doing their daily work ... The development of a science, on the other hand, involves the establishment of many rules, laws and formulae that replace the judgment of the individual workman and can be effectively used only after having been systematically recorded, indexed etc. (Taylor 1911: 26–9)*

Yet when we and our co-contributors started to investigate Taylor's management and the solutions proposed, comparing this with the way in which contemporary knowledge and professional workers are managed, we discovered some interesting paradoxes. Despite a key assumption by policymakers and employers of the increasing economic importance of intangible assets, hence requiring a more highly skilled and educated workforce, many contemporary knowledge workers find that they have increasingly less scope for exercising discretionary behaviour.

Brown and Hesketh (2004) are highly critical of the current preoccupation with high-skilled employment, arguing that the demand for high-skilled jobs (especially graduate-level jobs) has been exaggerated and question whether there are sufficient jobs for highly educated individuals to go into, and whether employers have sufficiently well-developed human resource management systems to utilize the diverse talents that these individuals bring into the workplace. Brinkley (2008) points out that although knowledge-based businesses are graduate-intensive, not all jobs in this sector are of graduate level. As will be discussed in Chapter 10, the adoption of standardized work routines introduced to improve efficiency and quality, for example Lean Six Sigma, in sectors that fall into the high-tech manufacturing sector, creates tensions for managers and employees alike, given that this is a sector that typically expects its employees to be of graduate calibre (Taylor's Principle Two).

Thus, despite the complexity and operational uncertainty that organizations now face, instead of designing work systems where knowledge and service workers have the freedom to apply knowledge and skills at the point where it is most needed, organizations have become obsessed with maintaining tighter control in the false assumption that this will be more productive. This is a managerial approach that seems to fly in the face of contemporary job design, which emphasizes the importance of viewing operational uncertainty as a contingency which requires structuring work to ensure maximum opportunities for shared learning (Parker et al. 2001).

One potential positive outcome of the expansion of the knowledge economy is that this appears to have created more opportunities for female graduates (Brinkley 2008). Yet despite this optimism, occupational segregation continues to affect women's longer-term employment and career prospects. Whilst women appear to be gaining parity with men in professional, associate professional and technical roles (Glover and Kirton 2006), they are still under-represented in senior managerial roles and in board-level positions (Broadbridge 2000, Sealy and Vinnicombe 2012). The latest Female FTSE Board Index indicates that although there has been a 25 per cent increase in the number of women on FTSE 100 boards, the picture regarding the extent to which organizations are making progress in developing the female managerial pipeline is still mixed (Sealy and Vinnicombe 2012).

There is clear evidence of occupational segregation in Taylor's era too: whilst men were employed in physically demanding work (such as pig iron handling and bricklaying), women (referred to as 'girls' by Taylor) were felt to be better employed in more delicate work (such as inspecting ball bearings used in the production of bicycles). Although not stated implicitly, there was an assumption that these girls were 'under-working'. But in contrast to their male counterparts, this was perhaps understandable as there were not the jobs available for 'these girls' to demonstrate that they could work at peak performance – a not too dissimilar experience, then, from that of women in contemporary society who choose to work part-time; as a consequence part-time workers invariably find that they are working below potential (Grant et al. 2006).

Taylor's scientific management 'Principle Three' refers to management's responsibility for the 'careful selection and subsequent training of the bricklayers into first-class men, and the elimination of all men who refuse or are unable to adopt the best methods' (Taylor 1911: 66). However, when trying to ascertain what constituted the 'best' worker for the role of inspector of ball bearings, Taylor was left with a bit of a conundrum. This was work that required 'the closet attention and concentration, so that the nervous tension of the inspectors was considerable' (Taylor 1911: 68): yet this was not men's work. However, the selection criteria were derived from experiments with male workers, using scientific methods conducted in a laboratory setting, that ascertained that the best person for the job of inspector of ball bearings was someone with a 'low personal coefficient', plus the 'ordinary qualities of endurance and industry' (1911: 70). Taylor then went on to state that for the good of the girls, and the company, any girls who could not meet this criteria would need to be laid off. The use of systematic and sophisticated selection methods has become a feature of many contemporary organizations. In Chapter 9, Yvonne Guerrier discusses the sophisticated selection methods adopted in consultancy firms (arguably an elitist type of knowledge company), yet the methods adopted seem designed to select individuals who are skilled at analysing in a particular type of way, rather than demonstrating any independent thought.

Drawing on insights from academics with diverse backgrounds and interests in management and organizational studies, we hope that this book will provide a thought-provoking read for professional managers and postgraduate students, as well as academics teaching and researching organizational studies and management. By adopting a historical perspective on management (past, present and future) it is intended that this book will appeal to the 'curious' management practitioner seeking something different from traditional management texts. We hope that it will encourage you to be more reflexive about what constitutes effective management in different contexts, rather than opting for the universalist one best way of managing, which Taylor clearly believed was the case:

> This paper [Principles of Scientific Management] was originally prepared for presentation to the American Society of Mechanical Engineers. The illustrations chosen are such as, it is believed, will especially appeal to engineers and to managers of industrial and manufacturing establishments ... It is hoped, however, that it will be clear to other readers that the same principles can be applied with equal force to all social activities: to the management of our homes ... our philanthropic institutions our universities and our governmental departments. (Taylor 1911: 3)

## Structure of the Rest of this Volume

The rest of this volume is structured into three main sections. Part I (consisting of three chapters) sets the scene for the nature of organizations and management in the twentieth century, drawing out the key influences of Taylor's principles of management, contrasting these with alternative perspectives on management. It will also provide a historical perspective on the effect and impact of Taylor's work on business and management education in the UK, as well the professionalization of management more broadly. Part II (consisting of five chapters) provides evidence that each of Taylor's five principles of management still exist in the contemporary knowledge and service economy, despite contemporary 'grand managerial discourse' of empowering the workers (Mabey 2009). Part III (containing the final three chapters) draws on some of the themes in Taylor's original work that have received less coverage in contemporary management writing. These include the notion of 'the biddable disciplined worker', hence the use of prescriptive recruitment and selection methods designed to select employees who demonstrate the right behavioural dispositions to remain 'fit for work' and the way that biddable workers are then shoe-horned into roles that threaten their identity (hidden voice – gender). In the final part, we draw together key continuities and change in management practice since Taylor's original work, before considering a future-orientated perspective on management, discussing what it might take for 'new' ways of managing (in other words, that reflect an increasing desire for workplaces with a strong purpose) to become as entrenched in management thinking as Taylor's principles of scientific management. An overview of each chapter now follows.

Colin Hales (Chapter 2) sets the scene by making the case for how Taylor's obsession with the notion of 'rationalization of work' reflects 'a continuing work in progress' in managerial work. He eloquently argues how Taylor's management ideology, that work and workers must be managed using rationale scientific methods, still underpins contemporary management thinking, despite the pathogenic flaws in this ideology. The twist, as Colin Hales points out, is that contemporary managers (specifically middle managers) now find themselves in a situation where an unquestioned adoption of scientific methods has robbed them of their discretionary elements; as Hales points out, 'the rationalizers are themselves being rationalized'.

Huw Morris (Chapter 3) compares and contrasts the spread of Taylorism within the US and in the UK, tracing the major influences on the take-up of Taylor's Shop Management and Scientific Management ideas in each of these contexts. He points out that whilst businesses in the US were quick to pick up on Taylor's principles of scientific management – an early form of 'best practice' management – businesses in the UK seemed more reluctant to adopt this rationale prescriptive approach. Several explanations are provided for this apparent difference: the speed at which industrialization took off in the US compared to the UK; greater receptivity by employers and managers to the management philosophy of Taylor and his followers, who appeared less concerned with the impact on workers from rationalistic management, and differences in the growth in consultancy and business schools in the US compared to the UK. In tracing the roots of Taylor and Taylorism, Huw Morris debates the role that business and management education has played in transmitting and possibly reinforcing the 'myths surrounding the "Taylorisation" of work in the USA and the UK'. Furthermore, he points out how 'Taylor's achievement was not the invention or identification of new management approaches, but rather the synthesis and documenting of established best practice'. Finally, this chapter surfaces tensions with the nature of managerial knowledge – codified, prescriptive – and the best place/way for such knowledge to be developed; as an abstract activity that occurs in educational institutions, or as a situated activity that is best located within the workplace: a debate that persists amongst contemporary management educationalists.

Leonard Holmes (Chapter 4) builds on Huw Morris's chapter by examining accounts of managerial expertise (knowledge, skill, competence, etc.) and of (purportedly) underpinning accounts of managerial behaviour/performance, and how these have been presented and evolved over the past century. Over this period the occupation of management has certainly grown in terms of economic, social and political significance, as has the numbers of people employed as managers. Accompanying the growth in the numerical size of the occupation, and of education, training and development, is the large-scale publication of textbooks and other literature, aimed at both students of management and practising managers. Underlying such provision, as with that of non-qualification-bearing training and development, is the assumption that there is some distinctive form of expertise (knowledge, skills, etc.) appropriate to managing. But to what extent is that assumption valid? This chapter then examines various attempts over the past century to present appropriate and valid accounts of the expertise of managing. In particular, it examines the types of such accounts, broadly classifying these into prescriptions, (claimed) descriptions, and ascriptions. The chapter argues that prescriptive and descriptive accounts have yielded problematic results. An approach based on the notion that expertise is *ascribed* is then elaborated through consideration of processes by which managers' behaviour is construed as managerial performance, implicating issues of identity and practices. Processes of identity construction and identity work are examined as inescapable aspects of modern forms of organizational life.

Shuchi Sinha and Yiannis Gabriel (Chapter 5) expose opportunities and tensions with managing in the contemporary service sector, drawing on empirical data from an investigation into management practices within call centres in India. Despite the facade of 'high-commitment' human resource management practices, the work in these environments is fragmented, standardized and closely monitored and controlled by team leaders, using different surveillance techniques (observational and technological). This chapter highlights an interesting paradox: the critical role that customers in the service sector play in the labour process can enable management to exercise greater control over their workers. In service environments, unlike in the industrial era, high performance requires 'emotional labour' (that is, aligning one's heart and mind with customer expectations and organizational interests). But as Shuchi Sinha and Yiannis Gabriel point out, call centre workers, like the workers in Taylor's era, appear to have found a way of duping management. So despite the proliferation of quality assurance and service level agreements, call centre workers have learnt how to use the power of the customer to disrupt the power of managers.

Judith Glover (Chapter 6) draws on research that investigated hybrid workers in the UK's ICT (information and communication technologies) sector, employed in roles that require them to demonstrate combined technical and soft skills. These workers are employed in roles that fit somewhere in between Brown et al.'s (2011) 'developers' and 'demonstrators' categories and Whitchurch's (2008) 'third space' professionals. Whilst hybrid workers bring considerable organizational value, as Judith Glover points out there are tensions relating to the management of this type of worker. First there are difficulties with classification. The hybrid workers that participated in her research felt their skills were unquantifiable: from a Taylorist perspective, then, this would make such skills difficult to routinize and standardize. Second, there were tensions from a performance perspective: evaluating 'soft' skills is problematic, involving perceptions, not hard measurements. From an individual career perspective, the fact that organizations may have difficulty in classifying hybrid roles could be to the former's advantage – there is less scope for standardization, and thus any attempts to remove 'permission to think' will be unsuccessful. However, there are longer-term career concerns: as technical skills become obsolete through lack of practice, the only career path open to these workers might be that of following the managerial ladder.

Tony Cutler (Chapter 7) discusses some interesting similarities and differences between the practice of 'systematic soldiering' in Taylor's era (that is, the collective attempt of workers to keep managers ignorant of how quickly work could be carried out) and the practice of 'gaming' under the contemporary New Public Management regime (that is, the manipulation of targets by management to give the impression of achievement). Both of these practices, Cutler suggests, represent a form of 'reactive subversion'. However, whilst scientific management offered a way of demonstrating the feasibility of meeting set production targets, there is a distinct lack of any attempt to link targets and methods under New Public Management. Tony Cutler highlights another fallacy of contemporary management too – the search for a single 'best way' of management: this is a theme that permeates much of the management literature and one that arises in other chapters.

Christopher Bond and Darren O'Byrne (Chapter 8) build on the theme of New Public Management with their critical appraisal of the implications of adopting an instrumental technical rationale approach to management, subsumed under the quality agenda, within the UK higher education sector. Several implications of this are discussed: standardization and commodification of learning and knowledge creation, resulting in an impoverished experience for both academics and students; an over preoccupation with the notion of 'best practice', assumed to be based on scientific rationality, yet lacking in any form of critical debate about 'best for whom'; and the de-professionalization of the role of academics. The unchallenged pursuit of a technical rationale agenda is likely to result in universities becoming factories for the production of 'technically useful knowledge', rather than a breeding ground for developing the sort of independent thinking that employers and governments claim are essential employability skills.

Yvonne Guerrier (Chapter 9) contrasts the work–life experiences of elite knowledge workers, drawing on the fictional character of Changez in Moshim Hamid's (2007) book *The Reluctant Fundamentalist*, with Taylor's (possibly fictional) 'high class' pig iron workers. Despite the very different types of work (cognitive versus physical), Yvonne Guerrier highlights the similarities in the expectations of workers by management: the need for workers to be self-disciplined, ensuring that they keep themselves 'fit for work'; docility, in the sense that they do not question the work routine and systems that they are expected to 'fit' into and that they are equally unquestioning of authority. In her conclusions, Yvonne Guerrier questions whether Taylorism and scientific management can be considered a modernist movement, despite its claims on rationality, suggesting that it is perhaps more akin to a 'fundamentalist' movement.

Christina Evans (Chapter 10) discusses whether, despite the growing importance of knowledge and service work, the theory and practice of job design has kept up with the realities and expectations of the twenty-first century workplaces. In post-bureaucratic organizations with the free flow of information supported by intelligent information systems, in principle it should be easier for employees to exert more discretionary behaviour. Yet, as Christina Evans discusses, despite the recent management preoccupation with the concept of employee engagement, organizations still want to exert tighter controls for a variety of reasons. The chapter begins by mapping out key historical developments in the theory and practice of job design, before moving on to consider whether the adoption of the concept of 'job crafting' could help reduce the tensions between employers' needs for efficiency and quality and employees' needs for meaningful work, that fits with invividuals' own sense of professional identity.

In the final chapter, Leonard Holmes and Christina Evans draw together some of the key continuities and discontinuities in management thinking and practice, drawn from the contributions in the previous chapters, before concluding with some thoughts on future prospects for management.

## References

Adler, P.S. 2007. The future of critical management studies: a paleo-Marxist critique of labour process theory. *Organization Studies*, 28(9), 1313–45.

BERR 2008. *Globalisation and the Changing UK Economy*. [Online: Department for Business Enterprise & Regulatory Reform.] Available at: http://www.bis.gov.uk/files/file44332.pdf [accessed 16 March 2012].

Brewster, C., Sparrow, P., Vernon, G. and Houldsworth, E. 2011. *International Human Resource Management*. London: CIPD.

Brinkley, I. 2008. *The Knowledge Economy: How Knowledge is Reshaping the Economic Life of Nations*. [Online: The Work Foundation.] Available at: http://www.workfoundation.com/assets/docs/publications/41_KE_life_of_nations.pdf [accessed 16 March 2012].

Broadbridge, A. 2000. Stress and the female retail manager. *Women in Management Review*, 15(3), 145–59.

Brown, P. and Hesketh, A. 2004. *The Mismanagement of Talent*. Oxford: Oxford University Press.

Brown, P., Launder, H. and Ashton, D. 2011. *The Global Auction*. Oxford: Oxford University Press.

Cooper, C. and Taylor, P. 2000. From Taylorism to Ms Taylor: the transformation of the accounting craft. *Accounting, Organization and Society*, 25(6), 555–78.

Gamble, J., Morris, J. and Wilkinson, B. 2004. Mass production is still alive and well: the future of work and organization in East Asia. *International Journal of Human Resource Management*, 15(2), 397–409.

Glover, J. and Kirton, G. 2006. *Women, Employment and Organizations*. Abingdon: Routledge.

Grant, L., Yeandle, S. and Buckner, L. 2006. *Working Below Potential. Women and Part-Time Work. Executive Summary.* [Online: Sheffield Hallam University.] Available at: www.shu.ac.uk/research/csi [accessed 10 February 2012].

Mabey, C. 2009. Review Section: Continuing the journey of reflexivity: responses to Scott Taylor's review. *Management Learning,* 40(3), 341–3.

Macleod, D. and Clarke, N. 2009. *Engaging for Success: Enhancing Performance through Employee Engagement.* [Online: Department for Business, Innovation and Skills.] Available at: http://www.bis.gov.uk/files/file52215.pdf [accessed 7 February 2012].

Parker, S.K., Wall, T.D. and Cordery, J.L. 2001. Future work design research and practice: towards an elaborated model of work design. *Journal of Occupational and Organizational Psychology,* 74(4), 413–40.

Sealy, R. and Vinnicombe, S. 2012. *The Female FTSE Board Report 2012. Milestone or Millstone?* Bedford: Cranfield School of Management.

Taylor, F.W. 1911. *The Principles of Scientific Management.* Reprinted by Forgottenbooks.org, 2010, http://www.forgottenbooks.org/info/9781606801123 [accessed 15 March 2011].

Tomlinson, J., Olsen, W., Neff, D., Purdam, K. and Mehta, S. 2005. *Examining the Potential for Women Returners to Work in Areas of High Occupational Gender Segregation.* [Online: University of Manchester.] Available at: http://lubswww2.leeds.ac.uk/fileadmin/user_upload/Documents/women_returners_dtinov2005.pdf [accessed 31 March 2011].

Tomlinson, M. 1999. *The Learning Economy and Embodied Knowledge Flows. CRIC Discussion Paper No 26.* [Online: Centre for Research on Innovation and Competition, The University of Manchester.] Available at: http://www.cric.ac.uk/cric/pdfs/dp26.pdf [accessed 16 March 2012].

Whitchurch, C. 2008. Shifting identities and blurring boundaries: the emergence of third space professionals in UK higher education. *Higher Education Quarterly,* 62(4), 377–96.

# PART I

# Management in an Historical Context

# Stem Cell, Pathogen or Fatal Remedy? The Relationship of Taylor's Principles of Management to the Wider Management Movement

*Colin Hales*

## Introduction

F.W. Taylor's ideas have, for good or ill, and despite persistent claims of their demise or contemporary irrelevance, cast a long shadow over the theory and practice of management and the management movement. Indeed, arguably, there would not be a 'management movement' to cast a long shadow over were it not for Taylor, since he first crystallized and articulated, even if he did not invent, the concept of 'management' as the systematic direction, organization, coordination and control of work on a large scale. However, Taylor's place in the great and the good of management thought is an ambivalent one: for some, an influential father figure, for others, the bogeyman (Rose 1988, Sheldrake 2000, Tillett et al. 1970).

To change the metaphor, Taylorist principles of management can be seen, variously, as the stem cell, pathogen and fatal remedy of management. They have, on the one hand, been the stem cell from which have grown, with some selection and adaptation, both subsequent approaches to management that have, in broad terms, applied Taylor's principles, and a set of general domain assumptions about management that have echoed Taylor's philosophy. On the other hand, Taylor's ideas have been regarded as the pathogen for which subsequent alternative approaches to management have sought some form of cure or alleviation. Finally and paradoxically, Taylor's principles have proved to be the fatal remedy for management in that the very ways in which they initially equipped and emboldened managers to manage the work of others have reacted back on the management process and work of managers itself such that the protagonists of 'scientific management' are now themselves increasingly managed along scientific management lines.

In this chapter, I want to examine, in turn, these three legacies of Taylor's principles. I will paint with a fairly broad brush since the developments which I seek to describe in general terms are exemplified in rich empirical detail in subsequent chapters by my co-contributors. I will show how Taylor's principles variously inspired a set of ideas and practices broadly clustered around the continuous *rationalization* of work; how they provoked other ideas and practices broadly clustered around the *humanization* and *de-specialization* of work; and how they came, paradoxically, to be applied to the very process of management to which they had given rise and to managers to whom they had given a function and a *raison d'être*. In all of these developments, Taylor's ideas are no historical curiosity but a continuing work-in-progress.

## Taylor's Principles of Management

Taylor's principles of management were derived inductively from the practical methods he had sought to apply at Bethlehem Steel and elsewhere and were set out in *Shop Management* (1903) and, in conjunction with his testimony to the US Congress Special House Committee, *The Principles of Scientific Management* (1911). They were, in effect, a systematic set of ideas about what 'management', as a process, entailed and what managers, as an occupational stratum, were for. As such, they were a description of and, crucially, advocacy for: first, management *per se*, the idea that work should be managed systematically and not left to chance, employee discretion or managers' rules of thumb; second, a particular approach to management based on scientific analysis of work, specialization of tasks and functions and centralization of direction and control; and, third, a clear role and rationale for managers as the instruments of that approach.

Taylor was at pains to emphasize that what made his system different and superior was that it confronted the management of work and the worker as something that should be undertaken deliberately and systematically, in sharp contrast to what he saw as the capricious, lax and haphazard ways in which work at the time was 'managed'. The objects of Taylor's scorn were various: the failure to wrest *de facto* management control of the labour process from skilled, craft workers such that work methods and, in particular, pace of work continued to be determined by workers themselves and characterized by inefficient custom and practice in the case of the former and 'systematic soldiering' in the case of the latter; the delegation of management to internal contractors or gang bosses applying crude, inconsistent and unsystematic methods; and the amateur application of rules of thumb and extemporaneous practices by those nominally designated as 'managers'. To be sure, there is some debate as to which of these were primarily in Taylor's sights and whether the central purpose of his ideas was that of attempting to break the power of, and wrest control of the labour process from, craft unions (Braverman 1974, Stark 1980, Stone 1974) or the abolition of the gang-boss system (Hill 1981, Littler 1982), and, relatedly, whether the Taylor system was essentially political, for establishing managerial control (Braverman 1974, Marglin 1976) or technical, for improving managerial effectiveness (Wood and Kelly 1983). Either way, Taylor's answer to these perceived deficiencies in work organization was systematic management exercised and monitored by professional managers.

Of what did this systematic management consist? Five central principles may be identified (even though Taylor did not number these consistently in his writing), together with the specific characteristic features of work organization which they entailed: scientifically determined work methods, a detailed division of labour, centralized planning and control, an instrumental, low-involvement employment relationship and the ideology of neutral technical efficiency.

Taylor's First Principle was that all work can and should be subject to systematic observation, measurement, tabulation and analysis in order to arrive at scientific 'laws' of work which identify and codify the essential components of work tasks and their optimum sequence and pace and to eliminate all unnecessary elements. The consequent reduction of a complex work process into a sequence of separate, individual tasks then forms the basis for standardizing work methods and times, determining pay, designing workflow and utilizing machinery.

Taylor's Second and Third Principles were, respectively, the scientific selection and training of workers for particular tasks and the 'bringing together' of scientifically analysed work and scientifically selected workers in an optimum allocation of work. Taken together, these principles implied a detailed division of labour where jobs are based on individual task elements of a work process and employees are allocated to those tasks for which they have been identified as most suited through recruitment and selection and for which they have been specifically trained. The skill to conceptualize and execute a broad range of tasks is replaced by a specialized dexterity to execute a specific task.

Taylor's Fourth Principle was that there should be a clear functional division between managers who manage and workers who carry out the work itself. This may be more generally rendered as the principle of centralized planning and control of the labour process, or, to use Braverman's felicitous phrase, 'the separation of conception from execution' (1974: 114), where responsibility for the systematic analysis and codification of work and the use of this knowledge to plan, coordinate and control is the exclusive prerogative of managers.

Although Taylor couched his next Principle in terms of 'the intimate co-operation of management with the workmen so that together they do the work in accordance with the scientific laws which have been developed' (1911: 115), he meant something rather specific by this. Since the management of work was to be attempted primarily through the rational ordering of the work system as a whole, what was asked of the individual worker primarily was a disposition and willingness to carry out their allotted task as required by management. Thus, the nature of the 'co-operation' between the two parties was very specific and single-stranded: managers would expect workers to carry out their tasks exactly as instructed and without demur, whilst employees in return could expect the promised level of reward commensurate with their effort. In effect, then, for all Taylor's robustly emollient language, he was proposing a purely instrumental, low-involvement employment relationship of pay in return for obedience and effort, with wider obligations of loyalty, commitment or job security regarded as extraneous. The idea was also implicit in Taylor's Principle of 'bringing together work and the workman', where workers' potential to work is translated into actual work performance (or, put another way, labour power is translated into labour) by, firstly, having work times determined by carefully selected 'first class men' (sic) capable of sustained effort and willing to carry out instructions to the letter, and, secondly, having rates of pay tied to performance.

Finally, underpinning all of Taylor's Principles was the pursuit of technical efficiency as the unequivocally desirable end to which management as the means should be directed. Efficiency constituted not only the central criterion for choosing particular methods of organization but also provided an apparently unassailable legitimacy for this choice, since the pursuit of efficiency is both rational and universally beneficial, serving the interests and enhancing the 'prosperity' of employer and employee alike. As Taylor put it: 'It would seem so self-evident that maximum prosperity for the employer, coupled with maximum prosperity for the employee, ought to be the two leading objects of management, that even to state this fact should be unnecessary' (1911: 9).

Taylor was also at pains to emphasize that the principal 'burdens and duties' of his system fell on 'the management side'. This meant that responsibility for developing and implementing a scientific work system, for recruiting, training and incentivizing workers to operate it and for directing, coordinating and controlling that work process lay squarely with managers. With this 'burden' came a clear opportunity, however, in that it gave managers a clear function and *raison d'être*. No longer were managers simply those who happened to oversee work in whatever way they saw fit by virtue of their position. Taylor gave managers the specific technical role of prosecuting efficiency through science, gave them the means, in the form of prescriptive principles, to do that and thereby provided them with justification not only for what they did and how they did it but for their very existence as 'managers'. What managers did was now driven by the dictates of science and the pursuit of neutral efficiency, rather than personal whim or preference (Bendix 1963, Anthony 1977). Their 'right to manage' no longer stemmed precariously from a potentially contested hierarchical position but flowed from the rational authority bequeathed by superior knowledge. Opposition to managerial direction and control, therefore, became, by definition, 'unscientific' and irrational. Managers became the technically necessary, decisive agents in the labour process, the guarantors of efficiency.

Moreover, Taylor justified the pursuit of technical efficiency on the grounds of both rationality and fairness. Efficiency was 'rational' because it embodied the objective logic of science in the unobjectionable pursuit of 'more from less'. It was 'fair', since by maximizing output, it served the interest of employers, managers and workers alike. Who could reasonably advocate inefficiency and on what grounds? Thus, Taylor offered a powerful *ideology of management*, a coherent rationale for the fact *that* work must be managed, not left to chance; that it must be managed externally, by those equipped intellectually to understand it, and that it must be managed in a particular way, 'scientifically'. It also offered a powerful *managerial ideology* in that it furnished a set of ideas justifying the need for and authority and, therefore, status of managers and a justification for what they were now asking workers to do (Merkle 1980, Rose 1988, Thompson 1983).

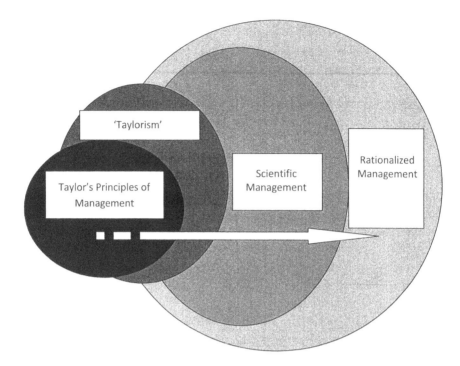

Figure 2.1     Relationship between Taylor's Principles, Taylorism,
               scientific management and rationalized management

## Taylor's Principles as the Stem Cell of Work Rationalization

The enduring legacy of Taylor's ideas has come more from the way that the
broad principles which he set out – the 'Taylor system' – have resonated in
later approaches to management, rather than through a wholesale adoption
of his specific proposals, some of which, even from the outset, were regarded
as excessively radical, unrealistic, not to say crackpot (Littler 1982, Palmer
1975). In that sense, Taylor's Principles represent, in effect, the stem cell
from which have grown selective extensions, adaptations and variants. It
is important, therefore, to make a distinction among the following: first,
Taylor's Principles (or System) *per se*; second, 'Taylorism' as their immediate,
often crude adoption; third, 'scientific management' as a broader adaptation
and extension of Taylor's ideas promulgated by his acolytes; and, fourth,
'rationalized management' as a suite of subsequent ideas and approaches
informed by Taylor's philosophy (see Figure 2.1).

The legacy of Taylor's principles of scientific work methods has been ever
more elaborate forms of work study and industrial engineering, embracing

techniques for deriving standard times, standard methods, job descriptions, planned workflow, mechanization and, ultimately, automation (Wood 1983, Kanawaty 1992). Although the essential purpose of work study has remained the same – to arrive at a technically best, or most efficient, way of performing a sequence of work tasks through objective scientific analysis – it has undergone considerable refinement and development beyond the simple time study proposed by Taylor (Davis et al. 1972, Taylor 1979). The search for different, and better, ways of working was the basic project of motion study pioneered by the Gilbreths (1911) and method study pioneered by Gantt (1919), where the emphasis shifted to observation of work, systematic and standardized analysis and the production of activity and process charts. These, in turn, facilitated 'motion economy' in which unnecessary movements are identified and eliminated, those that remain are combined, synthesized or replaced by simpler ones and rest periods are incorporated. This is most elaborately found in schemes such as the Bedaux system and its variants (Littler 1982) based on a unit of work measurement (the 'B') divided into work and rest periods or in the planning of shifts around 'circadian rhythms' (Folkard 1987). Recognition that improved work performance was also a function of improved work layout and equipment design led to the development of forms of operational research investigating problems of work allocation, sequencing and routing, and ergonomics, concerned with design of machine systems and work stations. Crucially, all these represent a shift from the contingent application of scientific insights to work systems to the systematic development of scientific techniques expressly to solve work system problems.

Application of these techniques has produced the standard work times and methods which are characteristic of contemporary rationalized work systems. Standard work times, with in-built relaxation and contingency, derived from such techniques as 'methods-time-measurement' and 'predetermined motion time systems' continue to be used retrospectively to monitor and evaluate individual work performance and determine rewards, discipline or training, and prospectively to determine performance norms through job cards, manuals, Gantt charts and product/service specifications. Now the key device for standardizing work has become mechanization or automation, replacing human labour by machines and, more recently, robots. Technology has become not simply an aid to the work process but, crucially, a key device for its organization and control. How work is carried out, at what pace and in what sequence is built into the machines or software with which workers interface (Callaghan and Thompson 2001).

The other key development of scientific work study has been the 'flow lines' (or production lines), which determine work pace and sequencing and thus effectively coordinate and control a series of disparate work operations. Flow lines developed in the mass consumer goods industries, the archetypes for which were meat-packing and automobile production, where the technique was developed by Ford from a simple, progressive shop layout to a power-driven continuous line where workers remained at their task and the *work* moved (Gartman 1979, Kelly 1982). Now, however, they are as much a feature of service industries and service work (Ritzer 1996).

Developments in work study have also been used to generate a system of job descriptions specifying the content, context and standards of performance of a job and used as a basis for recruitment/selection, training, job evaluation and remuneration. This increasing formalization of employee responsibilities has served to codify the detailed division of labour into the elaborate system of job grades found in many large organizations.

Equally definitive of the rationalized work systems which grew up first in mass production and later in large-scale service operations has been a high degree of job specialization, manifested variously in the separation of direct and indirect labour; the fragmentation and de-skilling of direct labour; specialized selection and training; and the treatment of workers/employees as impersonal 'factors of production'. In such systems, departments and work groups were based on functions, and jobs on specific tasks, a form of specialization intended to foster the expertise of departments, enhance the dexterity of workers on core tasks, eliminate time lost in moving between tasks and, crucially, facilitate close monitoring and control of work performance. The 'Babbage principle' (Babbage 1832) has resonated in the practice of reserving more complex, non-programmable tasks for more expensive skilled workers, whilst allocating simpler tasks or support activities to cheaper, unskilled labour. This has been extended into the geographical fragmentation of the labour process, with routine work located in areas of cheap labour, including, in particular, offshore (Beynon et al. 2002: 234)

The jobs created by work study and detailed specialization have, invariably, been undemanding and repetitive, with the creation of the 'detail worker' (Braverman 1974) reaching its most extreme on the Fordist material assembly lines associated with mass production and the informational assembly lines of mass service industries. In such systems, 'job training' takes a matter of minutes, workers are fragmented functionally and spatially and recruitment/ selection and training for these jobs are focused on the employee's physical and mental capacity to perform a given task, including, in contemporary echoes of Taylor's vignette of Schmidt the pig iron handler (Taylor 1912), a focus upon employee 'mentality', attitude, pliability and conformity (Smith 2000).

In the rationalized work systems that grew out of Taylor's principles, planning and control of work have been centralized and characterized by the separation and increasing elaboration of the management function as a whole; the removal of planning and control from junior managers and supervisors to specialist departments; and the increasing formalization of planning and control mechanisms. The resulting 'shadow' work process, once on paper, is now embodied in software systems (concerned with planning and control and embracing production engineering, organization and methods, logistics, cost accounting and human resource planning), which have given rise to new managerial/professional specialisms (Esland 1980) concerned with the production of 'representational outputs' such as blueprints, flow charts and work schedules (Hales 1980). In such systems, personal direction and control of work by supervisors has been replaced by more impersonal forms of control relying on formal, standardized feedback information, relating to production/ service quotas, scrap rates, customer complaints, overtime and so on. Further, centralized control operates through general and formalized mechanisms which focus primarily upon how work is carried out and takes the form of job specifications, blueprints, manuals and, increasingly, the characteristics of the technology with which employees work. The role of first-line supervisors shifts to monitoring and enforcing compliance with these rules through surveillance of workers and scrutiny of performance data.

Rationalized work systems exhibit a number of features which stem from Taylor's conception of the employment relationship as essentially an instrumental, low-involvement one in which the only strand linking employer and employee is pay in return for directed effort (Littler 1982). This 'cash nexus' is predicated on limited expectations about effort and reward, the freedom of either party to terminate the contract and, in particular, the desire to treat labour as a pliable 'factor of production'. At base, the employer promises no job security or career and makes no claim on employee behaviour outside the confines of work: the employer 'hires and fires' as purely economic considerations dictate and there is little or no job security (Burchell et al. 2002, Milkman 1998). In practice, however, concern with employee obedience and attitudes formed outside the workplace and the need for employee compliance has meant that the employment relationship may exhibit certain paternalistic or even 'totalizing' elements. Such has been the case in the 'Fordist' work organization with its emphasis on worker obedience and an intrusive managerial interest in employee behaviour in return for high wages, or the recent concern with 'monitoring' and 'counselling' employees over their health and 'lifestyle'. Such systems are also characterized by forms of appraisal and reward which focus primarily upon individual compliance and short-term performance and seek to harness individual self-interest, with problems of work performance seen as individual failures of competence, 'motivation' or 'attitude' and dismissal used as a central disciplinary device (Beynon and Nichols 2006).

The carrot to accompany this stick has usually been some form of payment by results (PBR) system, in which individual output is measured and rewarded directly and immediately. Whilst the general principle of PBR sits squarely with those of rationalized work organization, PBR systems take a wide variety of forms in practice (Bryson et al. 2008). Most are hybrids, combining some fixed 'time rate' element with variable bonuses for output or, more recently, outcomes. What they have all had in common is being not simply ways of rewarding past effort, but attempts to elicit and control future effort, by specifying the link between performance and reward, using rate setting to intensify effort and using diminishing bonuses to control labour costs.

Thus the stem cells of Taylorist principles have led to the growth of rationalized work in a more general sense, a plethora of cognate approaches, techniques and practices in which those principles have been extended, modified and refined. Rationalized work also extends Taylor's original system in four other key respects.

Firstly, the systematic, standard work methods, detailed division of labour, centralized planning and technological control have been extended from their traditional base in large-scale manufacturing to service *industries* – to the extent, indeed, that one particular service industry, fast food, and most specifically, McDonald's, has been considered the paradigm case of 'McDonaldization' (Ritzer 1996). Other services, such as retailing, banking/ insurance, health, education, leisure and tourism, the media and IT, have not been immune. This extension of rationalized work into services has corresponded with its retention in many manufacturing industries, with the consequence that many workplaces remain traditionally managed with de-skilling and work intensification rife, despite claims about the 'new workplace' (Gordon 1996, Warhurst and Thompson 1998).

Secondly, rationalization has spread into service *work*, in particular those tasks which involve interaction with customers. Standard work procedures and technological controls have not only been applied to what workers do but, increasingly, to what they say and feel (or, at least, what they are supposed to feel). Workers' dealings with customers are standardized in 'scripts' relating both to recurring interactions and more occasional, if predictable, contingencies. Nowhere is this more evident than in the various forms of call centre work. Further, there have been attempts to shape the emotions which workers display in their interactions with customers through training, surveillance and counselling (Hochschild 1983, Taylor 1998).

Thirdly and relatedly, the principle of separating out routine tasks and allocating them to cheaper, unskilled labour has been extended to include the allocation of work tasks to those whose 'labour' is entirely free: consumers. This often means customers operating or interacting with some form of automated systems, but may also include performing menial self-service tasks. Consumers have also been enlisted in the process of managerial control, particularly of 'front-line' service workers, by supplying information on worker behaviour to managers or by shaping worker behaviour through the kinds of demands and expectations which they have been encouraged to make upon service employees (Du Gay and Salaman 1992, Fuller 1991).

Finally, where control remains focused on how work is performed, the means for doing so has become ever more sophisticated and reliant upon technology. Much rationalized work is now carried out in ways determined by and built into the technology itself and/or is monitored by technological means. In that sense, control has become more intensive, not to say 'totalizing', in reducing freedom and choice in more and more aspects of workers' and, indeed, managers' lives. Employees have become subject both to the continuous 'carceral gaze' of panoptic technologies and systems (Jacques 1996, McKinlay and Starkey 1998). Where Taylor proposed 'fitting the man to the job' by selecting and training for specific physical and mental capacities, now attempts are made to mould workers' very being – their subjectivity – to fit the routines, systems and ethos of the organization.

As well as spawning the development and application of rationalized management, Taylor's principles have exercised a more diffuse but no less significant influence in that they have also led to the embedding of certain ideas both in certain strands of management theory and, more importantly, in managers' thinking, such that, in the case of the latter, they have assumed the taken-for-granted character of 'domain assumptions'. Firstly, there is the assumption that, despite its potential complexity and intractability, work not only *can* be subjected to 'scientific' analysis and construction without doing violence to its essential qualities but should be. In this purview, no form of work, whether manual, clerical, technical or professional, is regarded as so complex or nuanced that it is not amenable to systematic deconstruction, separation of its conceptual from its routine elements and fragmentation into task-based jobs. Moreover, the assumption is that work that is subjected to this analysis and reconstruction is perforce technically superior. Secondly, Taylor's ideas have spawned a managerial conceit that the efficiency of work is primarily dependent on how it is *managed* and that managers are the decisive agents in work since only they have the knowledge inclination and intellectual capacity to comprehend work. Organizations are 'well managed', rather than 'well worked'.

Thirdly and relatedly, Taylor's mindset resonates in a certain managerial contempt for workers, what they seek from work and of what they are capable. Perhaps Taylor's most enduring legacy is the absorption into managerial thinking of the belief that workers are an indolent rabble who must be coerced or bribed to comply and, since they are intellectually incapable of grasping the complexity of the labour process, are 'not paid to think'. Whilst managers' *espoused* views on motivation may have changed, with most well-versed in the anodyne rhetoric of 'empowerment' and people as 'our most valuable assets', many have continued to behave as if dangling carrots and, more especially, waving sticks is as sophisticated as worker motivation need ever get (Herzberg 1966, Gordon 1996). Fourthly, flowing from this is the assumption that, aside from physical fatigue, workers' subjective experience of work is largely irrelevant to the efficiency of a work system. Energy, enthusiasm, commitment and, indeed, pleasure in work do not count. Rather, what determines the efficiency of work is the technical sophistication of the *system*. Thus, workers can be hired and fired without apparent consequence for the quality of work, insecurity does not detract from workers' capacity to work (indeed, the threat may spur it) and labour is essentially a commodity that can be bought and sold as required. Technical (or cost) efficiency trumps all other criteria for judging the effectiveness of work systems.

## Taylor's Principles as Pathogen

It did not take long before others, even Taylor's immediate followers, began to recognize and decry the tendency for a system based on a detailed division of labour, rigidly imposed work methods and tight managerial control to create, first, narrow, de-humanized jobs which both under-utilized and debilitated those performing them and, second, over-elaborate, inflexible work systems prone to disruption and inflexibility in the face of external change (Gantt 1919, Mayo 1933). Since then there have been a succession of approaches to management which have addressed the perceived pathology of Taylor's ideas, seeing these as the malaise for which an organizational cure needed to be found. Whilst the specific concerns of these approaches have shifted between the attempt to humanize work, to make it more flexible and to supplant narrow efficiency by quality of output (Buchanan 1994), a common underlying theme, even if it has not been expressed as such, has been to regard some form of 'de-specialization' – reversing the tendency of work rationalization to specialize operational tasks and separate them from management – as central (Hales 2001).

Until the 1980s, the focus of concern was the 'de-humanized' character of rationalized work and the need to improve the quality of working life and work satisfaction of employees. However, even then these concerns had a more pragmatic side, focusing more on the waste and inefficiencies created by rationalized organization. This came to the fore in a concern with making work processes, and workers themselves, more flexible, most recently under the twin prompts of 'total quality management' and 'business process re-engineering'. Related to this has been a shift away from such changes as a defensive reaction to employee pressure and towards the de-specialization of work as a proactive initiative by managers designed to seize the opportunities offered by new technologies and to maintain, or enhance, organizational effectiveness.

At the level of ideas, the humanistic reaction to rationalized organization initially coalesced in the 'human relations' movement. This often amounted to little more than a demonstration of the existence of social relations at work and a plea for managers to recognize their importance. This only rarely translated into concrete prescriptions for reorganizing work and usually amounted to advocating a participative managerial 'style' sensitive to the sentiments of employees and group dynamics (Roethlisberger and Dixon 1939, Mayo 1933, Warner and Low 1947). If early human relations ideas were mainly concerned with warning of the possible consequences of rationalized and de-humanized work, later ideas focused on the 'quality of working life' (QWL) were prompted more by actual documented consequences. From the 1950s onward, evidence accumulated which suggested that routine manual, clerical and service work was chronically dissatisfying for those who did it. This evidence was rather piecemeal, ranging from case studies of particular work places (for example Beynon 1973) or accounts of individual occupations (Terkel 1973) to broader surveys, and complicated by the use of a variety of terms such as 'work dissatisfaction' and 'alienation' (Blauner 1964). Nevertheless, through this diversity of evidence ran a consistent theme: that satisfaction with work declines with occupational status and is coupled with expressions of particular dissatisfaction at work.

Advocates of QWL (such as Davis and Cherns 1975) pointed the finger of accusation firmly at rationalized organization and specifically at the principle of specialization. For them, excessive levels of horizontal and vertical specialization had created jobs lacking in content, personal control or autonomy and sense of context (how the job fitted in to a wider whole). Part of the argument for de-specialization was that work of this kind was undesirable *per se* (Argyris 1964, Maslow 1970, Hofstede 1979): for work to be little more than an unchallenging, unsatisfying deprivation represents a damning indictment of human beings capacity to organize their affairs humanely. This is all the more true if work deprivations spill over into non-work and reduce the quality of life generally (Faunce and Dubin 1975). However, a more pragmatic substrate asserts that jobs lacking in content, context and autonomy lead to sub-optimal employee performance and productivity. Narrow jobs diminish employee performance both directly, by under-utilizing human resources, and indirectly, by creating boredom and dissatisfaction at work which, in turn, create low employee morale and high levels of absenteeism, turnover and stress (Hackman et al. 1975). Thus employee deprivations and organizational inefficiency have a common origin in a low quality of work life.

A second wave of interest in rolling back Taylor-inspired work specialization sprang from evidence that, far from receding after the initial flush of enthusiasm for quality of working life in the late 1960s and early 1970s, the practice of work redesign and, to a lesser extent, employee participation persisted into the 1980s but appeared to do so less from a concern to humanize work and more from a need to make work systems and workers more flexible. 'Flexible specialization' became, not altogether accurately, the umbrella term to describe these changes which were a response to both pressures and opportunities (Kelly 1982, Wood, 1989). The pressures arise from the marketplace, in the form of more intense competition and shifts in consumer tastes away from mass, standardized products towards specialized, higher-quality products. This necessitated short production runs (or 'batch' production) and flexible operating systems, rather than flow lines. Mass production methods were becoming redundant because mass products had. The opportunities for introducing these changes took the form of technological developments, notably in computing, which facilitated the development of both information systems, for monitoring and controlling operations, and 'non-dedicated' production equipment. Flexibility was not exclusively sought through changes in work organization. Of course, this could, and did, entail *numerical* flexibility through the very Taylorist practices of hiring/firing workers as required, employing temporary and/or part-time workers or buying in services. However, *functional* flexibility involved creating working arrangements in which multi-skilled employees moved more freely between different tasks and this implied some form of horizontal and vertical de-specialization.

The most recent wave of interest in de-specialization through work redesign and participation has been as a key component of 'total quality management' (TQM) and 'business process re-engineering' (BPR), both managerially driven attempts to improve the quality and efficiency of products/services and processes of production and delivery in order to secure or maintain competitive advantage through superior quality or service. As well as re-conceptualizing 'quality' and moving from Taylorist quality *control* to quality *assurance*, TQM was concerned with a shift away from procedures and measurement embodied in 'hard' quality management to an emphasis on maximizing worker contributions to work and restoring some degree of worker control over it, in order to reclaim workers' inputs of skills and knowledge: this represented its key break with rationalized work organization.

In seeking radical reinvention of work processes 'from scratch', BPR rejected the notion of work as an assemblage of activities and sought to restructure work around the processes which create outputs of value to the ultimate consumer (Hammer and Champy 1995). The corollary was that anything which was unnecessary, did not add value or delayed core work processes should be eliminated. Further, work processes should occur in their natural, not imposed, order, with different stages occurring simultaneously if possible and could take multiple forms. Put like this, BPR seems little more than an extension and elaboration of Taylor's basic principles except, perhaps, with the addition of information technology as a key enabling factor. However, BPR was more than simply 'Taylorism with chips' since it saw the reinstatement of workers' knowledge, skill and capacity for self-management as central to the reorganization of work processes. Thus BPR advocated: recombining tasks and jobs into generalist roles, giving workers greater opportunity for self-management ('empowerment'); creating multi-function process teams; and permitting workers greater involvement in decisions relating to the immediate circumstances of their work and organizational strategy. Further, it suggested that necessary corollaries of de-specialization and increased involvement were greater emphasis on education and learning to equip workers for responsibility, rather than training for a task; reward systems based on results; and a change in the managerial role from 'command and control' to 'advise and facilitate'.

Throughout these various initiatives, intended as alternatives to rationalization, a number of key principles were evident. Firstly, work methods were to be flexible, with the work process conceived as a variable 'socio-technical system' (Miller and Rice 1967), rather than a fixed technical system, and with methods of work more the outcome of employee choice, rather than an imposed 'best' way. Secondly, worker motivation was seen as complex, with people wishing to fulfil a variety of needs at work, including, crucially, the social and psychological (Herzberg 1966, Schein 1979), and work organization had to provide for this.

Thirdly, horizontal de-specialization has meant reducing the degree of specialization of tasks and activities, whether at the level of the individual job, the work group, or the organization as a whole. At the level of the job, it has meant creating more task variety, a greater opportunity for the use of skills, a greater sense of task significance and a closer fit between the job and a 'whole' task or sequence (Hackman and Oldham 1980). At the level of the work group, horizontal de-specialization has meant giving a group collective responsibility for a discrete and substantial element of the work process, removing previous job demarcations and creating a multi-skilled group or team. Lastly, at the level of the organization, horizontal de-specialization has meant replacing a rigid system of functionally differentiated sub-units with sub-units based upon products, markets or projects, bringing together individuals with different specialisms to work on a task as a team. Vertical de-specialization *has* meant transferring management functions, such as planning, coordination and control, from managers to workers. At the level of the job, it meant giving workers a greater opportunity to plan, monitor and control their own work and to coordinate their efforts with others – in short, to manage themselves. At the level of the organization, it meant removing the rigid division between managers and managed by extending participation in organizational decision-making and shifting the role of managers away from direction and control towards technical advice and coordination.

Fourthly, a high-involvement employment relationship treated employment as a broadly based, long-term commitment, with loyalty and obligations on the part of both employers and employees, rather than as a purely contingent economic attachment. This implied not only fair pay to reward commensurable contributions equally but also the provision of non-material, psychological rewards such as recognition and praise for contributions, some form of security of employment, and opportunities for training and development. In short, employees are to be regarded not as commodities but as 'human capital'. Finally, linked to these proposals were two ideologies: 'quality of working life' – the conviction that work organization must strike a balance between the pursuit of efficiency and economic performance on the one hand and providing work which is fulfilling, satisfying and well-rewarded (Elizur and Shye 1990) on the other – and 'empowerment' – the conviction that workers should not be constrained by rules but enabled to do their job how they think best and to 'take charge' of the circumstances of their work by being given the freedom and resources to do so (Hales 2000, Wilkinson 1998).

These broad ideas have ramified in practice in diverse forms of job re-design, such as job rotation, job enlargement, job enrichment and job empowerment; forms of group working such as autonomous work groups and self-managing work teams; and structures of participation, such as formal employee consultation and co-determination (Hales 2001). In doing so, they have sought to address, in various ways, the pathologies of de-humanized work, sub-optimal performance, inflexibility and lack of employee involvement that have flowed from Taylor-inspired work rationalization.

## Taylor's Principles as Fatal Remedy

An enduring legacy of Taylor's ideas was the definition of what the process of management entailed, what managers were for and, by implication, what managers were to do – or, more strictly, what a particular *type* of management entailed and what particular managers were for, since Taylor's concerns lay primarily with management and managers at the 'shop' or operational level, rather than at the strategic level of the enterprise as a whole. (The complementary articulation of what 'administration' in its broader sense entailed and senior managers were to do came from Fayol.)

Application of Taylor's principles of the separation of conception from execution and the scientific analysis and reconstruction of work were at the heart of the development of operational management: the former crystallized it as a distinct function, the latter specified its central concerns and methods. Management became the mental labour of work system design, planning and coordination and the political work of directing, motivating and controlling labour. These two elements broadly ramified into the two types of managerial job which developed in conjunction with the growth of rationalized work.

Job and work system design – the 'shadow' labour process – became the province of a growing cadre of assorted work/time/method study, design and production engineers, operational researchers, and inventory, materials and quality controllers, supplemented by manpower planners and an array of personnel officers variously concerned with devising and implementing payment systems and systems of recruitment, selection and performance appraisal – a more sophisticated elaboration of the 'thinking department' that Taylor proposed. Although the occupiers of these positions were not always designated as 'managers', they were located firmly within 'management' in both senses.

Overseeing and enforcing compliance with specified work methods, production quotas, workplace rules and quality standards became the province of first-line managers and supervisors, concerned with the proximal and immediate direction, monitoring and control of operational work. In practice this meant some combination of planning, scheduling and allocating work; monitoring output and work conduct; checking equipment, safety and cleanliness; dealing with unforeseen staffing, equipment and production problems; maintaining discipline; handling disputes; record-keeping and assisting with operational work (Hales 2005).

Thus, the result of the application of Taylor's principles, or some variant of them, was to create, in effect, a *managerial* labour process, 'conducted for the purpose of control within the corporation and ... exactly analogous to the process of production, although it produces no product other than the operation and co-ordination of the corporation' (Braverman 1974: 267), in which 'management' as a whole became the outcome of the work of many individual 'managers'. Whether or not Taylor or his followers realized the implication of this – and his advocacy of specialist functional foremen for the work 'gang', work speed, inspection or repair respectively hinted at this – this managerial labour process was, of course, by Taylor's logic, itself going to be amenable, at least in principle, to rationalization, fragmentation, de-skilling, centralized control and standardization.

In practice, of course, the growth of production operations and of the enterprises in which they were located, particularly following Fordist versions of work organization, led to a burgeoning and elaboration of management as both a process and an organizational stratum and of managers as an occupation (Enteman 1993). The growing size and complexity of production (and later, service) operations led to the growth of middle management, responsible for the operational effectiveness of a meso-level organizational unit subsuming a number of smaller operational units and concerned with translating strategy and policy into operational objectives, directing, coordinating, controlling and deploying resources within that unit; managing junior managers within that unit; coordinating with other organizational units; and reporting and accounting for operational and financial performance. At the same time, increasingly large and complex enterprises, coupled with a shift of emphasis from the production to the realization and deployment of capital, meant the delegation of business management, concerned *inter alia* with strategic planning, investment decisions, finance, marketing and external relations, to middle manager specialists. As these activities burgeoned, so did the middle management specialisms and positions associated with them. In both cases, whilst the boundaries of managerial roles were usually circumscribed by designated areas of responsibility and lines of accountability, managerial work was characterized by some breadth and variety of activity, a degree of autonomy or choice over means if not ends, relatively generous salary and conditions, job security and the prospect of a career.

Despite periodic restructurings and occasional warnings about the impact of assorted technologies on managers' work, management structures flourished and managers' work continued to exhibit these characteristics into the 1990s: whether or not it was 'mean', management was not yet '*lean* and mean' (Gordon 1996). This did not imply that management had remained the capricious, unsystematic rule of thumb activity which Taylor had decried but, rather, that if management was systematic and efficient, it was so because of the choices made by managers themselves: management had not been subjected to serious external rationalization. Gradually, however, evidence began to emerge that de-layering of middle management was being accompanied by de-skilling of the middle manager role (Cascio 1993, Delbridge et al. 2000, Ehrensal 1995, Newell and Dopson 1996, Scarbrough 1998, Vouzas et al. 1997).

More recent evidence (Hassard et al. 2009) shows that, despite some inter-country differences, middle management work in the UK, US and Japan has been subject to work intensification and reduced job security and career prospects as corporations have, to the accompaniment of a rhetoric of unavoidable, ubiquitous change, taken to continuous de-layering in order to reduce costs in response to pressure from competition and financial markets. The resulting winnowed cadre of middle managers are subjected to more targets and pressure to perform, are offered fewer career opportunities and less job security and endure increased workloads, longer working hours and more stress. Equally, much managerial work has been routinized, stripped of its discretionary and judgemental elements, programmed by software systems through which much of this work is conducted, and subjected to 'speed-up' in the form of increased responsibilities and tighter deadlines, even if it has not yet been subject to the more extreme forms of de-skilling. Whilst *qua* managers, middle managers remain the agents of work rationalization, as the managed they have themselves become the target of rationalization. In short, the rationalizers are themselves being rationalized. Recent changes to the role of first-line manager reflect the way that middle management has been increasingly rationalized. The apparently indispensable first-line manager role has become the attractor around which additional responsibilities arising from a re-division of managerial labour have coalesced (Hales 2005, 2007). Consequently, some first-line managers have acquired management and HR responsibilities that were previously the province of middle management as perceived external pressures to reduce costs whilst satisfying more demanding customers/clients has intersected with a reduced number of middle managers to handle these pressures. Thus, in some organizations, there is more 'middle management' work to be done than there are surviving middle managers to do it, and these tasks, if not the authority to execute them, have fallen to first-line managers.

## Conclusion

Despite being redolent of a more robust, mechanical era, Taylor's principles continue to leave their mark on the body of management thought and practice. They have been the stem cell from which have grown the continuing applications and elaborations of rationalized work grounded in systematic methods, specialization and centralized control, with their concomitants of work fragmentation, de-skilling, automation, piece rates and contingent employment. Today the iPad is just as much a product of an extended application of Taylor's basic methods at FoxConn's Chengdu plant as the Model T was at Ford's River Rouge plant – and with similar consequences. Because of the perceived undesirability of some of those consequences, Taylor's principles also continue to be seen as the pathogen, giving rise to de-humanized work, inflexible workers and work systems and over-centralized decision-making with their concomitants of low quality of working life, poor work–life balance, wasted talent and potential contribution and an absence of worker commitment, responsibility and initiative. Consequently, much of the ongoing concern with re-skilling and 'empowering' individual workers and work teams, giving employees more say in organizational decision-making, making jobs and employment more flexible and widening and strengthening the mutual obligations entailed in employment is, wittingly or unwittingly, the search for cures to Taylorism or, if not cures, palliatives. The work–life balance initiatives of modern human resource teams are no less a reaction to Taylor than were human relations programmes of the old personnel departments.

Neither have those who were the primary beneficiaries of Taylor's principles – managers – been immune. At the outset, these principles were proposed and adopted as the remedy to capricious, inefficient or abdicated management by creating a cadre of professional managers with a clear function to perform and the means to perform it. However, the remedy has proved injurious, if not fatal, for these managers' successors as they have become increasingly subject to rationalization and centralized control of management processes, fragmentation, de-skilling, standardization and technicization of managerial work, payment by results and contingent employment. The occupation which Taylor charged with rationalizing work is itself, especially in its middle levels, being rationalized and, in turn, being offered similar palliatives for the effects.

Few occupations or spheres of work, with the exception of senior management, have been untouched by Taylor's ideas as stem cell, pathogen or fatal remedy.

## References

Anthony, P.D. 1977. *The Ideology of Work*. London: Tavistock.

Argyris, C. 1964. *Integrating the Individual and the Organization*. New York: Wiley.

Babbage, C. 1832. *On the Economy of Machinery and Manufacture*. London: Charles Knight.

Bendix, R. 1963. *Work and Authority in Industry*. New York: Harper.

Beynon, H. 1973. *Working for Ford*. Harmondsworth: Penguin.

Beynon, H. and Nichols, T. 2006. *The Fordism of Ford and Modern Management*. London: Edward Elgar.

Beynon, H., Grimshaw, D., Rubery, J. and Ward, K. 2002. *Managing Employment Change*. Oxford: Oxford University Press.

Blauner, R. 1964. *Alienation and Freedom: The Factory Worker and his Industry*. Chicago: University of Chicago Press.

Braverman, H. 1974. *Labor and Monopoly Capital*. New York: Monthly Review Press.

Bryson, A., Pendleton, A. and Whitfield, K. 2008. *The Changing Use of Contingent Pay at the Modern British Workplace*. NIESR Discussion Paper 319. London: National Institute of Economic and Social Research.

Buchanan, D. 1994. Principles and practice in work design, in *Personnel Management*, edited by K. Sisson. 2nd edn. Oxford: Blackwell, 85–116.

Burchell, B., Lapido, D. and Wilkinson, D. 2002. *Job Insecurity and Work Intensification*. London: Routledge.

Callaghan, G. and Thompson, P. 2001. Edwards revisited: technical control and call centres. *Economic and Industrial Democracy*, 22(1), 13–37.

Cascio, W.F. 1993. Downsizing: what do we know? What have we learned? *Academy of Management Executive*, 7(1), 95–104.

Davis, L.E. and Cherns, A.B. (eds). 1975. *The Quality of Working Life*, vol. I, *Problems, Prospects and the State of the Art*. New York: Free Press.

Davis, L.E., Canter, R.R. and Hoffman, J. 1972. Current job design criteria, in *Design of Jobs*, edited by L.E. Davis and J.C. Taylor. Harmondsworth: Penguin, 65–82.

Delbridge, R., Lowe, J. and Oliver, N. 2000. Shopfloor responsibilities under lean teamworking. *Human Relations*, 53(11), 1459–88.

Du Gay, P. and Salaman, G. 1992. The culture of the customer. *Journal of Management Studies*, 29(5), 615–33.

Ehrensahl, K.N. 1995. Discourses of global competition: obscuring the changing labour process of managerial work. *Journal of Organizational Change Management*, 8(5), 5–16.

Elizur, D. and Shye, S. 1990. Quality of work life and its relation to quality of life. *Applied Psychology: An International Review*, 39(3), 275–91.

Enteman, W.F. 1993. *Managerialism: The Emergence of a New Ideology*. Madison: University of Wisconsin Press.

Esland, G. 1980. Professions and professionalism, in *The Politics of Work and Occupations*, edited by G. Esland and G. Salaman. Milton Keynes: Open University Press, 213–50.

Faunce, W.A. and Dubin, R. 1975. Individual investment in working and living, in *The Quality of Working Life*, vol. I, *Problems, Prospects and the State of the Art*, edited by L.E. Davis and A.B. Cherns, 299–316.

Folkard, S. 1987. Circadian rhythms and hours of work, in *Psychology at Work*, edited by P. Warr. 3rd edn. Harmondsworth: Penguin, 30–52.

Fuller, L. 1991. Consumers' reports: management by customers in a changing economy. *Work, Employment and Society*, 5(1), 5–16.

Gantt, H. 1919. *Organizing for Work*. New York: Harcourt Brace Jovanovich.

Gartman, D. 1979. Origins of the assembly line and capitalist control of work at Ford, in *Case Studies on the Labor Process*, edited by A. Zimbalist. New York: Monthly Review Press, 193–205.

Gilbreth, F. 1911. *Motion Study*. New York: Van Nostrand Reinholt.

Gordon, D. 1996. *Fat and Mean: The Corporate Squeeze of Working Americans and the Myth of Managerial Downsizing*. New York: Free Press.

Hackman, J.R. and Oldham, G.R. 1980. *Work Redesign*. Reading MA: Addison-Wesley.

Hackman, J.R., Oldham, G.R., Janson, R. and Purdy, K. 1975. A new strategy for job enrichment. *California Management Review*, 17(4), 57–71.

Hales, C. 2000. Management and empowerment programmes. *Work, Employment and Society*, 14(3), 501–19.

Hales, C. 2001. *Managing Through Organisation*. 2nd rev. edn. London: Thomson Learning Business Press.

Hales, C. 2005. Rooted in supervision, branching into management: continuity and change in the role of first-line manager. *Journal of Management Studies*, 42(3), 471–506.

Hales, C. 2007. Moving down the line? The shifting boundary between middle and first-line management. *Journal of General Management*, 32(2), 31–55.

Hales, M. 1980. *Living Thinkwork: Where Do Labour Processes Come From?* London: CSE Books.

Hammer, M. and Champy, J. 1995. *Re-Engineering the Corporation*. Rev. edn. London: Nicholas Brearley.

Hassard, J., McCann, L. and Morris, J. 2009. *Managing in the Modern Corporation: The Intensification of Managerial Work in the USA, UK and Japan*. Cambridge: Cambridge University Press.

Herzberg, F. 1966. *Work and the Nature of Man*. Cleveland OH: World Publishing.

Hill, S. 1981. *Competition and Control at Work*. London: Heinemann.

Hochschild, A. 1983. *The Managed Heart*. Berkeley: University of California Press.

Hofstede, G. 1979. Humanization of work: the role of values in a third industrial revolution, in *The Quality of Working Life in Western and Eastern Europe*, edited by C.L. Cooper and E. Mumford. London: Associated Business Press, 18–37.

Jacques, R. 1996. *Manufacturing the Employee*. London: Sage.

Kanawaty, G. 1992. *Introduction to Work Study*. Geneva: ILO.

Kelly, J.E. 1982. *Scientific Management, Job Redesign and Work Performance*. London: Academic Press.

Littler, C.R. 1982. *The Development of the Labour Process in Capitalist Societies*. London: Heinemann.

McKinlay, A. and Starkey, K. (eds). 1998. *Foucault, Management and Organization Theory*. London: Sage.

Marglin, S.A. 1976. What do bosses do? The origins and functions of hierarchy in capitalist production, in *The Division of Labour*, edited by A. Gorz. Brighton: Harvester, 13–54.

Maslow, A.H. 1970. *Motivation and Personality*. 2nd edn. New York: Harper & Row.

Mayo, E. 1933. *The Human Problems of an Industrial Civilization*. New York: Viking Press.

Merkle, J. 1980. *Management and Ideology: The Legacy of the International Scientific Management Movement*. Berkeley: University of California Press.

Milkman, R. 1998. The new American workplace: high road or low road?, in *Workplaces of the Future*, edited by P. Thompson and C. Warhurst. Basingstoke: Macmillan, 25–39.

Miller, E.J. and Rice, A.K. 1967. *Systems of Organization: The Control of Task and Sentient Boundaries*. London: Tavistock.

Newell, H. and Dopson, S. 1996. Muddle in the middle: organizational restructuring and middle management careers. *Personnel Review*, 25(4), 4–20.

Palmer, B. 1975. Class, conception and conflict: the thrust for efficiency, managerial views of labour and the working class rebellion 1903–1922. *Review of Radical Political Economy*, 7(2), 31–49.

Ritzer, G. 1996. *The McDonaldization of Society*. Rev. edn. Thousand Oaks CA: Pine Forge.

Roethlisberger, F.J. and Dixon, W.J. 1939. *Management and the Worker*. Cambridge MA: Harvard University Press.

Rose, M. 1988. *Industrial Behaviour: Theoretical Developments since Taylor*. 2nd edn. Harmondsworth: Penguin.

Scarbrough, H. 1998. The unmaking of management? Change and continuity in British management in the 1990s. *Human Relations*, 51(6), 691–716.

Schein, E.H. 1979. *Organizational Psychology*. 3rd edn. Englewood Cliffs NJ: Prentice-Hall.

Sheldrake, J. 2000. *Management Theory. From Taylorism to Japanization*. London: Thomson.

Smith, T. 2000. *Technology and Capital in the Age of Lean Production*. Albany NY: SUNY Press.

Stark, D. 1980. Class struggle and the transformation of the labour process: a relational approach. *Theory and Society*, 9(1), 89–130.

Stone, K. 1974. The origins of job structures in the steel industry. *Review of Radical Political Economics*, 6(2), 113–73.

Taylor, F.W. 1911. *The Principles of Scientific Management*. New York: Harper & Row.

Taylor, F.W. 1903. *Shop Management*. New York: Harper & Row.

Taylor, F.W. 1912. Testimony to the House of Representatives Committee, in *The Principles of Scientific Management*. New York: Harper & Row.

Taylor, J.C. 1979. Job design criteria twenty years later, in *Design of Jobs*, edited by L.E. Davis and J.C. Taylor. 2nd edn. Santa Monica CA: Goodyear, 54–63.

Taylor, S. 1998. Emotional labour and the new workplace, in *Workplaces of the Future*, edited by P. Thompson and C. Warhurst. Basingstoke: Macmillan, 84–103.

Terkel, S. 1973. *Working*. Harmondsworth: Penguin.

Thompson, P. 1983. *The Nature of Work: An Introduction to Debates on the Labour Process*. London: Macmillan.

Tillett, A., Kempner, T. and Wills, G. (eds). 1970. *Management Thinkers*. Harmondsworth: Penguin.

Vouzas, F., Burgoyne, J.G. and Livian, Y.-F. 1997. Trends in European middle management: evidence from five countries, in *Middle Managers in Europe*, edited by Y.-F. Livian and J.G. Burgoyne. London: Routledge, 53–77.

Warhurst, C. and Thompson, P. 1998. Hand, heart and minds: changing work and workers at the end of the century, in *Workplaces of the Future*, edited by P. Thompson and C. Warhurst. Basingstoke: Macmillan, 1–24.

Warner, W.L. and Low, J.O. 1947. *The Social System of the Modern Factory*. Newhaven CT: Tale University Press.

Wilkinson, A. 1998. Empowerment: theory and practice. *Personnel Review*, 27(1), 40–56.

Wood, S. 1989. The transformation of work?, in *The Transformation of Work? Skill, Deskilling and the Labour Process*, edited by S. Wood. London: Hutchinson, 1–43.

Wood, S. (ed.). 1983. *The Degradation of Work? Skill, Deskilling and the Labour Process*. London: Hutchinson.

Wood, S. and Kelly, J. 1983. Taylorism, responsible autonomy and management strategy, in *The Degradation of Work? Skill, Deskilling and the Labour Process*, edited by S. Wood. London: Hutchinson, 74–89.

Wren, D. 2004. *The Evolution of Management Thought*. Chichester: Wiley.

# 3

# The Influence of Taylor on UK Business and Management Education

*Huw Morris*

## Introduction

The influence of Frederick Winslow Taylor on business and management education in the US and the UK has been profound and enduring. However, the history of this influence and its effects on business and management practice reveals significant differences between these two countries. There are differences in the scale of impact and the timing of these changes as well as variations in the methods through which Taylorist ideas were introduced in workplaces. This chapter considers these differences and reviews a number of strands in the story of Taylorism in the US and UK from the early 1900s to the present day. In pursuit of these objectives, this chapter builds on the outline of the five principles of Taylorism provided by Colin Hales in Chapter 2. The main focus of the chapter is the following three questions. First, what impact did Taylor's own early education and work experiences have on the development of the ideas underpinning what was initially called Scientific Management and later became known as Taylorism? Second, how did Taylorism spread within and between workplaces in the US? Third, how did the same ideas and practices spread in the UK? Having considered each of these questions in separate sub-sections the chapter concludes by commenting on how similarities and differences in the fortunes of Taylorism in the US and UK may have affected contemporary management practices in the two countries.

## Taylor's Life and Early Career

Taylor began his career as an apprentice pattern maker and machinist in Philadelphia at the Enterprise Hydraulics Works, also known as Ferrell &

Jones, in 1874. Taylor later described the informal and disorganized form of his apprenticeship in the following terms: 'We always used to say, "I'm picking up a trade"' (Kanigel 1997: 137). As he explained, he and his fellow apprentices literally picked up a trade by '[looking] at this fellow and that fellow to see what they [were] doing' (ibid). This experience was not untypical; several books from the period describe similarly disorganized approaches to the education and training of young apprentices (Rorabaugh 1988). This was, however, in marked contrast to the more organized and orderly apprenticeship systems which had operated in the UK and much of continental Europe, at least among established trades, for several centuries.

The lack of organization in the development of technical skills at Ferrell & Jones was something of a shock for Taylor. He came from a wealthy family and had grown used to a more orderly and rigorous approach to learning. The shock was all the more profound because Taylor and his family had thought that he would study law at Harvard University. It was only when his eyesight began to fail him towards the end of his studies at school that he decided to take up an apprenticeship rather than to accept the place he had been offered at university.

Taylor enjoyed his time as an apprentice and felt that he had gained a great deal from the experience. As he later wrote, the practical skills and understanding of work colleagues which can be gained from vocationally orientated courses and apprenticeships bring with them benefits which it would be difficult to provide through classroom-based teaching. In an essay he wrote in 1908 entitled 'Why manufacturers dislike college students', he observed that 'college-educated engineers were so spoiled by interesting studies, by the sheer pleasure of learning, [and] by their college freedoms, that shop life almost always disappoint[ed] them' (Kanigel 1997: 138–9).

The emphasis that Taylor placed on his early technical education is not to say that he did not also value higher education. In his late twenties Taylor completed a degree in mechanical engineering by correspondence course at Stevens Institute of Technology (Nelson 1992). His enrolment followed in the wake of the rapid increase in the number of universities in the US after the Morrill Act of 1862. This legislation and a similar law passed in 1890 provided land grants in each state of the US for one or more new higher education institutions focused on developing agricultural, technical and research skills. Following the foundation of these colleges and universities, the number of students expanded steadily and by 1900 two per cent of the US population had completed a college- or university-based higher education.

Having completed his apprenticeship at Ferrell & Jones, Taylor moved to become a machine shop labourer and then a machinist at the Midvale Steel Works. Over the next ten years he was promoted rapidly to positions as gang boss, machine shop foreman, research director and finally chief engineer. This experience and his subsequent work as a freelance consulting engineer between 1890 and 1898 and as a manager at the Bethlehem Steel Works between 1898 and 1900 provided the raw material for his first paper on piece rate systems and his first book, *Shop Management* (Taylor 1895, 1904). In 1901, Taylor set up as a consultant again, and over the next fourteen years he and his associates introduced 'scientific management' in 181 factories and other large commercial organizations (Nelson 1992). Over this period, Taylor and his colleagues developed and described the practices which would become known as 'shop management' and then 'scientific management' and ultimately 'Taylorism'.

Members of Taylor's entourage and the growing scientific management movement included industrialists like James Dodge, as well as the consultants Carl Barth, Morris Cooke, Frank Gilbreth, H.K. Hathaway, Robert Kent, Conrad Lauer and Dwight Merrick (Urwick 1949). Many of these individuals, like Taylor, had served apprenticeships and worked their way up into management positions within one or more companies, many of them aided by subsequent study at one of the growing number of universities and colleges. The experiences of these individuals in large industrial concerns formed the basis for the talks, papers and books that they produced. This combination of a number of colleagues writing up established practice, developing new ways of working and consulting with other companies meant that Taylorism had many sources and contributors. As Lyndall Urwick, the most influential champion of Taylorism in the UK, commented in the late 1940s:

> *'scientific management' [Taylorism] was not an invention, a new idea which occurred suddenly to the fertile brains of F.W. Taylor and his colleagues. It was merely the codification and restatement in coherent and logical form of the essence of a host of practices which had been developing in the best managed factories over a very long period.*
> *(Urwick 1949: 77)*

## The Spread of Taylorism in the US

In the US the writings of Taylor and many of his colleagues were initially popularized by the American Society of Mechanical Engineers (ASME). The ASME was founded in 1880 to promote the art, science and practice of mechanical engineering and the allied arts and sciences (Sinclair 1980). In pursuit of this aim the 80 or so founding members committed themselves to the collection and diffusion of existing knowledge about mechanical engineering as well as encouraging their colleagues to get to know one another and to engage in study visits in the US and occasionally overseas. Indeed, in the early 1900s, Taylor and his colleagues visited Birmingham in the UK to share their experiences and engage in debate about the research they had completed in the US.

Informal and loosely structured forms of learning, like those provided by the ASME, were a common feature of occupational organizations and professional associations at the end of the nineteenth century on both sides of the Atlantic. Samuel Smiles demonstrated in the 1850s through his description of the lives of famous engineers and innovators that they were all highly motivated learners and entrepreneurs who sought information from colleagues working on similar issues in other organizations. Smiles used these written histories, with their emphasis on the importance of the oral tradition in passing on innovations, to call on young apprentices and engineers to engage in their own self-help through meetings and discussions with others (Smiles 2008). It is a mark of the popularity of this form of self-improvement that by the time Taylor published *Shop Management* in 1904 Samuel Smiles' book *Self-Help* had already sold 250,000 copies in the UK and US.

By 1910, the ASME had begun to concentrate on manufacturing and production engineering issues. This narrowing focus of its activities prompted the formation by Taylor and his colleagues of the Society to Promote the Science of Management (SPSM) in 1912. After Taylor's death in 1915 this organization was renamed the Taylor Society in recognition of his pivotal role in the scientific management movement (Brown 1925).

The roots of Taylorism in informal exchanges between advocates of a more systematic approach to management were supported by the development of professional associations like the ASME, SPSM and Taylor Society. However, it was the development of university-based business schools in the US at the end of the nineteenth century and beginning of the twentieth century which provided the test bed and nursery within which the principles of Taylorism could be further developed, formalized and passed on to prospective and practising managers. As Daniel Nelson notes, the growing number of business and management lecturers and professors in the newly founded colleges and universities in the US were:

*intrigued by time study, wage incentives, cost accounting, and other features of Taylor's work, but especially by the idea that management techniques were the building blocks of a larger edifice, a body of theory applicable to any institution. [P]rofessors of business and engineering found scientific management highly useful. In the decade after Taylor's death [in 1915], they made it a notable feature of the practical curriculum. By 1930 they rivalled the consultants as promoters of scientific management. As the role of the university in business and society continued to grow, they became the leading interpreters of Taylor's legacy. (Nelson 1992: 118)*

The direct exposure of scientific management thinking to university students, as well as the broader commercial interest promoted by the ASME, Taylor Society and consultancy firms, helped to spread awareness of these techniques. Between 1904 (the date of the publication of Taylor's *Shop Management*) and 1920, the teaching of scientific management techniques became an element of the business and management curriculum at a range of US universities beginning with the elite schools at Harvard and Wharton on the East Coast and spreading through a range of technical schools like Carnegie, Drexell, Purdue and MIT to schools in the South and West, as indicated in Table 3.1 (see page 32).

The appetite of students for information about scientific management was satisfied by established tenured university academics – people like Harlow Parson (Dean at the Amos Tuck School of Administration and Finance at Dartmouth College) who placed a heavy emphasis on accounting and statistics and who ensured that the students' last year included work in the principles of scientific management, scientific management in distribution and scientific management in manufacturing (Pierson 1959. 42). Others influential in taking the message into universities included Carl Barth who delivered lectures on scientific management at Harvard Business School between 1911 and 1916 as well as at the University of Chicago between 1919 and 1923. Indeed, Taylor himself lectured at Harvard Business School occasionally, while another of his associates, Hathaway, taught regularly at Stanford University (Merkle 1980).

Although early interest in scientific management at the new university business and engineering schools in the US helped lay the foundations for the take-up of this technique in businesses, it was the Eastern rate case hearing before the Interstate Commerce Commission in Washington in 1912, and subsequent evidence given by Taylor to a Congressional Committee examining scientific management, which created the press coverage and public interest

Table 3.1    Introduction of management courses in selected American universities (1899–1932)

| Institution | Engineering | Business | Scientific Management | Personnel Management |
|---|---|---|---|---|
| Penn State | 1906 | *** | 1908 | 1915 |
| Cornell | 1905 | * | 1914 | 1920 |
| Purdue | 1908 | * | 1919 | 1932 |
| Carnegie | 1908 | * | 1910 | 1919 |
| MIT | 1899 | * | 1915 | 1920 |
| Drexel | 1919 | * | 1919 | 1926 |
| Harvard | 1914** | 1908 | 1908 | 1919 |
| Dartmouth | 1918 | 1904 | 1911 | 1915 |
| Chicago | * | 1913 | 1915 | 1916 |
| Ohio State | *** | 1911 | 1913 | 1923 |
| Wisconsin | 1909 | 1915 | 1910 | 1918 |
| Michigan | 1914 | 1914 | 1916 | 1918 |
| Iowa | 1905 | 1915 | 1915 | 1921 |
| Pennsylvania | *** | 1901 | 1914 | 1919 |
| NYU | 1914 | 1903 | 1915 | 1916 |
| Northwestern | * | 1908 | 1913 | 1912 |
| Pittsburgh | 1920 | 1911 | 1911 | 1920 |
| California | * | 1913 | 1918 | 1921 |
| Washington | 1924 | 1917 | 1917 | 1917 |
| North Car. | 1921 | 1919 | 1919 | 1921 |
| Vanderbilt | 1921 | 1919 | 1920 | * |

Source: adapted from Nelson, 1992: 83.

Notes: * inappropriate or unavailable, ** cooperative programme with MIT, *** cross-listed courses.

which fuelled greater commercial and industrial interest in these methods (Taylor 1911, Cooke 1914). The implementation of these methods was then taken up and led by a number of business consultancy firms.

According to Steven Kreis, Charles Bedaux was the most successful consultant following in the Taylorite tradition (Kreis 1992). Between 1918 and 1934 staff from Bedaux's company oversaw the introduction of his system of work study in over 230 large companies in the US. However, this is not to say that the take-up was quick. Dean Gay, head of the Graduate School of Business and Administration at Harvard University, estimated in 1910 that it would take two generations for the principles of Taylor's scientific management to be generally accepted and the methods widely adopted in any area of industrial activity in the US (Cooke 1914: 482). The expansion of university education, business school activity and the growing use of consultants in the inter-war period helped to ensure this steady progress did take place.

The importance of university business schools to the teaching of prospective and practising managers increased steadily after 1920 (Pierson 1959, AACSB 2011). Between the end of World War I in 1918 and the involvement of the US in World War II in 1940, almost every public university established a school of business (Khurana 2007). However, the content and quality of the courses on offer in these establishments and the extent to which there was formal provision for the teaching of scientific management varied. This variation in content and quality gave rise to repeated criticism by commentators and reviewers from other university disciplines and subject areas (Marshall 1928, Bossard and Dewhurst 1931, Gordon and Howell 1959, Pierson 1959). The Carnegie and Ford reports on business and management education in the late 1950s suggested that many of the junior colleges, extension programmes and four-year programmes on offer at state and other universities provided an education which was over-reliant on practising managers as educators and too close to the interests of business and the professions (Gordon and Howell 1959, Pierson 1959). As these studies sought to demonstrate, the business and management content of a four-year degree varied enormously from institution to institution. The range of courses on offer included what is now familiar in the form of accounting, economics and marketing, as well as what now might seem unusual, such as business letter writing, rates and regulation, salesmanship, transportation systems and rhetoric and themes (Pierson 1959: 43–4).

There was slightly greater coherence in the curriculum content of the growing number of MBA-providing institutions. Here the taught curriculum of these postgraduate awards was not untypically split between courses in business techniques (such as accounting and statistics); courses dealing with business operations and management (for example finance and marketing) and courses specializing in types of business (such as banking and transportation) (Aaronson 1992, Datar et al. 2010). This greater consistency was helped by the formation of a range of higher education regulatory bodies. These bodies included accreditation agencies like the Association of American Collegiate Schools of Business (AACSB) which was formed in 1916 by 17 leading US business schools and which in 1925 issued a list of the subjects which it would expect to see in a business degree, including accounting, statistics, business law, finance and marketing (Irwin 1966). This list was then expanded over the next fifty years to include organizational behaviour, international management, information systems and ethics, among other areas (Flesher 2007). Other bodies promoting the gradual standardization of faculty development in US business schools included the American Academy of Management, founded in 1936, as well as a number of other specialist research and scholarly societies in the field of business and management. As these groups developed and increased their influence through regulation and involvement in faculty education and training, explicit prescriptive reference to scientific management became less evident in business school curricula.

Inside universities, critiques of Taylorism became a more central focus of business school teaching in the US after the Hawthorne studies in the 1930s (Roethlisberger and Dickson 1939). From this point on, a new generation of social scientists with an interest in business and management issues popularized complex views of human motivation which challenged the economic and managerialist assumptions that underpinned Taylorism. As these assumptions began to change, they had significant consequences for the forms of job design, payment system, selection methods, management roles and approaches to planning advocated by business school researchers (Khurana 2007). With this change the following five patterns of management practice began to receive more attention from researchers: (i) group and team working, as well as schemes of job rotation, enlargement and enrichment; (ii) systems of measured day work payments and other hybrid combinations of time and performance-based pay; (iii) processes of employee selection, induction and development which emphasize the psychometric profile of employees and their socialization into the workplace, as well as their technical skills; (iv) employee and team self-management supported by centrally located functional specialists and external consultants; (v) shop floor continuous improvement processes in addition to central work planning. The researchers and movements which promoted these new approaches adopted or were ascribed the following names and labels: human relations, socio-technical systems, quality of work life, excellence, total quality management, lean production and business process re-engineering, among many others (Mayo 1933, Cummings and Molloy 1977, Peters and Waterman 1982, Juran 1989, Womack et al. 1990, Hammer and Champy 1993).

For many business commentators these new approaches marked a significant shift in management thinking, towards more humane and socially sensitive practice (Adler 1993). For others, these changes offered little more than a change in the terminology; the underlining capitalist rationale of increasing profits while reducing the costs of staff and equipment remained unchanged (Wilkinson and Willmott 1994). The form may have changed, but the processes remained unaltered as Taylorism was replaced by Neo-Taylorism (Boje and Winsor 2007). For yet another group, there was nothing inevitable about the effects of these changes. These new practices could temper some of the pressures revealed by traditional Taylorist methods by offering the possibility of greater job satisfaction while also providing for employer-encouraged innovation by workers (Jones 2000, Peaucelle 2000, Lomba 2005). Yet another perspective was provided by Michael Roper who argued that the shift from the practitioner-based management teaching advocated by Taylor towards business education informed by applied social science research was paradigmatic and reflected inter-generational rivalry and conflict between new and established members of faculty and reflected the incorporation of business schools within the broader university academic tradition (Roper 1999).

## The Spread of Taylorism in the UK

The publication of Taylor's books in Europe, Japan and Russia helped to spread the popularity of the management techniques he championed outside the US. The champions of these initiatives included Henri Le Chatelier and managers at the Michelin factories in France, Professor Georg Schlesinger and the Association of German Engineers in Germany, and Koichi Kanda in Japan (Kreis 1995, Kipping 1997). In the UK, business people in general and academics in particular were less easily persuaded of the merits of scientific management and as a consequence the take-up of these techniques relied more heavily on the work of a few prominent management consultancies and professional bodies interested in promoting Taylorism (Brech et al. 2010).

Many business owners, managers and engineers in the UK were aware of the contents of Taylor's *Shop Management* and the *Principles of Scientific Management* shortly after their publication (Whitson 1995, 1997, Brech 2002). However, leading industrialists, their suppliers and competitors were slow to introduce these techniques (Littler 1982, Locke 1984). This hesitance reflected the constraints imposed by the nature of the markets, industries and organizations within which these owners and managers worked, as well the established power and influence of craftsmen and their trade unions (Hoxie 1916). As Brech has demonstrated, British companies at the end of the nineteenth century and beginning of the twentieth century were predominantly small in size, reliant on batch production and overseen by self-taught owner managers (Brech 2002). Among the more paternalist of these employers the constraints preventing the adoption of Taylorism extended to include concern about the consequences of these forms of work organization for employee job satisfaction and morale. As Edward Cadbury indicated in his review of Taylor's principles of scientific management in an article for the *Sociological Review* in 1914:

> *The most important question of all is the effect of [scientific management] upon the personality and character of the worker ... one has to admit the justice of the criticisms of unskilled labour in its effect on personality and character. The work is monotonous and depressing, the sub-division of processes being carried to such an extent that there is a narrowing of interest, and automatic machinery almost eliminates any demand for initiative and adaptation ... Therefore any further sub-division of labour in the direction of eliminating any little judgement initiative as to methods of work, valuable as it might be in its immediate impact on production, would almost certainly in the long run produce effects which would lower the whole capacity of the worker. (Cadbury 1914: 105)*

In the face of this indifference, if not on occasion hostility, it fell to people like Lyndall Urwick to champion scientific management in the UK individually and to work with colleagues in business and professional associations to promote the case for this approach nationally.

Lyndall Urwick read Taylor's *Shop Management* in 1915 while an officer on the front line in France. After the First World War he began to work at the Rowntree factory in York and with others began to implement elements of Taylor's scientific management (Brech et al. 2010). As Urwick later described it, 'the Cocoa works at York in the early 1920s was a kind of practical university of management' (Urwick 1949: 38). Rowntree established a reputation as a progressive employer and set a standard for much business and management education at the time through its staff journal, its annual Oxford management conference at Balliol College and research-informed innovations to products, production and back office activities. These practices were further complemented by the creation in 1927 of management research groups which brought together managers from several firms in secret to exchange experiences and to learn from experience of change and development in each organization. The first of these groups brought together Rowntree, Dunlop Rubber and British Xylonite and spurred the creation of a further seven groups over the next three years.

Initial assessments of the take-up and popularity of shop management, scientific management and Taylorism in the UK tended to emphasize the lack of management, engineering and worker interest in these techniques, and the consequent low level of take-up of these new practices (Urwick and Brech 1947, Littler 1978). More recent studies have suggested that interest in scientific management and knowledge of these techniques was much more widespread than initially thought (Whitson 1995, Brech 2002). Indeed, detailed reviews of the contents of leading engineering magazines and newsletters from the early twentieth century have revealed that Taylor's papers were published in the UK shortly after they had first been presented and printed in the US (Whitson 1997). Meanwhile, interest in these methods in senior business and political circles was clearly evident. For example, in 1920 a recently formed organization of business people, the Industrial League and Council, arranged for Frank Gilbreth (one of Taylor's main disciples) to address a meeting at the House of Commons presided over by the Deputy Speaker of the House (Brech 2002: 55).

Between the 1920s and 1940s the steady increase in business consultancy activity in the UK appears to have provided the real spur to the introduction and wider adoption of Taylorism in the UK. This new branch of management practice was informed by scientific management and was undertaken by what became five major firms: (1) British Bedaux Ltd (the UK subsidiary of the US Charles Bedaux and Co. Ltd which became Associated Industrial Consultants in 1939), (2) Urwick, Orr & Partners, (3) Production Engineering (PE), (4) Harold Whitehead & Staff, and (5) Personnel Administration (PA) (McKenna 2006).

The Bedaux method relied heavily on work study and payment systems and drew inspiration from the earlier work of Taylor and his colleagues in the SPSM and Taylor Society. The same was true to a lesser extent at Urwick, Orr

& Partners where Lyndall Urwick joined forces with John Orr and a number of former Bedaux consultants. Through the work of these consultancies several hundred UK companies were reviewed and had new forms of work and task organization introduced as a consequence (Brech et al. 2010).

The implementation of management techniques associated with Taylorism received a significant boost during World War II when government ministries took control of an increasing number of factories and attempted to implement work study, production planning and the more systematic training of staff (Brech 2002). This work required the training of many managers and foremen and led directly to the establishment of the Bedford Work Study School which was set up in 1941 by William Lodge, a former Urwick, Orr & Partners consultant. Further training facilities dedicated to developing work study skills were set up in Slough by Urwick Orr in 1946 (Ferguson 2002).

Alongside the growth in management consulting to support the introduction of Taylorism in the UK, there was a steady increase in the number of professional associations with an interest in time, motion, method and work study as indicated in Table 3.2 opposite.

The Institute of Estimators, Planning and Time Study Engineers, founded in 1941, was the first British professional body concerned wholly with time, motion, method and work study as a means of increasing productivity. Over the course of the next forty years the Institute changed its name on nine occasions and combined with two other associations before becoming the Institute of Management Services in 1978. These changes of name reflected shifts in the focus of these organizations and their members, from time and motion study to work study and on to broader interest in productivity and quality assurance and management.

According to Kevin Whitson, the use of work study grew in the UK after World War II, reaching a peak of influence at the end of the 1960s. At the same time, a plethora of new management tools found other means to continue Taylor's work. Time study became one technique among many other forms of work study, workflow and process mapping. Payment systems, selection methods, management structures and planning operations proliferated and became more varied and complex so that Taylorism was effectively now one element of management practice which had long since developed beyond the point at which Taylor left it, but which rested on foundations he had laid (Whitson 1995).

Table 3.2     Professional associations specializing in time, motion and work study in the UK (1940–80)

| Year | Organization | | |
|------|------|------|------|
| 1941 | Institute of Estimators, Planning and Time Study Engineers | | |
| 1942 | Institute of Economic Engineering | | |
| 1944 | | Motion Study Society | |
| 1945 | | | Institute of Industrial Technicians |
| 1946 | Institute of Economic Engineering merges with the Production Control Research Group | | |
| 1953 | Society of Industrial Engineers | | |
| 1954 | | Work Study Society | |
| 1958 | Work Study Society (Society Industrial Engineers and Work Study Society) | | |
| 1960 | Institute of Work Study | | Institute of Incorporated Work Study Technologists |
| 1964 | Institute of Work Study Practitioners (Institute of Work Study and Incorporated Work Study Technologists) | | |
| 1975 | Institute of Practitioners in Work Study, Organisation and Methods (following merger with the Organisation and Methods Society) | | |
| 1978 | Institute of Management Services | | |

*Source*: Whitson 1995: 276 and IMS Archive, University of Warwick.

The effects of scientific management and Taylorism on management practice in the UK after 1980 is difficult to detect and comment upon. The development of new words, phrases and prescriptions for the management of work and employees, including quality of work life, total quality management, business process re-engineering and lean production, altered the terms of the debate and redefined the measures against which changes in the management of work and workers might be assessed (Gallie 2009). In the absence of comprehensive surveys using terms and measures which would enable us to assess the extent to which Taylorism had been adopted, we are forced to rely on very occasional surveys and the more frequent, but less representative case studies which have mapped these changes (Jones 1997, 2000, Glover and Noon 2005, Gallie 2005, 2009, Lloyd and Payne 2009). A common theme in these accounts is the replacement of traditional forms of Taylorism with new forms of work control. Under these arrangements there is less direct evidence of work study, narrow division of labour, piece rate payment systems, functional management and central work planning departments. Under these newer forms of work organization there is a greater reliance on work planning linked to computerized information systems, grade-related payment systems and socialization within teams and workplaces. There is also debate about whether direct interaction with customers in the service sector calls for higher levels of skill and emotional labour than the routinized arrangements evident in foundry, manufacturing or process production environments (Lloyd and Payne 2009). Meanwhile, in other parts of the world the division of labour, work intensification and anti-union motivations evident in the account of earlier critiques of Taylorism are apparent in case studies of new manufacturing environments in South East Asia and other parts of the newly industrialized world (Nichols et al. 2004).

Beyond the workplace the influence of shop management, scientific management and Taylorism on business and management education in the UK is difficult to clearly identify. British industry until the post-World War II period was made up of large numbers of small companies overseen by owner managers who had received little or no formal business or management education. As a consequence of this pattern of organization and management there was a heavy reliance on formal and informal workplace-based training and development and the parallel work of professional associations and industry bodies (Constable and McCormick 1987, Handy et al. 1988). This approach has been characterized as a professionally orientated system of business education in contrast with the university-based system evident in the US. For managers who developed their skills through the British professional-based system, qualifications studied at college or by correspondence course became progressively more important and structured during the twentieth century. The first of these professional associations in the UK was the Institute of Chartered Accountants in Scotland (ICAS) founded in 1850, followed thirty years later by the forerunner of the Chartered Institute of Accountants in England and Wales (ICAEW) in 1880 and the Chartered Institute of Public Finance and Accountancy (CIPFA) in 1885. The organization which would become the Institute of Chartered Secretaries and Administrators (ICSA) was established in 1891, followed at the beginning of the twentieth century by the Institute of Directors in 1903 and the forerunner of the Association of Chartered Certified Accountants (ACCA) in 1904. These early professional associations focused on board-level activities in companies, including finance, legal duties and obligations to shareholders. It was sometime later that the supporting functional areas of management began to become professionalized along similar lines. The forerunners of the Chartered Institute of Marketing and the Chartered Institute of Personnel and Development were established in 1913 and the forerunner of the Chartered Institute of Management Accountants (CIMA) in 1919 along with the Institute of Industrial Administration (an early attempt to establish a professional body for people in general management roles).

Few of the professional qualification syllabi adopted by accounting or management professional bodies during the 1920s and 1930s included extensive reference to the work of Taylor or the subjects and interests which he focused upon in his books (Guerriero Wilson 2011). Indeed, the first management textbook in the UK developed to support the curriculum and examinations of the Institute of Industrial Administration focused on commercial and company law, accounting and finance, statistics and principles of office organization. It made no reference to work study, payment systems, employee selection, functional management or the operation of planning departments (Elmbourne 1934).

The formation of the professional associations in key areas of business and management activity at the end of the nineteenth and beginning of the twentieth centuries ran alongside small-scale experiments with business education in at least three universities: Birmingham, Manchester and the London School of Economics. These experiments led to the establishment of a degree in commerce (BComm), new commerce departments and the appointment of professors in all three universities (Keeble 1992). By the end of the 1920s the BComm model had been adopted by 13 other universities in the UK – including Aberdeen, St Andrews, Belfast, Cardiff, Dundee, Durham, Edinburgh, Hull, Leeds, Liverpool, Nottingham, Sheffield and Southampton. The content of the BComm courses varied from place to place, but generally included subjects such as commercial law, economics, history and statistics, as well as general vocational topics including accounting, company management, works management and [hu]man management [*sic*] (Keeble 1992).

Despite the initial success of the BComm degree, employer demand for graduates declined and the interest of university academics waned in the 1930s. This decline in interest led to the closure of several of these degree courses and the non-replacement of academic staff when they retired or left. Retrospective comment on the failure of these experiments is consistent in drawing attention to the anti-intellectualism of business people and the anti-trade views of academics. In his history of the Institute of Industrial Administration, T.G. Rose illustrates the view of many business people in the first half of the twentieth century with the following quote from a speech by the Institute's first honorary director, Edward Elmbourne:

> *Out of war experience and out of other experience is the outstanding lesson that leadership is the necessary indefinable quality essential to the administrator [manager] it is something based as much on character as on knowledge, something that is not to be learned by educational courses at any university. (Rose 1954: 17–18)*

And commenting on views within universities, Lyndall Urwick made the following observation:

> *Those engaged professionally in teaching at the universities, particularly the older universities of Oxford and Cambridge which largely set the tone of the national educational life, have felt that this new field of knowledge [business and management] was too new and too unorganized to be regarded as a serious vehicle for education. This attitude has been reinforced by relics of the medieval contempt for trade based on the religious prejudice against usury. This developed into the unpleasant social snobbery characteristic of the nineteenth century. 'The best people', the gentry, did not go into business: as an occupation it was felt to be somewhat derogatory. (Urwick 1957: vii–viii)*

From the 1930s until the early 1960s formal business and management education was very limited in scale and confined to a few provincial university departments and fledgling professional bodies. It was not until after World War II that interest in larger-scale more formal business and management activity began to gather pace and gain government backing.

In 1945 Sir Stafford Cripps, President of the Board of Trade, appointed a Committee under the chairmanship of Sir Clive Baillieu, President of the Federation of British Industries (forerunner of the CBI), to formulate detailed proposals for the setting up of a central institute for all questions relating to management. The body formed as a consequence of these deliberations was originally named the British Institute of Management (BIM) and became the Chartered Management Institute in 1992. This Labour government-sponsored move to professionalize management activity in the UK met with limited success and was not actively supported by Conservative administrations in the 1950s and early 1960s.

It was not until the early 1960s that postgraduate business schools modelled, at least in part, on the leading US schools were set up (Williams 2010). The new schools, principally London and Manchester, with smaller sums of direct funding for departments at Aston, Bradford, Durham, Lancaster and Loughborough among others, adopted curricula for their programmes which focused on the established social sciences of economics, psychology and sociology, together with law and accounting, before moving on to consider the principal functional areas of management, including marketing, operations research, industrial relations and personnel management. As the number of institutions offering these courses increased over the next five decades, the scale and complexity of courses grew. With this expansion the volume of regulations governing this activity also increased.

National formats for three new college-based awards were introduced in the early 1960s, the Higher National Certificate (HNC), Higher National Diploma (HND) and the Diploma in Management Studies. The formation of the Council for National Academic Awards (CNAA) in the mid-1960s then provided the impetus for the development of a four-year BA in Business Studies degree and, over subsequent years, other specialist degrees in business and management (Morris 2010). Meanwhile, the Association of MBAs (AMBA) formed in 1967 began pushing for greater business understanding of the content and potential role of MBA qualifications.

From the mid-1960s to 2011, the number of students enrolled on undergraduate and postgraduate awards in business and management increased steadily, reaching 270,000 in 2011 (ABS 2012). On most of the courses studied by these students there was some obligatory reference to the work of Taylor in the opening sessions of organization behaviour and operations management courses, but rarely any direct tuition in work study methods, the mechanics of payment systems, functional management or the operation of work planning departments. On courses in industrial relations or employee relations, Marxian labour process accounts of Taylorism emphasized what it was suggested were the de-skilling, de-grading and anti-trade union instincts of Taylorism, drawing on examples from manufacturing firms and routinized service sector environments (Braverman 1974).

## Conclusion

The evidence presented in this chapter has demonstrated that Taylorist thought had a direct impact on management and working practices in both the US and the UK in the first half of the twentieth century. However, the scale of impact was greater and quicker in the US than in the UK. The reasons for these differences appear to be threefold. First, the rapid industrialization of the US in the second half of the nineteenth century was not constrained by established traditions of craft and guild organization and was able to develop to greater scale in larger companies and workplaces than was typically the case in the UK. Second, employers and managers in the US were more receptive to the ideas put forward by Taylor and his colleagues and less concerned about the impacts of these changes on employee work experience and morale. Third, the development of consultancy organizations and business schools in the US in the first quarter of the twentieth century supported the rapid diffusion of this new thinking among business owners and managers. In the UK it was not until the 1920s and 1930s that the consultancy industry began to establish itself. and the reliance on small professional associations of managers and work study engineers, rather than business and management schools, meant that the speed of take-up was much slower.

In the period after World War II Taylorist approaches to management became the subject of sustained critique in business schools in the US and in university social science departments in the UK. Despite this intellectual assault, the use of work study and piece rate payment systems, if not functional management and work planning departments, became more commonplace in many US and UK manufacturing firms and foundries. By the 1970s and 1980s this pattern of practice began to change. The decline in iron and steel industries and manufacturing companies in North America and Europe, the associated rise of the services sector and the promotion of other approaches to the organization of work challenged the Taylorist tradition. The quality of work life movement, total quality management, business process re-engineering and lean production built on and developed strands in Taylorist thinking, but adopted a language and method of exposition which disguised this intellectual ancestry. These new techniques were applied in the services sector as much as they were in manufacturing, but the success of these initiatives was by no means assured.

## References

AACSB (Association to Advance Collegiate Schools of Business). 2011. *Business School Data Trends and 2011 List of Accredited Schools*. Tampa FL: AACSB.

Aaronson, S. 1992. Serving America's business? Graduate business schools and American business, 1945–60. *Journal of Business History*, 34(1), 160–80.

ABS. 2012. *Data and Surveys*. [Online: Association of Business Schools.] Available at: http://www.associationofbusiness schools.co.uk [accessed 10 March 2012].

Adler, P. 1993. Time and motion regained. *Harvard Business Review*, January–February, 97–108.

Boje, D. and Winsor, R. 2007. The resurrection of Taylorism: Total Quality Management's hidden agenda. *Journal of Organizational Change Management*, 6(4), 57–70.

Bossard, J. and Dewhurst, J. 1931. *University Education for Business*. Philadelphia: University of Pennsylvania.

Braverman, H. 1974. *Labor and Monopoly Capital: The Degradation of Work in the Twentieth Century*. New York: Monthly Review Press.

Brech, E. 2002. *The Evolution of Modern Management: Productivity in Perspective, 1914–1974*. Bristol: Thoemmes.

Brech, E., Thomson, A. and Wilson, J. 2010. *Lyndall Urwick, Management Pioneer: A Biography*. Oxford: Oxford University Press.

Brown, P. 1925. The work and aims of the Taylor Society. *Annals of the American Academy of Political and Social Science*, 119(1), 134–9.

Cadbury, E. 1914. Some principles of industrial organisation: the case for and against scientific management. *Sociological Review*, 7(2), 99–117.

Constable, J. and McCormick, R. 1987. *The making of British managers*. London: British Institute of Management and Confederation of British Industry.

Cooke, M. 1914. The spirit and significance of scientific management. *Journal of Political Economy*, 21(6), 481–93.

Cummings, T. and Molloy, E. 1977. *Improving Productivity and Quality of Work Life*. Westport CT: Praeger.

Datar, S., Garvin, D. and Cullen, P. 2010. *Rethinking the MBA: Business Education at a Crossroads*. Boston MA: Harvard Business School Press.

Elmbourne, E. 1934. *Fundamentals of Industrial Administration*, vol. 1. London: MacDonald & Evans.

Ferguson, M. 2002. *The Rise of Management Consulting in Britain*, in the series *Modern Economic and Social History*. London: Ashgate.

Flesher, D. 2007. *The History of AACSB International*, vol. 2, *1966–2006*. Tampa FL: AACSB International.

Gallie, D. 2005. Work pressure in Europe 1996–2001: trends and determinants. *British Journal of Industrial Relations*, 43(3), 351–75.

Gallie, D. 2009. *Employment Regimes and the Quality of Work*. 2nd edn, Oxford: Oxford University Press.

Glover, L. and Noon, M. 2005. Shop-floor workers' responses to quality management initiatives – broadening the disciplined worker thesis. *Work, Employment and Society*, 19(4), 727–45.

Gordon, R. and Howell, J. 1959. *Higher Education for Business*. New York: Columbia University Press.

Guerriero Wilson, R. 2011. The struggle for management education in Britain: the Urwick Committee and the Office Management Association. *Management and Organizational History*, 6(4), 367–89.

Handy, C., Gordon, C., Gow, I. and Randlesome, C. 1988. *Making Managers*. London: Financial Times, Prentice Hall.

Hammer, M. and Champy, J. 1993. *Re-Engineering the Corporation*. London: Nicholas Brearley.

Hoxie, R. 1916. Scientific management and labor welfare. *Journal of Political Economy*, 24(9), 833–54.

Institute of Management Services. 2012. *Welcome to the Institute of Management Services*. [Online: Institute of Management Services.] Available at: http://www.ims-productivity.com [accessed 10 January 2012].

Irwin, R. 1966. *The American Association of Collegiate Schools of Business, 1916–1966*, Tampa FL: AACSB.

Jones, O. 1997. Changing the balance? Taylorism, TQM and work organisation. *New Technology, Work and Employment*, 12(1), 13–24.

Jones, O. 2000. Scientific management, culture and control: a first-hand account of Taylorism in practice. *Human Relations*, 53(5), 631–53.

Juran, J. 1989. *Leadership for Quality: An Executive Handbook*. New York: Free Press.

Kanigel, R. 1997. *The One Best Way: Frederick Winslow Taylor and the Enigma of Efficiency*. New York: Abacus.

Keeble, S. 1992. *The Ability to Manage: Study of British Management, 1890–1990*. Manchester: Manchester University Press.

Khurana, R. 2007. *From Higher Aims to Hired Hands: The Social Transformation of American Business Schools and the Unfulfilled Promise of Management as a Profession*. Princeton: Princeton University Press.

Kipping, M. 1997. Consultancies, institutions and the diffusion of Taylorism in Britain, Germany and France, 1920s to 1950s. *Business History*, 39(4), 67–83.

Kreis, S. 1992. The diffusion of scientific management: the Bedaux company in America and Britain, 1926–1945, in *A Mental Revolution: Scientific Management Since Taylor*, edited by D. Nelson. Columbus: Ohio State University Press.

Kreis, S. 1995. Early experiments in British scientific management: the Health of Munitions Workers Committee, 1915–1920. *Journal of Management History*, 1(2), 65–77.

Littler, C. 1978. Understanding Taylorism. *British Journal of Sociology*, 29(2), 185–202.

Littler, C. 1982. *The Development of the Labour Process in Capitalist Societies: A Comparative Study of the Transformation of Work in Britain, Japan and the USA*. London: Heinemann,

Lloyd, C. and Payne, J. 2009. 'Full of sound and fury, signifying nothing' – interrogating new skill concepts in service work – the view from two UK call centres. *Work, Employment and Society*, 23(4), 617–34.

Locke, R. 1984. *The End of Practical Man: Entrepreneurship and Higher Education in Germany, France and Great Britain*. Greenwich CT: JAI Press.

Lomba, C. 2005. Beyond the debate over 'Post' vs 'Neo' Taylorism: the contrasting evolution of industrial work practices. *International Sociology*, 29(1), 71–91.

McKenna, C. 2006. *The World's Newest Profession: Management Consulting in the Twentieth Century*, in the series *Cambridge Studies in the Emergence of Global Enterprise*. Cambridge: Cambridge University Press.

Marshall, L. 1928. *The Collegiate School of Business*. Chicago: University of Chicago Press.

Mayo, E. 1933. *The Human Problems of an Industrial Civilisation*. Cambridge MA: Harvard University Press.

Merkle, J. 1980 *Management and Ideology: The Legacy of the International Scientific Management Movement*. Los Angeles: University of California Press.

Morris, H. 2010. Business and management research in the UK from 1900 to 2009 and beyond, in *Challenges and Controversies in Management Research*, edited by B. Lee and C. Cassell. London: Routledge.

Nelson, D. 1992. Scientific Management and the transformation of university business education, in *A Mental Revolution Scientific Management since Taylor*, edited by D. Nelson. Columbus: Ohio State University Press.

Nichols, T., Cam, S., Chou, W., Chun, S., Zhao, W. and Feng, T. 2004. Factory regimes and the dismantling of established labour in Asia: a review of cases from large manufacturing plants in China, South Korea and Taiwan. *Work, Employment and Society*, 18(4), 663–85.

Peaucelle, J.-L. 2000. From Taylorism to post-Taylorism: simultaneously pursuing several management objectives. *Journal of Organizational Change Management*, 13(5), 452–67.

Peters, T. and Waterman, R. 1982. *In Search of Excellence: Lessons from America's Best Run Companies*. New York: Warner.

Pierson, F. 1959. *The Education of American Businessmen: A Study of University-College Programs in Business Administration*. New York: McGraw Hill.

Roethlisberger, F. and Dickson, W. 1939. *Management and the Worker*. Cambridge MA: Harvard University Press.

Roper, M. 1999. Killing of the father: social science and the memory of Frederick Winslow Taylor in management studies 1950–1975. *Contemporary British History*, 13(3), 39–58.

Rorabaugh, W.J. 1988. *The Craft Apprentice: From Franklin to the Machine Age in America*. New York: Oxford University Press.

Rose, T. 1954. *A History of the Institute of Industrial Administration, 1919–1951*. London: Institute of Industrial Administration.

Sinclair, B. 1980. *A Centennial History of the American Society of Mechanical Engineers, 1880–1980*. Toronto: University of Toronto Press.

Smiles, S. 2008. *Self-Help*. Oxford: Oxford University Press.

Taylor, F. 1895. A piece rate system – being a step toward partial solution of the labor problem. Paper presented to the American Society of Mechanical Engineers.

Taylor, F. 1904. *Shop Management*. Fairfield IN: First World Library, Literary Society.

Taylor, F. 1911. *The Principles of Scientific Management*. Fairfield IN: First World Library, Literary Society.

Urwick, L. 1949. *The Making of Scientific Management*. London: Management Publications Trust.

Urwick, L. 1957. Introduction, in H. Newman and D. Sidney, *Teaching Management: A Practical Handbook with Special Reference to the Case Study Method*. London: Routledge & Kegan Paul.

Urwick, L. and Brech, E. 1947. *The Making of Scientific Management*, vol. II. London: Management Publications Trust.

Whitson, K. 1995. *Scientific Management Practice in Britain, A History*. PhD thesis, Coventry: University of Warwick.

Whitson, K. 1997. The reception of scientific management by British engineers, 1890–1914. *Business History Review*, 71(2), 207–29.

Wilkinson, A. and Willmott, H. 1994. *Making Quality Critical: New Perspectives on Organizational Change*. London: International Thomson Business Press.

Williams, A. 2010. *The History of UK Business and Management Education*. Bradford: Emerald.

Womack, J. Jones, D. and Roos, D. 1990. *The Machine that Changed the World*. New York: Rawson Associates.

# 4

# Managerial Performance and the Expertise of Managing: Prescriptive, Descriptive or Ascriptive?

*Leonard Holmes*

In *The Principles of Scientific Management*, Taylor clearly sought to distinguish 'scientific management' from 'defective systems of management' (1967: 15), from 'old systems of management' (ibid.: 25), from 'ordinary management' (ibid.: 30), and so on. The purpose of the book, he states, was to 'try to convince the reader that the remedy for … inefficiency lies in systematic management …', and to 'prove that the best management is a true science …' (ibid.: 7). Elsewhere, Taylor tells his audience at a conference on Scientific Management, held in 1911 at Amos Tuck School of Administration, that the 'fallacy' that increasing output would result in increased unemployment (it 'would throw men out of work') 'lies in our own inefficient systems of management' (Taylor, 1912: 26). 'Principles', 'system', 'science', and similar terms, and the aim of 'convincing' readers, even 'proving', are all suggestive of Scientific Management lying outside and beyond individual persons.

Yet the 'system' requires such individual persons, managers, to put into effect the 'principles' specified. For 'engineers and managers … are more intimately acquainted with these facts than any other class in the community' (Taylor, 1967: 18), and so 'those in the management whose duty it is to develop this science should also guide and help the workman in working under it' (ibid.: 26). Taylor writes that whilst the 'scientific study' of a particular work task (loading pig iron onto railroad carriages) at Bethlehem Steel Company (at which Taylor had worked) had shown that 47 tons was the 'proper day's work', 'the task that faced us *as managers* under the modern scientific plan was clearly before us' (ibid.: 42, emphasis added). And under Scientific Management, he writes, 'it is the duty of the management to know what is the best, not to take what someone thinks is the best' (Taylor, 1912: 37). Clearly, Scientific Management as a system requires *managers*, a managerial labour force, individuals who engage in *managing*.

Of course, the 'story' of management over the past century has been told in various ways, largely as the 'unfolding' of ideas and practices (for example, Crainer 1999) but also more critically (for example, Diefenbach 2009). Taylor's work clearly has an important place in that history, with other key figures including, of course, Taylor's European contemporary Fayol (1949, originally published in 1916, in French). Along with that history, *managers* have been exhorted to engage in practices deemed appropriate to 'good' management, as this has been viewed at the time (or, at least, a version of what is deemed to be appropriate).

In the previous chapter, Huw Morris discussed developments in management education during the twentieth century in the UK and US, and Taylor's and other influences. Certainly by the beginning of the twenty-first century, management education has become 'big business', delivered mainly but not solely through business schools or similar faculty or departmental entities in universities, for which they represented major sources of funding in terms of student enrolment, research and 'knowledge transfer' (Association of Business Schools 2011). In addition to the provision at such institutions, management training and development activity takes place within employing organizations, by management development practitioners who may themselves employed within those organizations or may be external to them. To these may be added the large volume of articles, books, and multimedia purporting to be sources of instruction and guidance to managers and aspirants to managerial positions.

On the face of it, such management education, training and development would appear to have one overriding aim: to improve the abilities (competence, expertise) of those who occupy, or seek to occupy, managerial positions. This suggests a key question: what are the abilities, what is the expertise, that such individuals need? However, this chapter will examine a prior question: how are we to understand the nature of what we might term 'managerial expertise' (abilities, skills, competencies, etc), and it will suggest that there are different kinds of answers to that question. It appears to be an empirical question, one that can be answered by some form of observational investigation. Any answers would consist of *descriptions* of managerial expertise. Yet, for much of the writings on management, the question appears to have already been answered, for the main focus is on *prescribing* what managers should (be able to) do. In addition to such descriptive and prescriptive approaches, this chapter will suggest that we can consider a third: where expertise is *ascribed* to persons by virtue of their position *as managers*. This approach will be elaborated to show, it will be argued, how it can shed further light on the issues of managerial performance and expertise.

## Expertise: Competence and Performance

I have used the terms 'abilities' and 'expertise' so far. Other terms that have been used and are in use include 'competencies', 'capabilities' and, in education particularly, 'skills', 'knowledge' (or 'knowledge and understanding'). The terms 'competence', and 'competencies', became popular during the 1980s and 1990s, particularly following the publication of research in the US by McBer & Company (Boyatzis 1982) and a number of studies on perceived 'problems' with then-existing approaches in the UK (Silver 1991). The term 'expertise' is adopted here, as a general term, because it has not (yet) become associated with particular approaches in the way that 'competence' has.

The term 'expertise' has been associated particularly with those who would be referred to as 'professional experts' (for example, in courts of law or on special committees of inquiry, etc.) (see, for example, Selinger and Crease 2006, Ericsson 2009, Collins and Evans 2007). However, given that it is generally claimed that management is a field requiring a period of special education, training and development, as well as experience, we might well extend the term to cover this occupational area (see also Black 2005, Chipman 2006). It thus brings the claims made for management into scrutiny alongside those made for any other field of expertise, whilst avoiding the conceptual presumptions that might arise from deploying other, previously used, terms such 'effectiveness', 'competence'/ 'competency', and so on.

There is, of course, no shortage of *prescriptions* for managers, on how they should manage and, by implication or explicitly, what they should know, understand and *be able* to do, in order to manage. Those wishing to avail themselves of simple (or *simplified*) prescriptions may find a wide range in the continuing stream of the 'self-help' type of books that academics disparagingly term 'departure lounge literature'. Training courses are usually based on some assumption that those undergoing the training *need* and will benefit by learning the specified knowledge and skills. However, the basis for such prescriptions is usually based on very little sound enquiry. The study of managerial expertise, its analysis and *description* should, one would anticipate, provide better basis for *prescription*.

In general, we tend to think of expertise as (a) some quality or attribute of an individual that (b) is a necessary precursor to performance. That is, (consistently) good performance by an individual depends upon them 'having' relevant expertise. We tend to talk of an individual 'acquiring' knowledge and skill, competence (or competencies) during some process of education and development. Someone whose performance is deemed 'good' ('competent', 'excellent', etc.) is said to 'possess' certain abilities, competencies and so on. This language of possession might be taken as merely metaphoric, that it is just another way of saying someone is knowledgeable, skilful, competent. We might, however, note in passing that such language of possession is clearly an example of what Macpherson termed 'possessive-individualism', the view that each individual human being is the 'proprietor' of their 'own person and capacities, owing nothing to society for them' (Macpherson, 1962: 3). This view, argues Macpherson, arose within the development of the ideas of 'property rights' in political philosophy of the sixteenth and seventeenth centuries, and underpinned the development of capitalism.

## Managerial Effectiveness, Managerial Competence

Whether talk of 'possession' carries such ideological weight, as Macpherson might argue, or is merely a general, mundane way of speaking, we should note that the discourse of expertise carries normative weight. That is, expertise is regarded as related to some form of 'good', 'desirable' performance in a particular arena of activity; poor performance is taken as evidence of lack of expertise. In terms of management performance, a key criterion of what is 'good' is that of effectiveness. 'Managerial effectiveness' became a central theme in management literature in the mid-twentieth century (Drucker 1967), and various attempts were made to 'identify', and so *describe*, what constituted such managerial effectiveness in operational terms (Campbell et al. 1970, Reddin 1970, Brodie and Bennett 1979).

During the 1980s, particularly following the seminal study by Boyatzis and colleagues (Boyatzis 1982), the term 'management competencies' came into vogue. In the UK, the alternate spelling of 'competences' was used alongside the introduction of National Vocational Qualifications in management/managing (MCI 1989). Boyatzis subtitles his book 'a model for effective performance', and certainly the approaches to examining managerial effectiveness may be seen to accord with those concerning 'managerial competence'. The underlying assumption is that effectiveness/competence is amenable to empirical identification and description. In the case of Boyatzis and colleagues, extensive studies were undertaken, on a sample of over 2,000 individuals in over 40 different managerial jobs, in 12 organizations in various sectors. Boyatzis uses a definition by Klemp (1980) of a job competence as 'an underlying characteristic of a person which results in effective and/or superior performance in a job' (cited in Boyatzis 1982: 23). He and his colleagues used performance data, interviews and tests of various types, and sought to find statistical relationships between competencies and performance. Woodruffe (1992) and Kandola and Pearn (1992) present similar models, applied in a UK context. Such approaches to managerial expertise might therefore be seen as attempts at empirically based description.

However, we should note that the definition of competence relates to performance in a job. This does, then, raise the question: what is the managerial job? For much of the first part of the twentieth century, this may be seen to have been answered by the promoters of Scientific Management and by those who drew upon the work of Fayol (1949). For Fayol, there were five *functions* of management: forecasting and planning, organizing, commanding, coordinating, controlling. Alongside was a set of 14 principles of management. Although both Taylor and Fayol wrote on the basis of personal experience in management, neither writer can be seen as undertaking the kind of empirical investigations that characterized later studies into managerial effectiveness and managerial competence, outlined above. Indeed, as we have seen, Taylor was very keen to 'convince' others of the methods he proposed; Fayol put considerable emphasis on *teaching* management, stating that Part 1 of his book was on the '[n]ecessity and possibility of teaching management' (Fayol 1949: xxi). Fayol's main interpreter, Lyndall Urwick, played a significant role in the development of management education and development in the UK. Wheatcroft (1970: 87) states that, during the 1920s, he was '*preaching* ... that there *should be* more study of methods of organization and control in industry, more training and development of managers, as well as study of manual operating methods' (emphasis added). Their writings may thus be seen more as *prescriptions* for managers in terms of their work, and thus viewing managerial expertise in prescriptive terms.

## Managerial Work

Yet, these prescriptive accounts came under considerable scrutiny from mid-century by empirical studies of what managers *actually* did (for example, Carlson 1951, Sayles 1964, Stewart 1967a, 1967b, Mintzberg 1973, Kotter 1982). These used a variety of methods investigation, including self-record diaries, questionnaires, observation and interviews, over varying periods of time. The managers in the studies varied in a range between chief executives (for example, Mintzberg 1973) to middle and lower-level managers (for example, Sayles 1964).

There is no space here to engage in lengthy examination of these studies. For review of these, see Hales (1980, 2001); also Mintzberg (1973) provides an appendix summarizing 'major studies' of the manager's job. We may, however, note that such empirical studies seem to indicate that the classical view did *not* accurately describe what managers *actually do*. Mintzberg in particular critiqued the classical view, primarily inherited from interpretations of Fayol: 'If you ask a manager what he does, he will most likely tell you that he plans, organises, co-ordinates, controls. Then watch what he does. Don't be surprised if you can't relate what you see to those four words' (Mintzberg 1975: 49). Rather, managerial work is characterized by fragmentation; managers spend brief periods of time on any activity, relying mostly on spoken communication with a diverse network of subordinates and peers. Managerial jobs are highly heterogeneous, albeit that different 'patterns' of similarity and contrast may be identified (Mintzberg 1973, Stewart 1976). If we accept Lupton's statement that management is 'what managers do during their working hours' (Lupton 1983: 17), then empirical studies of managerial behaviour would challenge the notions of managerial expertise presented by prescriptive accounts.

However, these empirical studies, and their apparent conclusions, have themselves been subject to critical scrutiny. Hales (1986) subjects these to critical review, arguing that the richness of data is accompanied by diversity of categorization, preventing 'identification of conflicts of evidence' (107). It is necessary, he continues, to re-examine 'who 'managers' are', focusing on the work process in organizations and the function of management in that process. Carroll and Gillen (1987) likewise challenge that the work of writers in the empirical studies field 'do[es] not clearly differentiate activities by *purpose* or *function* in relation to the survival of the whole organization' (49; emphasis in original). They conclude that the classical management functions remain useful in describing a 'core' concept of the manager's job.

Burgoyne (1976) had earlier made similar arguments in relation to managerial effectiveness, stating that this term 'is useful and usable to the extent to which [it] indicates a clearly defined function or purpose which can be fulfilled or achieved effectively' (4).

We should also note that when we talk, in ordinary everyday speech, of someone 'managing', we generally mean something more than that they are engaging in certain activities: there is a normative aspect to our discourse. That is, *unless we make comment to the contrary*, we implicitly make a positive evaluative judgement. Indeed, we often use the term 'manage' in everyday speech, not related to organizational and workplace functioning, in the sense of 'achieve'. For example, we might say that we 'managed' to catch a particular timetabled train (for example, despite leaving home later than intended), or suggest that a retired couple cannot be expected to 'manage' on the current level of state pension. In an organizational context, when we talk of individuals 'managing', we generally imply that we mean 'managing well'. One of the criticisms made by Hales (1986: 107), of the empirical studies of managerial behaviour, is that they tend not to establish whether or not the behaviour identified is 'good' or 'bad' management.

## The Functions of Management?

One implication of these critiques would seem to be that effectiveness in managerial performance, and therefore of competence or expertise, is indeed a matter of prescription; or, at least, prescription of function or purpose forms part of their conceptualization. This may be seen as underpinning the approach to managerial competence developed in the UK by the Management Charter Initiative (MCI) and by successor agencies. MCI was established as the executive arm of the Council for Management Education and Development in 1987, which itself had been set up by the Confederation of British Industry, the Foundation for Management Education and the (then) British Institute of Management. This had followed in the wake of two major reports (Handy et al. 1987, Constable and McCormick 1987) on the shortcomings of UK management education and development (Banham 1991). Very soon after its launch, MCI was charged by government with developing the 'occupation standards' for management, within the programme for developing 'national vocational qualifications' (NVQs) set in train after the 'Review of Vocational Qualifications' report (De Ville 1986). In taking on this role, MCI was required to adopt a particular approach to analysis of occupation competence, that of functional analysis.

Functional analysis has been subject extensively to critique (for example, Burgoyne 1989, Stewart and Hamlin 1992, Stewart and Sambrook 1995, Grugulis 1997), and these critical arguments will not be rehearsed here. However, we can consider the description of functional analysis of an occupation, authoritatively presented by two of the key developers of the approach, who state that

> The process [of functional analysis] starts by developing a 'key purpose' – the answer to the 'definition' of the entire occupational area in outcome terms and it should be capable of describing the occupational sector, organisations which operate specifically within the sector, key groups or departments in organisations as well as the expectations of individuals. (Mansfield and Mitchell 1996: 6, emphasis added)

The guidance notes issued by the Training Agency, the arm of government responsible for development of NVQs, stated that:

> Within any organisation – whether business, commerce or public sector – each individual contributes to the organisation performing effectively. They do so by carrying out those functions which lead to the organisation satisfying its mission or purpose. Functional analysis is the process of identifying those functions and breaking them down until they are described in sufficient detail to be used as standards. (Training Agency, 1991: 8)

Yet despite the use of terms such as 'identifying', execution of the functional analysis for management proceeded more by task groups engaging in *deduction* of 'lower' level aspects of competence from the 'higher level, and testing validity by focus groups, rather than the kind of empirical work undertaken by Boyatzis and colleagues, or by those who undertook empirical studies of managerial work' (Stewart and Hamlin 1992). This seems to be more a case of *prescription* than *description*.

And yet, we might discern a different way in which managerial expertise may be conceptualized, a different form of discourse, in which expertise is *ascribed* to those who are managers. To explore this requires consideration of the relationship between expertise, competence, etc., and performance. Rather than these being seen as separate phenomena, capable of separate observation, we may perhaps see them as integrally related. The next section will elaborate on this.

## Ascription of Expertise: Managerial Identity

To start this part of the discussion, consider the following thought-experiment. Imagine that, whilst visiting a workplace for some reason, we wander upon a scene with just two persons, oblivious to our presence, one of whom is talking to the other in stern tones. You hear the speaker say: 'your work is well below what we expect; unless it improves quickly, your career here will be very short!'. How would we interpret this situation? What is taking place? Most probably we would view this as some form of disciplinary action being taken, a reprimand being given by the speaker to the other (albeit, perhaps, not in accordance with 'best practice'). That is, we assume that the speaker is a manager, the other is a subordinate employee. But what if we are then told that, in fact, the speaker is the subordinate, the other is that person's manager. How do we understand it now? Perhaps we would say that it is a case of gross insolence, or ask whether this is a role-play; for example, the manager is coaching the subordinate (a supervisor?) in how to give a reprimand. Whatever we decide, we would surely consider the matter to be puzzling, as breaching what we would normally expect. This not because we *rarely* witness, or hear of, subordinate employees reprimanding their managers, but rather because it does not make sense to talk of 'reprimanding' in such circumstances. That is, reprimanding is something that can only be done by someone to another where there is status difference in terms of one being socially or organizational superordinate to the other (for example, parent–child, teacher–pupil, manager–managed).

There have been, and no doubt will continue to be, attempts to develop frameworks for categorizing managerial behaviour capable of locating, by observation alone, specific items of behaviour by specific managers. However, such attempts, *even if* they include some criteria for judging whether the behaviour is 'good' (effective, competent, etc.) or 'bad', fall foul of the long-established recognition that all human behaviour may be viewed in fundamentally different ways; that is, any statement about the behaviour of an individual may be subject to different 'logical grammars'. Thus, 'we can talk of human beings in many different ways, at various levels of generality, with varying degrees of abstraction, with different points of view, or with the presupposition of different standards. *It is important not to confuse or run together these different modes of talk*' (Hamlyn 1953: 145, emphasis added). The importance of recognizing the meaningfulness of human behaviour is, arguably, central to most traditions within the social sciences which seek to address the 'problem of order' without resorting to an 'oversocialised conception' of human beings (Wrong 1961).

Amongst these traditions we may note symbolic interactionism (Mead 1934/1962, Blumer 1969), interpretativism and social constructionism (Berger and Luckmann 1966, Schutz 1967), the 'micro-sociological' studies (Goffman 1967) and ethnomethodology (Garfinkel 1967). Within psychology we may note the ethogenics approach (Harré and Secord 1972), discursive psychology (Potter and Wetherell 1987), and various forms of social constructionism, including the rhetorical-responsive version (Shotter 1993) and relational-constructionism (Gergen 1994, Hosking et al. 1995). A key issue for our considerations here is that, in such perspectives, broadly, meaningfulness does not lie *merely* in the intention of the actor. An individual's behaviour has social significance and consequence to the extent that others attribute meaningfulness and they themselves act in a way that is related to the meaning attributed.

This recognition is central to Austin's exploration of performative utterances (Austin 1962), which Harré and Secord (1972) draw upon to distinguish between movement, actions and acts. An action is a movement or set of movements which we take to be meaningful which, if it meets certain criteria, may be taken to be the performance of an act; for example, a promise, apology, greeting, threat, marriage. So, they argue, a movement 'is given meaning as an action by being identified as the performance or part of the performance of an act' (Harré and Secord 1972: 166). And there is no one-to-one correspondence between movements, actions and acts: thus smiling is a physical behaviour which may be taken as a greeting, a threat, an apology, and so on. Which act it represents on a particular occasion will depend on the overall definition of the encounter into which it fits and the kind of actions by which we can perform the same act (Harré et al. 1985: 83). This poses a challenge for studies that seek to identify the components of managerial behaviour by observational methods.

Managerial behaviour is not 'just there', capable of being unequivocally observed, but arises within particular contexts through the meanings ascribed by a range of social actors, some of whom may be present (such as the manager, subordinate employees), others distant (such as senior management, customers, suppliers). Those meanings are not predetermined, nor fixed, but contingent and emergent, through processes of construal or interpretation of some specific activity or activities as the *performance of behaviour-of-a-particular-kind*.

The question may then be asked about how activity becomes interpreted or construed as performance. From the theoretical approaches indicated above, two 'standing conditions' would appear to be highly significant: (a) there is some set of *practices*, deemed by the relevant parties to be appropriate to the situation, such that the activity may be construed as the instantiation of an item from the set of practices; and (b) there is a set of *identities* deemed to be appropriate to the situation, such that the person whose activity is in need of interpretation may be taken as 'having' a particular identity.

In the case of the imaginary workplace in our previous thought-experiment, we can say that we initially drew upon notions of workplace practices (one being that of reprimanding) and of a set of identities in workplaces (managers, employees). When our perception of the speaker's identity is changed, we must then change our understanding of what practice was being instantiated; for instance, no longer reprimand but perhaps insolence. Garfinkel's (1967) famous breaching studies may be viewed in a similar light, whereby apparent breakdown in the identity-practice matching required 'repair'.

## PRACTICES

In much recent philosophy and social science, the term 'practice' has taken prominence over terms hitherto used, such as 'conventions', 'typifications', 'norms', 'customs' and 'rules', and modes of framing such as 'structures', 'systems', 'meaning', life world': this has been referred to as the 'practice turn in contemporary theory' (Schatzki et al. 2001). Limitations of space prohibit an extensive discussion here of this notion, and of debates concerning its validity and utility: however, a few comments are pertinent for the issues under consideration here. First, the concept of 'practices' as a 'primary social thing' (Schatzki et al. 2001) may provide for a more sociologically robust consideration of the matters which are often addressed through notions of 'skill' and 'competency' conceived as entities possessed by individuals and as causally related to behaviour (Holmes 2000).

Secondly, we may note Schatzki's useful distinction between 'dispersed' and 'integrative' practices. Examples given of the former include describing, ordering, following rules, explaining, questioning, reporting, examining, imagining: '[t]heir 'dispersion' consists simply in their widespread occurrence across different sectors of social life ...' (Schatzki 1996). In contrast, 'integrative practices' are 'the more complex practices found in and constitutive of particular domains of social life. Examples are farming practices, business practices, voting practices, teaching practices, celebration practices, cooking practices, recreational practices, industrial practices, religious practices, and banking practices (ibid.: 98). This distinction helps in addressing the notion that, because people mundanely talk of 'managing' various activities in their daily lives, they may be said to be managing in the same sense as managers do (cf. Grey 1999). Against that claim, we may say that 'managing' in the mundane sense is a form of dispersed practice, whilst in the latter sense it is an integrative practice.

Thirdly, it need not be necessarily the case that all or any of the parties to a situation are explicitly aware of and can articulate the practices relevant to the situation. Not only may they remain tacit to the actor concerned (Polanyi 1967), they may remain 'enigmatic' (Harré and Secord 1972) to the significant others. Nor is it necessary that all parties agree on what is the 'proper' construal of what practice is being instantiated: the construal may be subject to contestation. The arena of practice which constitutes management in work organizations implicates issues of power and control, and so should be regarded as a 'contested terrain' (Edwards 1979). These issues of the tacit dimension, enigmatic activity and contestability lead us on to issues relating to the notion of emergent identity.

## Identity

As with the notion of 'practices', 'identity' has 'become one of the unifying frameworks of [recent] intellectual debate' (Jenkins 1996: 7). The term 'identity' is deployed with a diverse, rather fragmented, range of conceptualizations within differing fields of social enquiry, with the differing problematization and theorization that form the analytical frameworks adopted (Wetherell and Mohanty 2010). The discussion here will be limited to a perspective on identity which draws upon a well-established body of social theory and research that seeks to explore the processes that emerge through social interactions within institutional settings (Jenkins 1996).

'Identity' has the related verb 'identify' and verbal noun 'identification' which are capable of allowing a more dynamic understanding. 'Identifying' and 'identification' provide for an interactional, relational conceptualization, such that various parties to a situation may identify an individual in various ways. Although we may talk of someone 'having' a particular identity, the interactional conceptualization reminds us that such idiomatic expression should not lead us into confused thinking that an identity is something which may be possessed in the way that a car, watch, book, etc., may be possessed. This accords with the conceptualization of 'self' in the symbolic interactionist tradition, in contrast with the 'modernist/humanist' conceptualization of the monadic sovereign self. Jenkins adopts such a conceptualization in his model of the internal–external dialectic of identification (Jenkins 1996).

## IDENTITY AND PRACTICES

The argument here is, then, that issues of *both* identity *and* practices are implicated in any attempts to make sense of meaningful human behaviour; and, presumably, we *do* work from the assumption that managerial behaviour is meaningful. Figure 4.1 attempts to indicate the coupling of practices and identity. Identities carry, or are associated with, certain kinds of practices, such that someone with a certain identity is generally deemed to have, or not have, certain rights and/or a duty to engage in certain kinds of practices. Similar analyses are made by others in terms of role-rule models (Harré and Secord 1972) and of member-categorization and category-bounded activities (Sacks 1972).

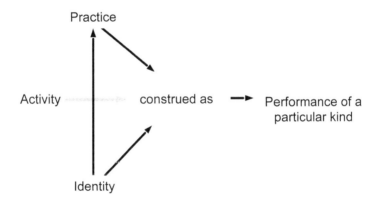

**Figure 4.1  Identity and practice in the construal of activity as performance**

However, although both issues of identity and practices are implicated, they are not necessarily of equal importance. In some areas of human life, it may be necessary for both to be 'correct'. This is particularly the case in rites and rituals, where the 'officiator(s)' must be the 'right' (kind of) person, and they must perform the relevant practices 'correctly'. Thus in a marriage ceremony, the question of which persons may be officiants is prescribed by law, and there are key parts of the ceremony that must be performed as prescribed. In most areas of social life, however, different levels of importance may be placed on *either* identity (who may legitimately engage in particular practices) *or* practices (in terms of the degree to which these are specified, even codified).

The suggestion here is that, in context of managerially organized structures of social and economic affairs in modern society, and the institutionalization of work as employment, identification *as a manager* is necessary for a person's behaviour to be construed as *managing*; that is, the instantiation of managerial practices. In that sense, only managers *can* manage, management *is* what managers do, to quote Lupton again (Lupton 1983: 17).

## Emergent Identity

Of course, managers are not (literally) born (as managers); individuals *become* managers, they become identified *as* managers. As discussed above, we may view identity, or *identification*, in terms of interaction between the various parties to a social setting in which a particular identity is salient. Identification is always a negotiated process, between an individual and those with whom they interact, by (and of) self and by others. In that sense, managerial identity is emergent; indeed, it has been argued that no unique individual ever becomes a manager (or anything else) but is always in a process of 'continually becoming' (Watson and Harris 1999). The sense in which 'emergent' is used here is somewhat stronger: a person's identity within a particular context is always and continually the subject of the interaction between that which the person themselves wishes to be seen as, and that which significant others ascribe to the person. Identification takes place synchronically as well as diachronically.

The two separate aspects of identification, by self and by others, may be developed further. As identity is negotiated, it is therefore essentially contestable, 'fragile', subject (always temporally) to success or breakdown. The individual may be taken as claiming a particular situated identity; the corresponding ascription by others that accords with the individual's claim may thus be taken as affirming that claim, whereas an ascription that does not so accord may be taken as a disaffirmation of the claim. An ascription by others to an individual of a particular identity may be contested by the individual, which may be taken as a disclaim. This interaction between claim or disclaim by the individual and the affirmation or disaffirmation by others thus give rise to what we may term different 'modalities of emergent identity', different degrees of stabilisation' of identity (Holmes 2000, see also DeRue and Ashford 2010, Lord and Hall 2004, for similar discussion regarding leadership).

There is, then, clearly a considerable amount of 'identity work' (Sveningsson and Alvesson 2003, Beech 2008, Watson 2008, Ybema et al.

2009) taking place in managed workplaces; a manager must engage in such identity work to 'become' and 'be' a manager. But it is not only individual managers who engage in this: within the contemporary form of managed organizations, such identity work must form part of organizational processes. That is, managerial positions, and their attendant rights (and responsibilities), including managerial prerogative, the 'right to manage' (Storey 1982), are inescapable aspects of the continuing construction of organizations as institutionalized forms. Whilst individual managers may encounter contestation from others, disaffirmations of their identity claims, the managerial position itself must be uncontested if the very organizational 'logic of action' is to be sustained. Indeed, even where there is 'resistance' by employees within a workplace, this often takes a localized form, such that workers continue to 'manufacture consent' to the managerial organizational form (Burawoy 1979). Perhaps, rather than 'consent', we might talk of 'assent', in a similar way to the notion that a constitutional monarch gives 'assent' to legislation passed by the democratic legislature, without necessarily agreeing with such legislation. Indeed, as Grieco and Lilja (1996) argue, 'opponents' in any particular institutionalized social setting are likely to act in ways that enable the continuation of that setting, to avoid the destructive consequences in terms of their energies and resources: 'synchronization of opponents'.

## Managerial Expertise as Ascriptive

It is on such understanding, then, that we can reconsider managerial performance and managerial expertise as *ascriptive*. The notion that managerial performance *is* an arena of human activity, requiring that those who are identified as managers be capable of engaging in managerial practices, is necessary for management to be separated from 'non-managerial' work. This is part of the logic of action of Scientific Management and of the main developments of approaches to management in the century after Taylor's seminal text. This requires that managerial identity be distinguished from non-managerial identity, 'manager' and 'managed' – and, increasingly, 'leader' and 'follower' (DeRue and Ashford 2010). The 'right to manage' may previously be warranted (Draper 1988) in terms of ownership rights, represented through management but, increasingly, expertise has become the basis for such warranting. Management as expressed in managerial performance is thus taken to be a field of expertise, one founded on rationality ('scientific' in Taylor's terminology) providing confidence that all will benefit from its exercise.

Underpinning such a rationale is the management education and development 'industry', particularly where managerial expertise may be codified, transmitted and endorsed. Thus the curricula of management education courses, at undergraduate and at postgraduate and/or post-experience levels, sustain the institutionalization of expertise-ascription. Regimes of assessment of individuals undertaking such courses further reinforce this. Such regimes include various modes of standardization and quality assurance, from external examiner systems to accreditation of courses and/or course providers (usually business schools) such as the Association of MBAs (AMBA), the Association to Advance Collegiate Schools of Business (AACSB) and the European Quality Improvement System (EQUIS). There are also other agencies, including professional bodies such as the Chartered Management Institute in the UK, that act as awarding and accrediting bodies, and include options for managers to gain a qualification on the basis of 'assessment of learning' through experience. Indeed, the Chartered Management Institute effectively took over the purportedly competence-based 'occupational standards' work initiated by MCI, discussed earlier. Such agencies and their activities may be viewed as part of what might be termed the 'governance of managerial expertise', actively producing the social form that this takes rather than merely reflecting some 'natural world' phenomenon, capable of objective identification, analysis and description.

Managers who go through the processes established within such governance processes thereby acquire a useful and useable warrant for their personal claims on the managerial identity. The possession of a management qualification such as an MBA enables the manager to 'call upon' others (usually unnamed and unseen), often with high reputation and prestige, as supporters of (affirming) the identity claim. It is virtually impossible to reasonably conceive that all parties engaged would know what a particular manager has done to gain the qualification, the basis on which her or his 'competence' has been assessed. Possession is more than 'nine tenths of the law' in such a case; it is an almost unassailable warrant on the expertise claim. It is not surprising, then, that in a survey of over 4,000 managers by the UK's Chartered Management Institute, business school qualifications were rated as by far the most important 'management learning and development' activity (McBain et al. 2012). Even in processes that are not qualifications-bearing, internal to an organization, including mentoring and coaching schemes, we may see expertise-ascription taking place, in that eligibility for and participation in such processes and schemes publicly affirms the identity claim.

This is not to say that MBA and other business school programmes, or other forms of 'management learning and development' activity, do *not* have any effect on some 'real' expertise: knowledge and skills. Clearly, in various walks of life we note that some people 'perform better' than others. Indeed, as this chapter was being completed, preparations for the London Olympics 2012 were nearing completion, and by the time of the book's publication, differences in performance of the athletes will be publically known, with the highest performers gaining medals. In the rhetoric in support of the competence movement of the 1980s and 1990s, proponents would often ask whether one would prefer to be treated by an 'educated' doctor (such as a brain surgeon) or a 'competent' one. However, it is difficult to justify comparisons with sports and athletics, or with high-stakes surgery, where the outcomes are very visible to all, mostly without dispute. The arena of management expertise and its relationship to performance lacks such criterial support, based on empirically based descriptions of managerial expertise and its relationship to managerial performance.

Before concluding this chapter, we should note that identity work also implicates negotiation around the multiple identities that we each have, in the multiplicities of social contexts and arenas in which we live our lives. Gender and ethnicity continue to be major modalities of identification in contemporary society, manifested particularly in terms of employment and career patterns. This is particularly so in respect of management (Schein et al. 1996, Powell et al. 2002, Gatrell and Swan 2008, Roberts et al. 2008). The ascription of managerial expertise is socially patterned, most especially along lines of gender and ethnicity. Examination of what we might term the 'social morphology' of managerial expertise is hardly available to descriptive and prescriptive accounts, but *may* be afforded by its framing within an understanding of its ascriptive nature.

## Conclusion

This chapter has explored issues relating to the notion that managerial performance is based on, or in some way manifests, managerial expertise, specialized knowledge, understanding, skill, competence. Taylor and his contemporaries, and later writers, have exhorted managers to follow their prescriptions for effective management. By the middle period of the century after *Scientific Management* was first published, efforts were made to 'locate' such expertise, to identify and so describe the 'components' of managerial effectiveness or managerial competence. However, also in that period, a range of studies of what managers actually do seemed to suggest the originating 'classical' conceptualizations of management were not accurate or adequate descriptions. Such studies were later critiqued for lack of a framework for determining what *function* management should perform, to enable 'good' managerial performance to be distinguished from 'poor' performance. An impasse seems to have been reached in these various studies. To help overcome that, it has been suggested that we might regard managerial expertise as *ascriptive*, part of the 'identity work' not only undertaken by managers themselves, but also unavoidably part of the social processes by and through which the organizational world is constructed. A century has passed since the publication of *Scientific Management*, and it seems that there is yet more to be understood about this major facet of modern life.

## References

Association of Business Schools. 2011. *Pillars of the Sustainable Economy, 2010/11.* London: Association of Business Schools.

Austin, J.L. 1962. *How to Do Things with Words.* London: Oxford University Press.

Banham, J. 1991. On professionalism and professions: the Management Charter Initiative, in *Competent to Manage: Approaches to Management Training and Development*, edited by M. Silver. London: Routledge.

Beech, N. 2008. On the nature of dialogic identity Work. *Organization*, 15(1), 51–74.

Berger, P. and Luckmann, T. 1966. *The Social Construction of Reality.* Garden City NY: Doubleday.

Black, J. 2005. Facilitating the development of the organizational competence: managerial expertise, in *Competence Perspectives on Resources, Stakeholders and Renewal*, edited by R. Sanchez and A. Heene. Amsterdam: Elsevier, 81–101.

Blumer, H. 1969. *Symbolic Interactionism: Perspective and Method.* Chicago: University of Chicago Press.

Boyatzis, D. 1982. *The Competent Manager: A Model for Effective Performance.* Chichester: Wiley.

Brodie, M. and Bennett, R. (eds). 1979. *Perspectives on Managerial Effectiveness.* Slough: Thames Valley Regional Management Centre.

Burawoy, M. 1979. *The Manufacture of Consent: Changes in the Labor Process under Monopoly Capitalism.* Chicago: University of Chicago Press.

Burgoyne, J. 1976. *Managerial Effectiveness Revisited.* Mimeo. Lancaster University.

Burgoyne, J. 1989. Creating the managerial portfolio: building on competency approaches to management. *Management Education and Development*, 20(1), 56–61.

Campbell, J., Dunnette, M., Lawler, M. and Weick, K. 1970. *Managerial Behavior, Performance and Effectiveness*. New York: Wiley.

Carlson, S. 1951. *Executive Behaviour*. Stockholm: Strömbergs.

Carroll, S. and Gillen, D. 1987. Are the classical management functions useful in describing managerial work? *Academy of Management Review*, 1238–51.

Chipman, S. 2006. Expertise in the management of people: a new frontier for research on expert performance, in *Development of Professional Expertise*, edited by K. Ericsson. New York: Cambridge University Press, 470–93.

Collins, H. and Evans, R. 2007. *Rethinking Expertise*. Chicago: Chicago University Press.

Constable, J. and McCormick, R. 1987. *The Making of British Managers: A Report for the BIM and CBI into Management Training, Education and Development*. Corby: British Institute of Management.

Crainer, M. 1999. *The Management Century*. Chichester: Jossey Bass Wiley.

DeRue, D. and Ashford, S. 2010. Who will lead and who will follow? A social process of leadership identity construction in organizations. *Academy of Management Review*, 35(4), 627–47.

De Ville, O. 1986. *Review of Vocational Qualifications in England and Wales: A Report by the Working Group*. London: Manpower Services Commission/Department of Education and Science.

Diefenbach, T. 2009. *Management and the Dominance of Managers*. New York: Routledge.

Draper, S. 1988. What's going on in everyday explanation?, in *Analysing Everyday Explanation: A Casebook of Methods*, edited by A. Antaki. London: Sage, 15–31.

Drucker, P. 1967. *The Effective Executive*. London: Heinemann.

Edwards, R. 1979. *The Contested Terrain: The Transformation of the Workplace in the Twentieth Century*. London: Heinemann.

Ericsson, K. (ed.). 2009. *The Development of Professional Expertise*. New York: Cambridge University Press.

Fayol, H. 1949. *General and Industrial Administration*. London: Pitman.

Garfinkel, H. 1967. *Studies in Ethnomethodology*. Englewood Cliffs NJ: Prentice-Hall.

Gatrell, C. and Swan, E. 2008. *Gender and Diversity in Management*. London: Sage.

Gergen, K. 1994. *Realities and Relationships*. Cambridge MA: Harvard University Press.

Goffman, E. 1967. *Interaction Ritual: Essays on Face-to-Face Behaviour*. New York: Doubleday.

Grey, C. 1999. 'We are all managers now'; 'we always were': on the development and demise of management. *Journal of Management Studies*, 36(5), 561–85.

Grieco, M. and Lilja, K. 1996. 'Contradictory couplings': culture and the synchronization of opponents. *Organization Studies*, 17(1), 131–7.

Grugulis, I. 1997. The consequences of competence: a critical assessment of the Management NVQ. *Personnel Review*, 26(6), 428–44.

Hales, C. 1980. *Managerial Effectiveness and its Determinants: Golden Fleece or Chimera?* London: Training Services Division, Manpower Services Commission.

Hales, C. 1986. What do managers do?: a critical review of the evidence. *Journal of Management Studies*, 23(1), 88–115.

Hales, C. 2001. *Managing through Organization: The Management Process, Forms of Organization and the Work of Managers*. London: Business Press.

Hamlyn, D. 1953. Behaviour. *Philosophy*, 28(April), 132–45.

Handy, C., Gordon, C., Gow, I., Randlesome, C. and Moloney, M. 1987. *The Making of Managers*. London: National Economic Development Office.

Harré, R. and Secord, P. 1972. *The Explanation of Social Behaviour*. Oxford: Blackwell.

Harré, R., Clarke, D. and De Carlo, N. 1985. *Motives and Mechanisms: An Introduction to the Psychology of Action*. London: Methuen.

Holmes, L. 2000. What can performance tell us about learning? Explicating a troubled concept. *European Journal of Work and Organizational Psychology*, 9(2), 253–66.

Hosking, D., Dachler, H. and Gergen, K. 1995. *Management and Organization: Relational Alternatives to Individualism*. Aldershot: Avebury.

Jenkins, R. 1996. *Social Identity*. London: Routledge.

Kandola, R. and Pearn, M. 1992. Identifying competencies, in *Designing and Achieving Competency*, edited by R. Boam and P. Sparrow. London: McGraw-Hill.

Klemp, G. (ed.). 1980. *The Assessment of Occupational Competence*. Washington DC: National Institute of Education.

Kotter, J. 1982. *The General Managers*. New York: Free Press.

Lord, R. and Hall, R. 2004. *Leadership Processes and Follower Self-Identity*. Mahwah NJ: Lawrence Erlbaum Associates.

Lupton, T. 1983. *Management and the Social Sciences*. Harmondsworth: Penguin.

Macpherson, C. 1962. *The Political Theory of Possessive Individualism: Hobbes to Locke*. Oxford: Oxford University Press.

McBain, R., Ghobadian, A., Switzer, J., Wilton, P., Woodman, P. and Pearson, G. 2012. *The Business Benefits of Management and Leadership Development*. London: Chartered Management Institute.

Mansfield, B. and Mitchell, L. 1996. *Towards a Competent Workforce*. Aldershot: Gower.

MCI. 1989. *Management Competences: The Standards Project*. London: MCI.

Mead, G. 1934/1962. *Mind, Self and Society*. Chicago: Chicago University Press.

Mintzberg, H. 1973. *The Nature of Managerial Work*. New York: Harper & Row.

Mintzberg, H. 1975. The manager's job: folklore and fact. *Harvard Business Review*, 53(4), 49–61.

Polanyi, M. 1967. *The Tacit Dimension*. London: Routledge & Kegan Paul.

Potter, J. and Wetherell, M. 1987. *Discourse and Social Psychology*. London: Sage.

Powell, G., Butterfield, D. and Parent, J. 2002. Gender and managerial stereotypes: have the times changed? *Journal of Management*, 28(2), 177–93.

Reddin, W. 1970. *Managerial Effectiveness*. London: McGraw-Hill.

Roberts, C., Campbell, S. and Robinson, Y. 2008. *Talking like a Manager: Promotion Interviews, Language and Ethnicity*. London: Department for Work and Pensions.

Sacks, H. 1972. On the analyzability of stories by children, in *Directions in Sociolinguistics*, edited by J. Gumperz and D. Hymes. New York: Holt, Rinehart & Winston.

Sayles, L. 1964. *Managerial Behaviour*. New York: McGraw-Hill.

Schatzki, T. 1996. *Social Practices: A Wittgensteinian Approach to Human Activity and the Social*. Cambridge: Cambridge University Press.

Schatzki, T., Knorr Cetina, K. and Von Savigny, E. (eds). 2001. *The Practice Turn in Contemporary Theory*. London: Routledge.

Schein, V.E., Mueller, R., Lituchy, T. and Liu, J. 1996. Think manager – think male: a global phenomenon? *Journal of Organizational Behavior*, 17(1), 33–41.

Schutz, A. 1967. On the methodology of the social sciences, in *Collected Papers I*, edited volume. The Hague: Martinus Nijhoff, 3–96.

Selinger, E. and Crease, R. (eds). 2006. *The Philosophy of Expertise*. New York: Cambridge University Press.

Shotter, J. 1993. *Conversational Realities: Constructing Life through Language*. London: Sage.

Silver, M. (ed.). 1991. *Competent to Manage: Approaches to Management Training and Development*. London: Routledge.

Stewart, J. and Hamlin, B. 1992. Competence-based qualifications: the case against change. *Journal of European Industrial Training*, 16(10), 21–32.

Stewart, J. and Sambrook, S. 1995. The role of functional analysis in national vocational qualifications: a critical approach. *British Journal of Education and Work*, 8(2), 93–106.

Stewart, R. 1967a. *Managers and their Jobs*. Maidenhead: McGraw-Hill.

Stewart, R. 1967b. *The Reality of Management*. London: Pan.

Stewart, R. 1976. *Contrasts in Management*. London: Pan.

Storey, J. 1982. *Managerial Prerogative and the Question of Control*. London: Routledge & Kegan Paul.

Sveningsson, S. and Alvesson, M. 2003. Managing managerial identities: organizational fragmentation, discourse and identity struggle. *Human Relations*, 56(10), 1163–93.

Taylor, F. 1912. The Principles of Scientific Management, in *Addresses and Discussions at the Conference on Scientific Management*, edited by Amos Tuck School of Business Administration. Hanover NH: Dartmouth College, 22–56.

Taylor, F. 1967. *The Principles of Scientific Management*. New York: Norton.

Training Agency 199. *Development of Assessable Standards for National Certification: Guidance Note 2 – Deriving Standards by Reference to Functions*. Sheffield: Training Agency.

Watson, T. 2008. Managing Identity: identity work, personal predicaments and structural circumstances. *Organization*, 15(1), 121–43.

Watson, T. and Harris, P. 1999. *The Emergent Manager*. London: Sage.

Wetherell, M. and Mohanty, C. (eds). 2010. *The Sage Handbook of Identities*. London: Sage.

Wheatcroft, M. 1970. *The Revolution in British Management Education*. London: Pitman.

Woodruffe, C. 1992. What is meant by a competency?, in *Designing and Achieving Competency*, edited by R. Boam and P. Sparrow. London: McGraw-Hill.

Wrong, D. 1961. The oversocialized conception of man in modern sociology. *American Sociological Review*, 26(2), 183–93.

Ybema, S., Keenoy, T., Oswick, C., Beverungen, A., Ellis, N. and Sabelis, I. 2009. Articulating identities. *Human Relations*, 62(3), 299–322.

PART II

# Taylor's Legacy in the Contemporary Knowledge and Service Economy

# 5

# Call Centre Work: Taylorism with a Facelift

*Shuchi Sinha and Yiannis Gabriel*

## Introduction

The last two decades have witnessed extensive technological, economic and social changes that have transformed the way work is organized and executed. New products, new markets, new technologies, new ways of doing business, new political, financial and organizational forms as well as the emergence of China, India and other countries as major industrial powers have prompted many scholars to argue that the fundamental nature of capitalism is changing. 'Terms such as "structural crisis", "transformation", and "transition" have become common descriptors of the present, while new epithets such as "post-Fordist", "post-industrial", "post-modern" and "fifth-Kondratiev", and "post-collective" have been coined by the academic prophets of recent times to describe the emerging new age of capitalism' (Amin 1994: 1). Several definitional and conceptual difficulties characterize the diverse models and frameworks offered to explain the massive changes in the structure and organization of modern Western economy and society. Prominent among these is the debate whether the new emerging trends represent a break from the past or modification of old patterns. 'New or not, it seems indisputable that the salience of so many of the icons of the age of mass industrialization and mass consumerism appears to be diminishing' (ibid.: 2).

A prominent icon of the mass industrialized era that has undergone considerable reconfiguration is the conception of the manager as a heroic figure who exercises control over productive operations through technical mastery (MacIntyre 1981). During the era of mass industrialization, the concept of management became synonymous with obsessive control and measurement, partly due to the efforts of Frederick Winslow Taylor (1856–1915), generally regarded as the founder of 'Scientific Management'. Taylor believed that management could and should stay in control, viewing the workers as pure pawns carrying out management's instructions. He made it his life's ambition to replace the variability in workers' performance with standardization and predictability. Through rational calculations and precise measurements, Taylor identified optimal ways of doing different tasks in order to enhance efficiency and control every aspect of workers' performance. Taylor's obsession with controlling workers in the name of efficiency found its apotheosis in 'the hero of the mass-production saga' (Beynon 1975: 17) – Henry Ford, who is well known for his innovations that revolutionized production in the early part of the twentieth century. Ford believed in similar principles of standardization and regimentation, as did Taylor, but he signed up to technological euphoria. Deploying technology in production would augur in a new conception of *consumption*, as a social sphere which promised everyone, not just the rich, happiness, meaning and fulfilment beyond their wildest dreams. Technology also allowed Ford to control his workers indirectly, thereby reducing their awareness of being controlled. The divorce of conception from execution, thorough planning, the fragmentation of production, constant measurement and de-skilling were the core principles behind the rise of mass production, prompting Braverman to argue in 1974 that 'Taylorism dominates the world of production' (Braverman 1974).

Today, such an unequivocal statement would be contested, as late modernity has prompted a rethinking of management. Contemporary capitalism is believed to have come a long way from the Fordist factories. Today's global economy is characterized by technological advancements resulting from extensive use of information and communication technologies (ICTs), the emergence of new looser organizational structures and networks, permeable trade borders, rise of the service sector and the inclusion of customers into the labour process. Together these changes have intensified competition and require organizations to respond quickly and flexibly. The rigidity of scientific management and the cold logic of bureaucracy constrain flexibility and are often found to be 'insufficiently responsive and adaptable' to these intensifying competitive pressures (Alvesson and Willmott 2002: 621). Contemporary capitalism, with uninhibited flow of information and use of ICTs at its core, appears to be better supported by a degree of employee initiative and autonomy.

Consider for instance the growing service sector, which is infused with variability and unpredictability caused by the growing centrality of customers in the labour process. Traditional forms of bureaucratic controls may be less effective in such work contexts. Front-line workers, who are the main point of contact for customers, need to use their discretion and judgement in dealing with the variability of everyday customer interactions. Allowing scope for worker autonomy undermines the traditional conception of management, where managers tightly controlled the content and process of work. Korczynski et al. (2000: 671) argue that, in service industries, the traditional command and control form of management is 'likely to be supplemented by the use of customer-related normative values, in which management seeks to make use of customer authority and identity at the societal level'. Using customers to control the workers substantially alters the previous relationship between managers and workers (Korczynski 2001, Gabriel and Lang 2006). It tips the power balance in unexpected and ambiguous ways, sometimes drawing worker and manager in opposition to 'unreasonable customers', at other times drawing the customer as an extra form of discipline over the workers, and at yet other finding the customer and the worker 'conspiring' and using up company time at the expense of the manager (Gabriel 2008).

Effective management in contemporary workplaces, notably in the service sector, places a high premium on the employee's ability to satisfy the customer by drawing on a wide range of emotional and aesthetic resources. Unlike Henry Ford's workers who were just expected to follow orders and work fast, today's service sector employees are expected, in addition to physical labour, to perform intellectual, emotional (Hochschild 1983) and even aesthetic (Hancock and Tyler 2000, Warhurst et al. 2000) labour. To this end, since the 1980s, an emphasis has been paid to aligning workers' hearts and minds with the organization's interests and values. This can hardly be done through coercive domination. Positive management practices, characterized by employee involvement, participation and welfare, are more likely to strengthen employee commitment and enhance organizational effectiveness (Whitener 2001). High-commitment management conveys a more humane orientation on the organization's part and may help to establish greater trust in management, facilitating employee identification with the organization and its interests (Casey 1999, Sturdy 1998). For some scholars this approach represents a genuine shift in management thinking towards increasing employee participation, especially in knowledge-intensive industries (McClean and Collins 2011). For others (Jermier 1998), adoption of high-involvement approaches is simply a façade intended to make organizational controls more invasive and inconspicuous.

In this chapter we direct attention to the nature and practice of management in call centres in India, which, as several researchers have documented, 'adopt HCM practices that resemble those in the West in terms of sociotechnical systems and HR practices' (see Carroll and Wagar 2009 and Russell and Thite

2009 in D'Cruz and Noronha 2011: 3). We draw on the findings of a qualitative study conducted in four call centres in India to interrogate whether control continues to lie at the heart of management or whether new patterns of employee engagement and commitment are emerging. The focus on call centres is highly appropriate since such workplaces have become arenas of intense debate as to whether they represent continuity with or discontinuity from Taylorist management models, with strong arguments piled on both sides of the debate (Taylor and Bain 1999, Frenkel et al. 1999, Taylor et al. 2002, Russell 2009). While acknowledging the importance of innovative human resource (HR) practices used to distract workers from the work standardization and regimentation that characterize call centre work, and while recognizing that today's capitalism involves various important discontinuities from its Fordist and Taylorist past, we also observe very pronounced similarities in modes of control and core management practices. Insights drawn from an appreciation of call centre work, we argue, offer glimpses into the future of work and its continuities with the past.

The rest of this chapter is structured as follows. In the next section, we offer an overview of the growth of call centres with specific focus on call centres in India, highlighting the host of challenges that make Indian call centres unique research sites for investigating a range of diverse topics. This is followed by an overview of the qualitative study from which data for this chapter is drawn. In the next section we present and discuss a selection of data to lay bare the nature and practice of management in Indian call centres. We conclude the chapter by arguing that while the institution of management has been transformed by the prominent changes in the world of work, it continues to be preoccupied by control.

## Call Centres – an Unprecedented Growth Story

Call centres, which broadly refer to 'dedicated operation[s] in which computer utilizing employees receive inbound – or make outbound – telephone calls with those calls processed by automatic call distribution (ACD) system, or perhaps by a predictive dialing system' (Taylor and Bain 1999: 102) constitute a young sector. Typical call centres in most countries across the globe are only 10–12 years old. In this short span, call centres have redefined and globalized service work (Holman et al. 2007). Since their appearance on the scene in the early 1990s, 'call, contact and "customer care" centres have become the most important single source of customer contact in the developed information economies' (Russell 2008: 195).

It is now well established that call centre work is far from uniform. There exist various sub-species of call centres, varying from Taylorized mass production to professional services to hybrid mass customization (Batt and Moynihan 2002, Taylor and Bain 2005). Despite these differences, Taylor and Bain (1999) argue, the integration of computer and telephone technologies leads to considerable similarities within call centres. Importantly, the pressures for cost containment and the Taylorization of work circumscribe the amount of variation that is possible within the call centre and its management (Taylor et al. 2002, Baldry et al. 2007). Holman et al. (2007), in the first large-scale international study of call centres, report that a majority of call centres across the 17 countries they studied predominantly serve mass-market customers (therefore, are highly standardized and regimented). Their study also shows that the offshored work tends to be most routinized as it allows for better monitoring.

India is a prominent destination of offshored call centre work, occupying 51 per cent market share of the market (NASSCOM 2010: 9). Despite its prominence, the Indian business process organization (BPO) sector faces several unique challenges. A large number of BPO firms in India handle mostly back office work that tends to be standardized, regimented and peripheral (Taylor 2010). Such mundane work offers minimal opportunity for upgrading skills and easily frustrates the well-educated and well-qualified workforce that is employed by the Indian BPO firms. In addition, everyday interactions with Western customers present unique challenges to Indian employees, accentuated by cultural differences and demands on the workers' identities. Indian front-line workers are often allocated Western pseudo-names or aliases to establish better rapport with the Western customers and facilitate efficient task completion (Poster 2007). Customer sovereignty is emphasized at every stage of the extensive induction training that front-line agents are put through. These agents regularly face discrimination, racism and abuse from customers which threaten their self-esteem (Cohen and El-Sawad 2007, Mirchandani 2008). Prohibited from reacting to such abuses, front-line employees are trained by the organization to endure them with acceptance and servitude. Maintaining their own dignity in the face of such conditions requires these workers to perform extensive identity work (Stein 2007).

How do the call centre workers in India cope with these everyday demands? How do they make sense of these experiences? What role do managers play in supporting employees through some of these problematic experiences? And what is, more widely, the function of management in call centres? These were some of the questions that were examined by the study from which data is drawn for this chapter.

## Method

A two-phase qualitative study, with onsite observations, 62 interviews and documentary analysis was conducted in four call centres in Delhi and Noida in India. Phase one of this study was exploratory in nature and was designed to increase familiarity with call centre work, workers' experiences of call centre work and the key HR challenges and opportunities facing call centres. During this phase, the first author spent four weeks (in August 2007) at three call centre units of a third-party BPO in Noida (referred to here as INT-A), spending an average of 35 hours a week onsite, observing the day-to-day working of Indian call centre employees. Phase two of the study was aimed at investigating the findings from phase one in detail and was carried out in June 2008 and September 2008 at the other three research sites – a call centre unit of a leading third-party BPO in Noida (referred to here as INT-B) and two domestic call centres serving the Indian domestic markets (referred to here as DOM-A and DOM-B). In phase two, focus was directed towards capturing the interactions between key workplace actors, the meanings workers ascribed to call centre work, the ways in which workers incorporated the idea of working in a call centre into their sense of self and the different coping techniques they adopted to deal with everyday workplace experiences. Data analysis for this study was carried out in an iterative fashion by going back and forth between the data and emerging themes (Miles and Huberman 1994).

Data for this chapter is drawn from the call centre units of INT-A and INT-B. Both INT-A and INT-B were viewed as being among the highly ranked BPOs in India and adopted several innovative HR practices to manage their front-line employees. They were similar on many counts, such as size, process mix, systems of control, the HR practices adopted and the customer base (both were third-party BPOs which served international clients in countries such as the UK, the US and Australia). They employed between 9,000 and 10,000 employees, most of whom were well qualified.

## Work Reality and Management in Practice

Work at INT-A and INT-B was highly repetitive, standardized and regimented. The typical inbound calls handled included routine billing-related queries, change of address, service cancellation or service help. Some of the customer service agents (often referred to as front-line executives (FLEs)) were responsible for making outbound calls to new customers to familiarize them with the different aspects of their service. Some informants at INT-B were responsible for debt collection.

In both companies, management exerted considerable efforts to control and monitor front-line interactions between call centre agents and their customers. Detailed step-by-step protocols were offered to guide front-line agents through a call. Customer service agents could only respond to customer demands by choosing from a pre-decided range of options available on computer menus. Agents were expected to follow conversation scripts, including opening and closing lines. The pace of work was dictated by the use of automated call-distribution systems, which continuously directed incoming calls to the next available agent in order to maintain a continuous call flow. A predictive dialler provided similar facility for outbound calling at INT-B. In all these aspects, work at Indian call centres entailed many of the signature marks of classical Taylorism – standardization, fragmentation and constant monitoring of performance.

Customer service agents were divided into teams based on the processes they worked for and these teams were made to sit together in clusters. One team leader was assigned to each of these process clusters. The team leaders worked the same shift as their teams, sat close to their team members and were responsible for overseeing their team's performance. Specific targets were set for each worker, which were closely monitored by the team leaders. The usual work shift at both the call centres was nine hours, during which each agent was allowed a one-hour or one-hour-and-fifteen minute break, which included lunch/dinner and two tea breaks. Every front-line agent was expected to adhere strictly to a work schedule, which was prepared based on actual and projected call flow. They did not have the freedom to alter these schedules by taking unplanned breaks. Any change in the daily routine needed a team leader's approval. The team leaders at INT-A were observed walking up and down the operations floor, checking/ensuring that all the agents logged into the system without any delays. Agents caught 'hanging around' and chatting with co-workers, were nudged verbally to return to their seats and immediately log into the system. Team leaders represented a managerial echelon whose purpose was almost entirely that of monitoring, controlling and chivvying the workforce.

In addition to managerial and technological controls, customers were made an integral part of the control system by frequently collecting their feedback on service quality and call experience. Even when absent, customers became authority figures – guiding training and performance assessment.

Elaborate and rigorous induction trainings were offered to the newcomers, in an attempt to establish customer supremacy and emphasize the importance of customer service. Voice and accent training and cultural training were used to equip the front-line agents with an understanding of their customers' culture and to ensure they sounded right when interacting with the customers. Once on the job, every call was recorded and a sample of calls, per front-line agent, was assessed on qualitative and quantitative parameters. Quality assessment was carried out by the Quality Assurance (QA) team and the Customer Experience Analysis (CEA) team. While the QA team assessed agents on parameters mentioned in the service level agreements and parameters, such as adherence to schedule (including call handling time, wrap time, etc.), adherence to scripts, voice quality, pitch and so forth, the CEA team assessed agents on listening skills, rapport formation, enthusiasm and warmth, among others.

## Call Centre Dynamics: Shifting Power Relations

### CUSTOMERS SEEK TO ENFORCE THEIR INTERESTS AND RESISTED BY WORKERS

Management's detailed attempts at standardization, efficiency and monitoring were often thwarted by the presence of customers who were aware of their importance and primacy. Desirous of greater choice and frustrated by scripted interactions, customers used their power to demand individualized experiences and time-devouring explanations. At times, customers made unreasonable demands, directly threatened front-line agents with poor performance evaluation or asked to be transferred to the managers. A front-line agent at INT-A shared one such call:

> Once this lady called … and was very irate. She wanted to cancel her dial-up connection after a month and was insisting that the advisor should make a note of the cancellation date right away. She said, 'Do whatever you want to – put the date into your system, make a note of it, try and remember it, do anything, but I will not call again to remind you about the cancellation'. My friend who was taking the call tried to explain that it was not possible and that it was against the company policy. But the lady was very irate and said, 'I want to speak to your manager'. My friend put the call on hold and told me that the lady was very irate and wanted to speak to the manager. So my friend asked me to speak to the lady as if I were the manager. (Simran, FLE, INT-A)

Such demands for escalation were common and undermined the front-line agents' ability to deal with customer needs. While on this occasion, Simran helped her friend by posing as a manager and convincing the customer to accept organizational rules, such manipulation was not possible on the majority of occasions. Frequent demands for escalation threatened to undermine the agents' performance in the managers' eyes.

## WORKERS CONSPIRING WITH MANAGERS TO RESIST CUSTOMERS AND DEFEND THEIR PROFESSIONALISM

Customer-generated stress was reported to be a prominent source of pressure on the job. Customer rejection, discrimination and abuse, following the customers' assumption that call centre work required no training or expertise and that UK- or US-based operators would deal with the customers' requests more effectively and professionally, were commonly reported as recurrent sources of frustration by the informants at INT-A and INT-B. Negative customer exchanges undermined the workers' sense of professionalism and professional identity sustained by the extensive training they had undergone prior to starting their jobs. These exchanges were particularly upsetting for the workers, many of whom, unlike their Western counterparts, had university degrees.

Front-line agents adopted a range of techniques – some studied and well-thought through, others reactive and risqué – in order to cope with the frustration and anger resulting from such negative customer interactions. On some occasions, the team leaders were called upon to act as allies to accomplish revenge against a rude customer. Stalin, an FLE at INT-A recalled:

> *There was once this time when I had been in the outbound process for three months and I had not even managed to do a single sale, not a single sale! Then one day, I made a call to some Mr. Ruth in UK and tried to sell the internet connection to him. I told him that in case a sale happened then he would be my first customer. I was trying to gain his sympathy. He was listening carefully for some time and then said, 'Ok Stalin, I will buy your product if you play one game with me'. I felt weird that he is asking me to play a game, but I continued and said 'Ok sir, I will play the game with you'. So, he said 'Ok Stalin, that is good. So now, in this game you will do exactly what I do, alright? Ok, so, one, two, three ...' and he banged down the phone!!! [Stalin dropped his jaw and opened his palms in disgust, indicating that he felt insulted by the customer.] I was so upset that I went to my TL [team leader]*

*and told him about the incident. Actually, when that fellow had banged down the phone, I had quickly put the call on hold and taken down his number. I told my TL that I wanted to call this person back. My TL told me, 'Leave it buddy, just forget about it'. But I said to my TL, 'I think I will manage to make this sale, so I want to call this person back'. My TL was not very happy, but agreed reluctantly. I quickly called Mr. Ruth back and said, 'Sir I am Rocky calling from <company name>, we have some great internet offers for you'. He immediately recognized my voice and said, 'That is not Rocky, that is Stalin, right?'. I said, 'Yes sir, it is me. You were playing a nice game with me and I just wanted to know, who taught you this game?'. Actually, I wanted to insult him by asking him who had done something similar to him [smiles]. That man went completely quiet. He was too embarrassed. Then he said, 'This is my wife's game'. Even though I could not manage to sell anything to him, I accomplished what I had wanted to. I wanted to insult him and that I managed to do!*

Such act of retaliation reinforced Stalin's belief of not being servile to 'nasty' customers. By engaging in revenge, Stalin hoped to induce similar feelings of insult and embarrassment in the customer that had been generated within him. Stalin used his team leader as an ally to bend the organizational rules and 'get back' at the customer.

## TIPPING THE BALANCE: WORKERS USING CUSTOMERS AS ALLIES

Not every agent was able to enlist his/her team leader's support to cope with work pressures. In fact, team leaders were persistently experienced as chief causes of dissatisfaction and frustration. Front-line agents expected team leaders to protect and support them when faced with discordant workplace demands; however, the agents often felt betrayed by their team leaders' obsession with standardization, efficiency and control.

Interestingly, while customer-generated frustrations were rationalized to be a part of the job, team leader-generated frustrations were less tolerated and met with active resistance. Responses to frustrations caused by team leaders were more explicit and often more aggressive than those to frustrations caused by customers. Hostility towards team leaders was consistent and predominantly expressed through 'retaliation' or 'silent rebellion'. At INT-A, a team member recalled feeling extremely angry at not getting 'deserving' incentives promised to her by the team leader after her 'outstanding performance' at meeting targets. In retaliation, she came to work but did not log into the system for three days.

Despite her team leader 'requesting' her to resume work, she insisted on speaking to a senior manager. In another act of rebellion, she decided to opt out of the 'fast promotion policy' offered by the management to outstanding performers because she did not trust the fairness of the process. Throughout the fieldwork, it was apparent that the biggest leverage available to the workers was the threat to quit; this was frequently used to get their team leaders to 'listen' to them.

Customers, as important authority figures, were often used as allies to undermine a team leader's position. As the following quote highlights, front-line agents sometimes dismissed their team leader's authority by evading their suggestions and aligning with customer interests instead:

> Our team leaders know nothing. Though they are supposed to update themselves, they do nothing. If you go to ask them something then they don't know how to handle the situation. Like once, I got a call from a customer who was asking for his phone bill, which was many months old. I did not know how to access that bill and how to help him, so I put him on hold and asked my TL (team leader). Imagine, my TL said: 'Tell him that we cannot do it. We cannot give him such an old bill. It's against our policy'. I was not satisfied with the answer and was very keen to help the customer, so I called up the client representatives. This lady who picked up the call had been working with <client's name> for twenty years and she knew everything about the policies. She explained to me the process to access the old bill and said that she would like to speak to my TL, who had said that this is not possible. I did not tell her my TL's name as that's not right but imagine, he did not know anything!! Then I went back to the call and told the customer about the bill etc. and he was so happy. (Suman, FLE, INT-A)

Events such as these dislocated the power relations between the worker and the management. As consciously chosen techniques, these gave workers a sense of active agency and a much greater sense of control over their work lives. Importantly, these reactions gave critical messages to the managers about the workers having *choices* rather than being trapped in a job from which they cannot escape.

## Management in Practice: Innovative or Distractive?

Aware of the constant tension among team leaders, employees and customers, company management exerted immense effort to monitor and control workplace interactions. Remote call recordings, live call barging and screen capture technology were used to monitor agents' actions and interactions. Such intensive and pervasive surveillance stifled the workers and several of them, interviewed for this study, reported experiencing work as suffocating and monotonous. Despite adopting a range of coping techniques, sometimes the pressures became too much to handle and agents resorted to fleeing the situation by absconding or quitting the organization.

Attrition was a major concern of call centre managers, as it had been in the early days of Henry Ford. To monitor and prevent attrition, team leaders at INT-A were expected to carry out a weekly analysis, categorizing their team members into Red, Amber or Green category, based on their assessment of how likely they were to quit. Agents categorized as Red were, in the team leaders' assessment, expected to quit within the next 0–7 days. Agents categorized as Amber were assessed as intending to quit between 7 and 20 days. Agents allocated to the Green category were considered 'safe' and were expected to continue working for more than 21 days. Following such assessments, the team leaders were expected to devise means to retain the 'Red' and 'Amber' team members.

Retention tactics involved the use of innovative HR practices to enhance the image of call centres as positive and progressive workplaces. Some of the prominent practices involved introducing fast-track promotion policies, teambuilding activities, creation of a 'fun' culture at work (see also Kinnie et al. 2000). These were used to set call centres apart from the traditional organizations in India that relied more on socially driven and ad hoc HR practices (see also Budhwar et al. 2006, D'Cruz and Noronha 2011). State-of-the-art buildings and high-quality infrastructure (such as an in-house gym, pool tables, cafeterias, etc.) were used to lure existing employees and potential candidates (as also noted by Ramesh 2004, Mirchandani 2004). High wages, higher incentives and an informal organizational culture were among the key aspects highlighted to entice workers.

Front-line agents were also reminded of their role in the organization's growth story. Some of the managers referred to them as the 'real breadwinners' responsible for representing the organization and contributing to customer satisfaction. Front-line agents were regularly encouraged to behave like 'professionals', who were expected to keep aside personal problems and behave rationally and objectively at all times while maintaining the expected levels of customer service (also see D'Cruz and Noronha 2006). They were expected to accept organizational monitoring without resistance (for it helps to ensure consistency of customers' experience) and take greater responsibility of representing organizational values to the customers (ibid.). Micromanagement of employees, however, severely undermined this very aspect of professionalism that management aimed to encourage – namely, self-discipline.

These innovative practices, though ostensibly aimed to enhance high involvement and commitment, were patently underpinned by managerial desire to limit attrition and enhance efficiency. Adoption of such innovative HR practices did not emanate from a sudden change of heart by the management to make provisions for worker autonomy and welfare, but from a need to reconcile the contradictory logics of customer orientation and efficiency that underpin service work. As Fleming and Sturdy (2010: 177) argue, these seemingly progressive management practices are intended to direct workers' attention away from work monotony and regimentation and 'capture employees' sociality, energy and "authentic" or "non-work" personalities as emotional labour' (also see Houlihan 2000).

Wallace et al. (2000: 10) argue that several of these management practices adopted by call centres have a sacrificial quality, whereby 'the enthusiasm of the front-line is sacrificed to provide efficient service without the costs the organization would otherwise have borne'. The strategy involves hiring agents with an intrinsic motivation for customer service and assigning them tasks that demand high efficiency, often at the expense of customer satisfaction. This deliberate 'misalignment between the task demands and employee intrinsic motivation' pushes 'the management of the efficiency/service tension' onto the front line, resulting in employee stress, burnout and turnover (ibid.: 10).

## Conclusion

As we are now aware the word 'management' derives from the French word *manège*, itself a derivative of the Italian *maneggiare*, the training of a horse in its paces. Management originates in taming and domesticating a wild force of nature and turning it into a useful resource for humans. One of its affinities lies in control – controlling a horse is a necessary part of training it. But there are other affinities. To manage also means to treat with respect, to handle as well as to control. It also means to unleash a hidden potential – just as the potential of each horse is developed through its training, management aims at developing the potentials of ideas, of resources and, of course, people. Yet, nearly all of these resonances in the word have been lost or subordinated to control (Gabriel 2012).

Despite the popular belief that the rise of service economy or the knowledge economy has compelled management to discard its traditional coercive garb and adopt participative shades, an obsession with control remains its defining feature. Some of the extreme methods for controlling workers, as popularized by Taylor and Ford, have been 'softened' by the introduction of flexible working, autonomous work groups and team working, among others. These, however, have by no means dampened management's desire or even enthusiasm to monitor, measure and control performance. In fact, scholars writing from a critical management perspective argue that the contemporary management controls are far more complex and invasive. Aided by various means – technological, bureaucratic, normative and a combination of these – today's management colonizes the very identity of the employee, whose emotions, commitment and private thoughts end up being controlled by the invisible hand of management (Casey 1999, Knights and Vurdubakis 1994, Sturdy and Fineman 2001). Inspired by the work of Foucault (1977), some contemporary thinkers have gone as far as to view the contemporary worker as colonized through and through by managerial and entrepreneurial discourses, not only unable to resist but unable to even conceptualize what resistance may entail (Alvesson and Willmott 2002). Findings of our study indicate that such a view may be too bleak and that requiems for worker resistance may be premature.

Investigations into the organization, management and experience of work in the prototypical growth sectors of the new economy – call centres – lend support to the view that the fundamental nature of management remains firmly rooted in the tradition of control pioneered by Taylor and Ford. Of course, many other things have changed – the nature of work that many people do, the structure of organizations, the rise of the cult of the consumer and the increasingly global dimension of competition and innovation may be worlds apart from a century ago. People who act as managers today may also be worlds apart from their predecessors of a century ago, not least because many of them are liable to find themselves on the receiving end of downsizing or outsourcing, spending time unemployed or downshifting. In its fundamental positioning with regard to the labour process, the experience of call centres indicates that the continuities far outweigh discontinuities.

## References

Alvesson, M. and Willmott, H. 2002. Identity regulation as organizational control: producing the appropriate individual. *Journal of Management Studies*, 39(5), 619–43.

Amin, A. 1994. Post-Fordism: models, fantasies and phantoms of transition, in *Post-Fordism: A Reader*, edited by A. Amin. Oxford: Blackwell, 1–39.

Baldry, C., Bain, P., Taylor, P., Hyman, J., Scholarios, D., Marks, A., Watson, A., Gilbert, K., Gall, G. and Bunzel, D. 2007. *The Meaning of Work in the New Economy*. New York: Palgrave Macmillan.

Batt, R. and Moynihan, L. 2002. The viability of alternative call centre production models. *Human Resource Management Journal*, 12(4), 14–34.

Beynon, H. 1975. *Working for Ford*. East Ardsley (UK): EP Publishing.

Braverman, H. 1974. *Labor and Monopoly Capital*. New York: Monthly Review Press.

Budhwar, P., Luthar, H. and Bhatnagar, J. 2006. The dynamics of HRM systems in Indian BPO firms. *Journal of Labour Research*, 27(3), 339–60.

Casey, C. 1999. 'Come join the family': discipline and integration in corporate and organizational culture. *Human Relations*, 52(2), 155–78.

Cohen, L. and El-Sawad, A. 2007. Lived experiences of off-shoring: an examination of UK and Indian financial service employees' accounts of themselves and one another. *Human Relations*, 60(8), 1235–62.

D'Cruz, P. and Noronha, E. 2006. Being professional: organizational control in Indian call centers. *Social Science Computer Review*, 24(3), 342–61.

D'Cruz, P. and Noronha, E. 2011. High commitment management practices re-examined: the case of Indian call centres. *Economic and Industrial Democracy*, 185–205.

Fleming, P. and Sturdy, A. 2010. 'Being yourself' in the electronic sweatshop: new forms of normative control. *Human Relations*, 64(2), 177–200.

Foucault, M. 1977. *Discipline and Punish*. London: Allen Unwin.

Frenkel, S., Korczynski, M., Shire, K. and Tam, M. 1999. *On the Front Line: Organisation of Work in the Information Economy*. Ithaca NY: Cornell University Press.

Gabriel, Y. 2008. Latte capitalism and late capitalism: reflections on fantasy and care as part of the service triangle, in *Service Work: Critical Perspectives*, edited by M. Korczynski and C. MacDonald. London: Routledge, 175–90.

Gabriel, Y. 2012. Under new management: Subjects, Objects and Hubris, New and Old. *Nouvelle revue de psychosociologie*, 13(1): 241–64.

Gabriel, Y. and Lang, T. 2006. *The Unmanageable Consumer*. London: Sage.

Hancock, P. and Tyler, M. 2000. 'The look of love': gender and the organization of aesthetics, in *Body and Organization*, edited by J. Hassard, R. Holliday and H. Willmott. London: Sage.

Hochschild, A.R. 1983. *The Managed Heart: Commercialization of Human Feeling*. Berkeley: University of California Press.

Holman, D., Batt, R. and Holtgrewe, U. 2007. *The Global Call Center Report: International Perspectives on Management and Employment*. Report of the

Global Call Center Network [Online: Global Call Center Project.] Available at: http://www.ilr.cornell.edu/globalcallcenter/upload/GCC-Intl-Rept-US-Version.pdf [accessed 22 March 2011].

Houlihan, M. 2000. Eyes wide shut? Querying the depth of call centre learning. *Journal of European Industrial Training*, 24 (2/3/4), 228–40.

Jermier, J.M. 1998. Introduction: critical perspective on organizational control. *Administrative Science Quarterly*, 43(2), 235–56.

Kinnie, N., Hutchinson, S. and Purcell, J. 2000. 'Fun and surveillance': the paradox of high commitment management in call centres. *International Journal of Human Resource Management*, 11(5), 967–85.

Knights, D. and Vurdubakis, T. 1994. Foucault, power, resistance and all that, in *Resistance and Power in Organizations*, edited by J. Jermier, W. Nord and D. Knights. London: Routledge, 167–98.

Korczynski, M. 2001. The contradictions of service work: call centre as customer-oriented bureaucracy, in *Customer Service: Empowerment and Entrapment*, edited by A. Sturdy, I. Grugulis and H. Willmott. London: Palgrave, 79–102.

Korczynski, M., Shire, K., Frenkel, S. and Tam, M. 2000. Service work in consumer capitalism: customers, control and contradictions. *Work, Employment and Society*, 14(4), 669–87.

McClean, E. and Collins, C.J. 2011. High-commitment HR practices, employee effort, and firm performance: investigating the effects of HR practices across employee groups. *Human Resource Management*, 50(3), 341–63.

MacIntyre, A. 1981. *After Virtue*. London: Duckworth.

Miles, M.B. and Huberman, A.M. 1994. *Qualitative Data Analysis: An Expanded Sourcebook*. Thousand Oaks CA: Sage.

Mirchandani, K. 2004. Practices of global capital: gaps, cracks and ironies in transnational call centres in India. *Global Networks*, 4(4), 355–73.

Mirchandani, K. 2008. Enactments of class and nationality in transnational call centres, in *The Emotional Organization: Passions and Power*, edited by S. Fineman. Malden MA: Blackwell, 88–101.

NASSCOM. 2010. *Executive Summary: NASSCOM Strategic Review* [Online: National Association of Software and Services Companies]. Available at: http://www.nasscom.in/upload/SR10/ExecutiveSummary.pdf [accessed 22 March 2011].

Poster, W.R. 2007. Who's on the line? Indian call center agents pose as Americans for US – outsourced firms. *Industrial Relations*, 46(2), 271–304.

Ramesh, B.P. 2004. 'Cyber coolies' in BPO: insecurities and vulnerabilities of non-standard work. *Economic and Political Weekly*, 39(January), 492–7.

Russell, B. 2008. Call centres: a decade of research. *International Journal of Management Reviews*, 10(3), 195–219.

Russell, B. 2009. *Smiling down the Line: Info-Service Work in the Global Economy*. Toronto: University of Toronto Press.

Stein, M. 2007. Toxicity and the unconscious experience of the body at the employee–customer interface. *Organization Studies*, 28(8), 1223–41.

Sturdy, A. 1998. Customer care in a consumer society: smiling and sometimes meaning it? *Organization*, 5(1), 27–53.

Sturdy, A. and Fineman, S. 2001. Struggles for the control of affect: resistance as politics and emotion, in *Customer Service: Empowerment and Entrapment*, edited by A. Sturdy, I. Grugulis and H. Willmott. London: Palgrave, 135–57.

Taylor, P. 2010. The globalization of service work: analysing the transnational call centre value chain, in *Working Life: Renewing Labour Process Analysis*, edited by P. Thompson and C. Smith. Basingstoke: Palgrave Macmillan, 244–64.

Taylor, P. and Bain, P. 1999. 'An assembly line in the head': work and employee relations in the call centre. *Industrial Relations Journal*, 30(2), 101–17.

Taylor, P. and Bain, P. 2005. 'India calling to the faraway towns': the call centre labour process and globalization. *Work, Employment and Society*, 19(2), 261–82.

Taylor, P., Mulvey, G., Hyman, J. and Bain, P. 2002. Work organization, control and the experience of work in call centres. *Work, Employment and Society*, 16(1), 133–50.

Wallace, C.M., Eagleson, G. and Waldersee, R. 2000. The sacrificial HR strategy in call centers. *International Journal of Service Industry Management*, 11(2), 174–85.

Warhurst, C., Nickson, D., Witz, A. and Cullen, A.M. 2000. Aesthetic labour in interactive service work: some case study evidence from the 'new' Glasgow. *Service Industries Journal*, 20(3), 1–18.

Whitener, E.M. 2001. Do 'high commitment' human resource practices affect employee commitment? A cross-level analysis using hierarchical linear modeling. *Journal of Management*, 27(5), 515–35.

# 6

# Digital Taylorism: Hybrid Knowledge Professionals in the UK ICT Sector

*Judith Glover*

## Introduction

Developing the concept of 'Digital Taylorism', Brown et al. (2011) argue that many jobs held by highly qualified workers are now over-categorized and routinized. Few are now in jobs that give 'permission to think'. This chapter is based on research that examined a particular type of knowledge worker in the ICT (information and communication technologies) sector: 'hybrid' professionals. These are workers with high levels of qualification who combine technical expertise with prosocial behavioural competences, popularly known as 'soft' skills.[1] Their role is to liaise between technical colleagues and customers. They could therefore be seen as working in an area located between 'different sources of knowledge' (Hulme et al. 2009). They could be seen as 'third space professionals' with fluid identities that are valuable to organizations (Whitchurch 2008).

The way that IT professionals in hybrid positions perceived their work and the skills involved are the focus of this chapter. The conclusion points to a dilemma for the concept of digital Taylorism: whilst categorization and routinization of jobs may indeed detract from 'permission to think', the research

---

[1] In the chapter I use the term 'soft skills', but I note Jubas and Butterwick's view: 'The use of the words hard and soft is insidious … as the former term implies skills that are solidly entrenched and evident, while the latter implies a lack of definition and reliability' (Jubas and Butterwick 2008: 521). The term may therefore reinforce a perception of such skills as inferior to 'hard' technical skills. My perspective is that these are strong arguments against its use and that perhaps another term could be adopted. This is not the focus of this chapter, however.

subjects felt that categorization was required in order to gain recognition for the hybridity of their jobs. Without this categorization, advancement in the organization was unlikely. Advancement was only likely to be achieved by abandoning a hybrid role and embarking on the management ladder, thus risking the atrophy of their technical skills. The value for the organization of translating between the technical world and that of clients would thus be lost.

## A Growth of Hybrid Jobs in ICT

Two shifts have led to a growth in hybrid jobs in ICT (Glover and Guerrier 2010). First, the 'technicization' of the ICT sector (Darr 2002) has created a demand for technical experts who can also sell products and services. This has led to an increased emphasis on social and interactive skills, since technical experts are increasingly dependent on contextual knowledge held by the client. Product development in ICT depends on close interaction with customers, since the way that they use the firm's products is key to further development (Ruiz Ben 2007). This client focus has led to the IT sector being seen as a 'new service sector' and software developers as 'service workers' (Loogma et al. 2004: 323). Increased emphasis on offshoring and outsourcing has added a global and increasingly complex dimension to the emphasis on clients.

A second key change relates to new organizational forms. Work in knowledge-intensive firms primarily takes place in multi-functional and multi-skilled project teams, where traditional hierarchies are kept to a minimum (Johnson et al. 2009). As the IT sector has globalized, these teams are increasingly multi-site, involving complex management with cross-cultural dimensions. Yet, despite flattened hierarchies, teams need to be managed and held together. Communication skills are therefore fundamental. This requirement has been further strengthened in the IT sector by the growing use of methods of working such as 'agile computing', the basis of which is good inter- and intra-team communication (Abrahamsson et al. 2002, Smite et al. 2010).

In view of these fundamental shifts, much work in the IT sector, whether client-facing or team-facing, or a combination of the two, requires a mix of technical and communication skills. This mix has taken the form of what has become known in the academic literature (but generally not in the practitioner literature) as 'hybrid' jobs. Woodfield (2002) argues that these changes have led to the emergence of new hybrid roles in ICT – for example in consultancy, client services and project management. There is furthermore a perception that skills other than technical skills are needed in order to improve graduate employment: hence the integration in some science, engineering and technology (SET) degrees of 'professional skills' training, to include communication and teamwork (Engineering Council 2011). The implication is that students of SET should aspire to a professional identity that encompasses both technical skills and non-technical behavioural ones. On a more general level, and based on the writings of Zeldin (1995), there is the view that postgraduate business programmes should teach the skill of *savoir-relier*: the ability to build bridges between people, generations, cultures and ideas (Reisz 2011: 41).

In this post-bureaucratic model of flexible specialization (Clegg 1990, Piore and Sabel 1984), the concept of hybridity has resonance with the longstanding literature on functionally flexible workers (see Blyton and Jenkins 2007). The hybrid worker could be seen as the ideal worker in a post-Fordist context, since workers with roles that can be changed and expanded are seen as best able to meet complex dynamic economic environments (Woodfield 2002, Whitchurch 2008). Labour market rigidities can thus be undermined.

Hybrid roles in the ICT sector have attracted attention from researchers. For example, there has been a focus on the employer perspective, showing that employers value such roles (Evans et al. 2007). There have also been attempts to identify different types of hybrid jobs in ICT (Whitehouse and Diamond 2005, Loogma et al. 2004). There has been a particular focus on the issue of women's position in IT, where there is a body of literature on the gendering of IT jobs (for example Guerrier et al. 2009, Kelan 2008, Webster 1996).

## Digital Taylorism

Brown et al.'s (2011) concept of 'Digital Taylorism' sheds new light on the employment of knowledge workers in the first decade of the twenty-first century. Knowledge work – often carried out by well-qualified workers – is rationalized in the same way as at the beginning of the twentieth century. The task of business in contemporary times remains the capturing and controlling of the individual, tacit, nature of knowledge in order to standardize it. The argument is that the standardization of production associated with F.W. Taylor's bid to raise productivity through 'scientific management' (Taylor 1911) can be observed in a contemporary form in many of the industries associated with the knowledge economy.

Brown et al. suggest three broad types of knowledge workers: 'developers', 'demonstrators' and 'drones'. Developers, representing no more than 15 per cent of an organization's workforce, are those who are given 'permission to think' (Brown et al. 2011: 81). Typical roles would be senior researchers, senior managers and professionals. Demonstrators, on the other hand, implement existing knowledge, which is standardized and pre-packaged. The implication is that they do not have 'permission to think'. Typical roles include consultants, teachers, technicians. Their unifying function is 'effective communication with colleagues and customers' (Brown et al. 2011: 81). These are highly qualified workers whose individual, tacit, knowledge has been standardized. Drones, typically in call centre and data entry jobs, are not expected to 'engage their brains', although they may be well qualified.

The implication is that the standardization and routinization of the demonstrator and drone categories will have effects on the way that they view their jobs, presumably lowering their job satisfaction because, despite their high levels of qualification, they do not have 'permission to think'.

## Methods and Methodology

The research that underpins this chapter aimed to fill a gap in the literature by exploring highly qualified ICT workers' constructions of the concept and nature of hybrid jobs. Thus the research explored their perceptions of 'soft' skills, the career consequences of hybrid jobs and whether there was a distinct hybrid skill set that operated in a space between two sets of discourse and knowledge: on the one hand that of technical colleagues and on the other that of clients.

The focus of the work was to explore workers' constructions of their hybrid jobs, and qualitative methods were therefore appropriate. A call was put out to the Young Professional Group of the British Computer Society (now known as BCS, the chartered institute for IT) in early summer 2010 for research subjects who saw themselves as being in hybrid (technical/soft skill) jobs in ICT. The Young Professional Group was targeted because one aim of the research was to explore employees' perceptions of their career paths; thus it made sense to focus on those who were in early or relatively early stages of their employment (35 is the age limit for the Young Professional Group). In-depth semi-structured phone interviews lasting between 30 and 45 minutes were carried out with 15 people (13 men and 2 women) in the period June–August 2010. The interviews were fully transcribed and participants were given the opportunity to review their transcriptions so that they could clarify points if they wished to. Anonymity was promised, through the use of pseudonyms. Quotations refer to pseudonyms without reference to job titles, discussed in more detail in the following section on the profile of participants. A decision to omit job titles was taken because in the context of a small-scale study involving 15 research subjects, the job title could identify the source of the quotation.

## Hybrid Workers in ICT

### PROFILE OF PARTICIPANTS

Because they were members of the Young Professional Group of the BCS, it is reasonable to assume that participants were in the early or fairly early phases of careers. Almost all had a strong technical background, with technical degrees and/or substantial experience in technical roles. Most participants were from the private sector.

Job titles included IT business analyst, business systems analyst, lead engineer, third line support, technical project manager, consultant, business relationship manager. A defining feature was that a key element of the jobs was effective communication between technical colleagues and clients. Some participants gave two or more job titles, perhaps underlining the difficulty in pinning down their work identity in conventional organizational terms.

The participants had a largely even split between the technical and the 'soft' side of their work, and typically described their work as 60 per cent technical, 40 per cent soft. There were a few outliers – for example, one person had more of a 70/30 split (technical/soft) and another 30/70. But some made the point that this split can vary from day to day and according to the stage of the project, underlining their flexibility. Some pointed out that it was not just a question of splitting time, but more a judgement about criticality and complexity.

> *Some weeks can be 80 per cent soft skills and only 20 per cent technical, other times it can be 70 per cent technical. It varies in what's going on and what's on my plate as it were. (Giles)*

Many participants felt that all jobs in the IT sector are now to some degree hybrid, thus:

> ... the business on the left ... the tech on their right, they can glue the two together and I'd say that's definitely the way things are going. (Jack)

Even highly technical jobs such as developer were thought to need some form of soft skills, specifically communication skills needed for teamwork. A small number of participants had experience of agile computing (referred to in the introductory section) and made the point strongly that colleague/colleague and employee/client communication skills are key to this approach.

## ROLE CONSTRUCTIONS

Participants talked about being a 'middle man', a 'go-between', liaising between different types of stakeholders, acting as a bridge. A common theme was to refer to a role as an intermediary – moving between different worlds of team and client and acting as 'the lynchpin' between the two. One referred to his role as a 'point man' – an expression with military origins that describes a person who takes up the first and most exposed position in a combat military formation. Another described his role as a 'filter', where he protected his team from being given tasks that might detract from the task at hand. One description was a 'conduit type of person', another constructed himself as a 'buffer' between client and team, with the role of sometimes needing to shield his team from demands. One saw the role as 'wanting the best for the client but also representing the company's needs'. Only one participant rather more negatively referred to being 'stuck in the middle'.

Almost all participants presented themselves as satisfied with their hybrid jobs. Job satisfaction was talked about by almost everyone. They enjoyed the technical and the soft side. Hybrid jobs' potential for creating future opportunities and keeping options open was mentioned.

> 'It's the ideal mix.' (Giles)

> 'There is a middle ground here that sits very well.' (Ian)

> 'It gives freedom, autonomy.' (Sean)

> 'Carrying on doing technical work but appreciating not being squirreled away.' (Alex)

Analysis of the interviews indicated that the participants saw themselves as adaptable, versatile, flexible – all ideal characteristics for organizations in a post-Fordist context (Whitchurch 2008). Participants came across as creative and active:

> *Having a conversation with a business person early on in the morning and the following afternoon sat down producing a code to meet whatever the topic of discussion was with that person in the morning. (Ian)*

## THE 'IDEAL' WORKER: SELF-PROVISIONING

The 'self-provisioning' of the research subjects was evident. This was particularly obvious when participants talked about the risk of losing the technical side of their expertise. They made the assumption that it was up to them as individuals to maintain and update technical knowledge. There was no suggestion that there were organizational imperatives to keep the technical side going.

> *I tend to get involved in what my [technical] team are doing … I don't just sit there and just do the non-technical stuff because I want to keep some of my technical knowledge and it helps me in other situations. (Maggie)*

> *I experienced that [lack of technical expertise] in my role, just for myself some of the knowledge that I didn't have I had to read up on it myself. (Sean)*

> *I actually schedule time into my weekly schedule, to do technical development stuff … I'm really lucky that I'm able to do this … I don't know what I'd do if I couldn't. (Larry)*

There was a clear sense of participants making their own way:

> *You have to sell yourself to people and you're the only one in there. You have to manage yourself in the relationship. (Sean)*

> *They needed more people in as well and so I got one or two others onto the team and ended up managing the team and I think it just progressed from there … working out what the requirements are and how we can meet them … it was really quite organic development. (Maggie)*

*It's exciting because I set my own career path. It's like I said, when you do strict technical work, you're very much this is what you're doing, or this is the technology you are working on. Whereas with what I'm doing, I'm making decisions, I'm changing the direction of things. (Ben)*

## MOVING BETWEEN TWO WORLDS: TRANSLATING AND INTERPRETING

It was striking that almost all participants talked about their role in linguistic terms. They talked about translation and interpretation; about adjusting their vocabulary and manner of speaking to address different audiences. Thus:

*I talk about a technology using the language of the audience. (Ollie)*

*If you try using the same communication style with technical colleagues that you do with customers, it's actually ineffective. (Giles)*

*Speaking two languages and translating between the two. (Susan)*

*Being able to talk as though you are the mirror image of that other person. So if somebody starts talking to you in a very very basic language then you respond in a very very basic way so that you develop a rapport with that person. (Martin)*

*So it lets me talk to the managerial people, I can get along roughly on their level, and I'm also able to talk directly to the architects or the technical people. (Larry)*

*There's quite a lot of translation, so I'll quite often be expected to translate from IT technical language and jargon to something which is a bit more business focussed. But also, on the flipside, part of my role is to understand the business's jargon ... So, [putting] their jargon back into something that the IT teams can understand. (Dan)*

These are key skills in the linguistics-based professions of translation and interpretation. A particular facility that was evident was moving between registers: having a deep knowledge of the subject matter that can be expressed in terms that are appropriate for different audiences; changing meaning into appropriate terms (Halliday 1978). Linguists refer to a source language and a target language: in the source language the skills are listening, understanding, memorizing, editing, mentally translating. In the target language the skill is to verbalize in different ways to different audiences. Working in both directions between source and target is also needed. Such skills are recognized as being demanding and difficult to achieve; they require high-level and long-lasting training – and they typically attract high salaries and prestige.

It was evident from participants that they saw these navigational and conversational skills (Hulme et al. 2009) as key to their jobs, perceiving them as a distinct set of blended skills:

> *Two previously distinct sets, now seen as a combination into a new set of skills that encapsulates a bit of both. (Ollie)*

This idea of a new set of skills that derive from two distinct sets has much in common with Whitchurch's (2008) idea of third space skills, defined as movement between functional and organizational boundaries, creating in so doing a new professional space. The implication in Whitchurch's work is that this has considerable organizational value. In the research, there was clear recognition of the productive role of translation and interpretation. For example, they were seen to be key to negotiating large public sector IT projects. In addition some participants felt that such skills could have helped avoid large public sector IT disasters. They have the vital function of keeping the technical employees in touch with customers, and vice versa, probably in repeated iterations.

> *I'll attend those [customer] meetings, get some requirements together and then translate those requirements into something I can tell the developers. The developers will develop and then I'll go back to the customer and say, this is what we've done, and talk about changes and things like that. (Sean)*

In an era of globalization, largely involving offshoring and outsourcing, good communication skills are self-evidently important and are key to productivity.

> *If you have people who are customer facing, who are uncomfortable about that experience, who don't know how to handle it and who do not understand why they are doing it, you're putting your whole business in jeopardy. (Martin)*

> *They [the customers] will be approaching things in their business-oriented way but I'm looking for the technical reasons behind the issues that they're finding and trying to define a solution for those. (Susan)*

*They [the customers] will be approaching things in their business-oriented way but I'm looking for the technical reasons behind the issues that they're finding and trying to define a solution for those. (Mark)*

Yet some concerns surfaced. Several participants also talked about the possible risk of allowing the technical side of their jobs to diminish. This was seen as a possibility if advancement could only be achieved by joining the management career ladder. Furthermore, there was quite a degree of uncertainty amongst the participants about whether their hybrid skills were formally recognized and rewarded.

In a Taylorist vision, these skills would be routinized and standardized, yet several participants felt that they were unquantifiable and that this posed a problem in terms of their career progression.

## QUANTIFYING SOFT SKILLS

Employers in the ICT sector value workers who combine technical and soft skills, but there is less evidence that they have a mechanism for rewarding them (Evans et al. 2007). Many of the participants thought that reward would follow from a quantification of hybrid skills, but they had a perception that this was a hard thing for employers to do. Other ways of bringing attention to soft skills – typically through client evaluations and informal feedback – were identified. One participant talked about providing employers with examples where project outcomes had changed because of soft skills. But there was concern that these were perceptions, not hard measurements, something that was seen to be unsatisfactory in terms of providing evidence that could be used with employers to gain advancement. For example:

*I'm not sure that they do reward soft skills adequately and my experience is that it's a problem of measurement. For example, in my organization, when I do my appraisals, there is a measure of soft skills in there, but it's based purely on perception. So my customers get a 360 degree feedback form, and the extent to which I'm good at my soft skills is based entirely upon their perception. Now, I have problems with that. (Dan)*

## HYBRID PROSPECTS?

Many of the research participants felt that their effectiveness was strongly related to maintaining their technical expertise, operated in the context of behavioural competences:

*If I get too soft, how could I possibly tell a customer how long something's going to take? (Larry)*

There was also the perception that not keeping up with the latest technology was a risk in terms of losing face with customers, who themselves might be very technologically aware.

*That's a risk for somebody like myself as well, the market's always moving forward. I've got intelligent customers who are playing the latest consumer tools. (Ben)*

And losing face with the technical colleagues due to a diminution of technical skills was also a concern:

*I think so yes [would lose the respect of the team]. You need to know some fundamental things, not the nitty gritty down to every line up code, but you need to know what's actually happening. (Maggie)*

A very clear majority planned to go on to a management job; the hybrid role was talked about as a stepping stone for moving onto other job ladders, usually the management one – which was typically described as 20/80 technical/soft, or even 10/90.

*The job ladder tends to move you more away from the technical to a management perspective, so it's a feeder process. (Alex)*

*If I intend to expand my career upwards in terms of seniority, then my direct (technical) competence will become less of an issue and what will be expected is an understanding and an appreciation of the strategic concerns around technology deployment. (Alex)*

Going back to purely technical roots was not a possibility, because technical knowledge would have moved on. The hybrid role was therefore largely perceived as a one-way street, leading in all likelihood to a management job.

Thus, there was the implication that the research participants enjoyed both sides of their jobs and not being able to use these could lead to a lack of job satisfaction.

## Discussion

In terms of Brown et al.'s (2011) categories, hybrid workers would probably fall into the middle category of 'demonstrator', where the major emphasis is on communication between colleagues and clients. Demonstrators are not seen by Brown et al. to fall into a 'permission to think' category. The argument is that under Digital Taylorism only 'developers' are able to do this.

Yet the evidence from this research is that hybrid workers in ICT are going beyond a demonstrator role. They talked about the way in which the distribution of technical and soft skills could vary from day to day, and about how they made decisions about the split between the two on the basis of judgements of criticality and complexity. They navigated between different discourses and communities and interpreted between them; they translated competing knowledges, showing characteristics of what Hulme et al. (2009) term 'third space working'. This suggests that they might constitute a particular sub-category of demonstrators: their technical knowledge had been routinized and systematized, but their 'third space' skills had not been – and perhaps could not be.

It might be expected that the combination of roles would have caused stress for employees. Goffman (1961) predicted that workers who had to combine roles that combined both front region (clients) and back region (colleagues) would experience role strain. Yet this did not come across in the research. Instead the research subjects' view was that they had a skill set that involved a rather unproblematic movement between clients and colleagues. This adds to the view that they could be seen by organizations as ideal workers in a post-Fordist context.

These are flexible workers who crafted a role that matched their needs and those of others; they actively changed roles, expanded and contracted them in tune with a dynamic economic environment. The research suggested that these were creative employees, able to act and react autonomously; they were self-provisioning in the sense of not expecting organizations to provide solutions to what they saw as their own development issues.

There were clear indications that these hybrid workers experienced job satisfaction. Yet there was an undercurrent of concern, particularly in relation to career advancement. The perception was that staying in a hybrid job could only be achieved by making sideways moves. More traditional advancement could only be achieved by climbing the management ladder –

which would imply reducing the technical aspects of their jobs, something that these employees felt reluctant to do:

> *If you go laterally into a different role, you'll tend to find the 80:20 split still stays 80 technical, but as you move up towards the managers' level, the 80 become the soft skills rather than the technical. (Ian)*

There was thus recognition, and a fear, that success on the management ladder would be likely to involve a diminution of technical skills.

## Conclusion

Hybrid workers, as the label suggests, are difficult to classify. They probably fall somewhere in between Brown et al.'s categories of developer and demonstrator but perhaps ironically their greatest strength may be that organizations will have difficulty in classifying them; any bid to standardize them has the potential to lead their roles to routinization and away from 'permission to think'. Whilst the research participants discussed in this chapter felt that their hybrid skills should be recognized, it may not be in their interest to have this happen. Nevertheless, a failure to formally recognize hybrid skills has negative consequences for individuals since there is no obvious job ladder for hybrid workers; the participants felt that the only way to advance was to climb the management ladder, thereby risking the atrophy of their technical expertise. This would also be a loss for the organization, since the skills of translating and interpreting between the technical and the client worlds are likely to underpin productivity.

The knowledge workers in this study wanted their roles to be categorized more clearly. They believed that this would create possibilities for career advancement that did not involve an inevitable transfer to the management ladder where they would lose much of their technical skills. Yet in seeking to pin down and describe the roles more fully – thus bringing about routinization – there is the possibility, according to Digital Taylorism, that 'permission to think' roles become rarer.

Future work could extend the research to IT professionals over the age of 35 who have a background in hybrid jobs. It seems likely, given the research reported in this chapter, that there are few hybrid jobs at a more senior level, suggesting that they are merely stepping stones to management positions. If they have largely disappeared, then future work could provide evidence that valuable hybrid skills were being lost to individuals, organizations and the ICT sector as a whole.

A further issue was that women were poorly represented. ICT remains an area that is dominated by men in most Western societies, but even so, their representation in this self-selected sample was less than would have been expected. Future work could extend the research to women in hybrid jobs in the IT sector with a view to exploring whether women and men perceive hybrid jobs in different ways and/or do different types of hybrid jobs. This could suggest an explanation of women's and men's different employment outcomes and gender pay gap in IT (Glover and Guerrier 2010).

Lastly, future work could examine the growth of hybrid working in other sectors and occupations where communication between clients and colleagues is key. Hybrid skills are likely to be needed in almost all aspects of the knowledge economy; thus similar issues of categorization and management are likely to arise, although their nature may vary between sectors and occupations.

The research suggests challenges for management. If employees are forced onto either a technical or a managerial ladder, then the organization risks not having senior people who have the ability to operate in both worlds. There is a risk to the organization if that particular kind of flexibility is lost. Having little choice but to move onto the managerial ladder also has costs for organizations that have invested in technical training; that investment could be lost if employees then leave the technical behind as they progress in the organization.

These are organizational risks, but risks for employees were also pointed out. People in hybrid roles enjoy both sides of their jobs; not being able to use these could lead to a lack of satisfaction – something that is not in the organization's interest either:

> *If you've got the kind of personality whereby you do enjoy chatting people and talking, presentation skills and things like that, and you're technical, you're going to want to use them both ... and if you don't then you might become unhappy and feel undervalued. (Jack)*

The implication of the research for managers is that fluid roles need to be institutionally recognized both for the good of the organization and for employees. However, such recognition needs to be carefully thought through:

flexible roles and personalities should not be 'shoehorned' into job schemas in such a way that quantification triumphs over the qualitative aspects that appear to be so important both for the organization and for employees.

## References

Abrahamsson, P., Salo, O., Ronkainen, J. and Warsta, J. 2002. *Agile Software Development Methods: Review and Analysis*. Espoo (Finland): VTT Publications, 478.

Blyton, P. and Jenkins, J. 2007. *Key Concepts in Work*. London: Sage.

Brown, P., Lauder, H. and Ashton, D. 2011. *The Global Auction*. New York: Oxford University Press.

Clegg, S. 1990. *Modern Organizations*. London: Sage.

Darr, A. 2002. The technicization of sales work: an ethnographic study in the US electronics industry. *Work, Employment and Society*, 16(1), 47–60.

Engineering Council. 2011. *The Accreditation of Higher Education Programmes* [Online: Engineering Council]. Available at: http://www.engc.org.uk/ecukdocuments/internet/document%20library/AHEP%20Brochure.pdf [accessed 22 March 2011].

Evans, C., Glover, J., Guerrier, Y. and Wilson, C. 2007. *Effective Recruitment Strategies and Practices: Addressing Skills Needs and Gender Diversity in the ITEC and Related Sector*. London: DTI.

Glover, J. and Guerrier, Y. 2010. 'Women in hybrid roles in IT employment: a return to 'nimble fingers'? *Journal of Technology Management and Innovation*, 5(1) 85–94.

Goffman, E. 1961. *Encounters: Two Studies in the Sociology of Interaction*. Indianapolis: Bobbs-Merrill.

Guerrier, Y., Evans, C., Glover, J. and Wilson, C. 2009. 'Technical, but not very …': constructing gendered identities in IT-related employment. *Work, Employment and Society*, 23(3), 494–511.

Halliday, M.A.K. 1978. *Language as Social Semiotic: The Social Interpretation of Language and Meaning*. London: Edward Arnold.

Hulme, R., Cracknell, D. and Owens, A. 2009. Learning in third spaces: developing trans-professional understanding through practitioner enquiry. *Educational Action Research*, 17(4), 537–50.

Johnson, P., Wood, G., Brewster, C. and Brookes, M. 2009. The rise of post-bureaucracy: theorists' fancy or organizational praxis? *International Sociology*, 24(1), 37–61.

Jubas, K. and Butterwick, S. 2008. Hard/soft, formal/informal, work/learning. *Journal of Workplace Learning*, 20(7/8), 514–25.

Kelan, E.K. 2008. Emotions in a rational profession: the gendering of skills in ICT work. *Gender, Work and Organization*, 15(1), 49–71.

Loogma, K., Ümarik, M. and Vilu, R. 2004. Identification-flexibility dilemma of IT specialists. *Career Development International*, 9(3), 323–48.

Piore, M. and Sabel, C. 1984. *The Second Industrial Divide*. New York: Basic Books.

Reisz, M. 2011. Leading questions. *Times Higher Education*, 21 April 2011.

Ruiz Ben, E. 2007. Defining expertise in software development while doing gender. *Gender, Work and Organization*, 14(4), 312–32.

Smite, D., Moe, N. and Agerfalk, P. 2010. *Agility Across Time and Space*. Berlin: Springer.

Taylor, F.W. 1911. *Principles of Scientific Management*. New York: Harper & Row.

Webster, J. 1996. *Shaping Women's Work: Gender, Employment and Information Technology*. London: Longman.

Whitchurch, C. 2008. Shifting identities and blurring boundaries: the emergence of third space professionals in UK higher education. *Higher Education Quarterly*, 62(4), 377–96.

Whitehouse, G. and Diamond, C. 2005. 'Hybrids' and the gendering of computing jobs in Australia. *Australian Journal of Information Systems*, 12(2), 79–89.

Woodfield, R. 2002. Woman and information systems development: not just a pretty (inter)face? *Information Technology and People*, 15(2), 119–38.

Zeldin, T. 1995 *An Intimate History of Humanity*. New York: Harper Collins.

# 7

# 'Taylorism' without 'Taylor'? Some Reflections on 'Taylorism' and New Public Management

*Tony Cutler*

## Introduction

The object of this chapter is to discuss the appropriateness of applying the concept of 'Taylorism' to 'new public management' (NPM) as a public management reform programme. The focus is predominantly theoretical. However, the argument is illustrated by reference to an important, though not universally used form of NPM, the idea of managing public services by 'numbers' and particularly by reference to 'targets' and the conclusion discusses some practical implications of the argument.

NPM can be broadly seen as promoting the view that the performance of public sector services can be radically improved by the adoption of 'management' techniques (Hughes 2003: 32). The use of the adjective 'new' stems from the assumption that this public management reform programme is relatively recent. Thus, while there is no precise consensus on the dating of this phenomenon, it has been frequently seen as operating since the 1980s (Aucoin 1990, Hood and Peters 2004; for a discussion of earlier examples of techniques associated with NPM see Cutler 2011). NPM has been associated with a variety of techniques: the use of performance measurement and management (including the use of targets), quasi-markets which separate 'purchaser' and 'provider' roles, and contracting out of services/competitive tendering. An important aspect of NPM has been 'devolved' management (Hood 1991: 4–5) where organizations providing key services like schools and hospitals are treated as 'provider' units whose 'performance' is measured, and a number of such practices will be discussed below.

NPM has been embraced across a number of national jurisdictions but support for such programmes has not been universal in the developed capitalist world. The authoritative comparative study by Pollitt and Bouckaert (2004: 98) identified a 'core' NPM group of Australia, New Zealand, the UK and the US. In contrast NPM has been much less significant in the major continental European economies such as France and Germany (Pollitt and Bouckaert 2004: 247). The principal focus for the illustrative material will be on the UK as one of the 'core' NPM jurisdictions. A feature of the British case, noted by Pollitt and Bouckaert (2004: 293), is the continuity of a broad commitment to NPM and although there are differences in emphasis an important element of continuity can be traced from Conservative administrations before New Labour and on to the current UK Coalition government.

The view that at least certain features of NPM have 'Taylorist' aspects can be found in the work of two of the leading scholars in the field. Christopher Hood, the Director of the ESRC Public Services Programme (for a brief account of the scope of this major research programme and a relevant link see Hood 2007: 95), postulates a link between Taylor and the use of performance 'targets' in managing public sector services. While he raises the caveat that the use of performance indicators as target systems 'no doubt has an earlier history', he goes on to point that they are associated with 'Frederick Winslow Taylor's approach to "scientific management" by setting production quotas linked to individualized payment systems' (Hood 2007: 98). Christopher Pollitt, the co-author of the major comparative study of NPM cited above, argued that 'the particular species of managerialism which Reaganite Washington and Thatcherite Whitehall sought to introduce to the public services in the 1980s has a certain 'neo Taylorian' character' (Pollitt, 1993: 15) and elements postulated as 'neo Taylorian' included 'the development of performance indicators to measure the achievement of … targets' (Pollitt 1993: 56).

The question addressed in this chapter is how far in particular the use of quantitative targets to 'manage' public services can be seen as following the precepts of Taylor. In this respect it is sought to make a distinction between supposed 'Taylorism' in the application of performance management techniques in public services and the management framework which Taylor advocated. The chapter is divided into five sections: the first discusses the case for significant parallels between elements of NPM and 'Taylorism'; the second examines Taylor's 'scientific management' framework and the character of some of the illustrative evidence used to support his claims; the third examines the use of quantitative targets to improve public service performance in the

UK and seeks to show that they are, in certain key respects, radically different from the Taylor framework; the fourth section considers the relationship between the phenomenon of 'gaming' in public services and contrasts this with Taylor's analysis of 'systematic soldiering'; and a conclusion seeks both to draw the elements of the argument together and to consider some of the practical implications of the differences between putative 'Taylorism' in the public sector and the 'Taylor' framework.

## New Public Management and 'Taylorism'

In this section the aim is to discuss how certain techniques of public sector management associated with NPM could be viewed as 'Taylorist'. It might be thought that there is one immediate objection. Taylor's exemplary material is usually drawn from manufacturing processes. Thus, for instance, in Taylor's *Principles of Scientific Management* (1913) attempts to demonstrate the efficacy of 'scientific management' are illustrated with the famous and much-quoted example of pig iron handling (Taylor 1913: 43–7, 54–63), bricklaying (Taylor 1913: 79–85), quality control in the production of steel balls used in bicycle bearings (Taylor 1913: 86–97) and optimum use of metal cutting equipment (Taylor 1913: 105–13). In contrast, particularly following extensive privatization of manufacturing and utilities, the sphere of application of NPM is predominantly in services. However, Taylor claims that the sphere of application of 'scientific management' is general and he states that 'the best management is a true science ... and that the fundamental principles of scientific management are applicable to *all* kinds of human activities' (Taylor 1913: 7, my emphasis, see also Pollitt 1993: 14).

If, however, there are potential parallels between NPM and aspects of Taylor's work this raises the question of their precise form. One supposed similarity relates to the salience of 'managing by numbers'. Taylor's attempts to demonstrate the efficacy of 'scientific management' are dotted with examples of either production targets which are claimed to be realizable on a sustained basis or increases in productivity seen as effects of 'scientific' methods. In the case of pig iron handling it was claimed that it was possible to raise output per man-day from 12.5 to 47 tons (Taylor, 1913: 46–7); that productivity in bricklaying could be increased from 120 to 350 bricks per man-hour (Taylor 1913: 81); and that in the work of inspecting balls used in bicycle bearings, 'thirty-five girls did the same work formerly done by one hundred and twenty' (Taylor 1913: 95). This approach can be compared with 'managing by numbers' as it has been manifested under NPM.

Hood (2007) has pointed out that public sector 'managing by numbers' can take three broad forms. The first he terms 'intelligence systems' which are characterized as measuring 'performance for background information' but involving no 'fixed interpretation of the data' (Hood 2007: 95). The second is the use of 'ranking systems' which 'measure current or past performance of comparable service units against one another' (Hood 2007: 95). Such rankings are intended to have a 'fixed interpretation' since it is assumed that the ranking is a measure of comparative performance. In turn they can operate as a putative means of improving 'performance'. In this respect Hood (2007: 95) identifies three potential uses – to 'inform consumer choice', 'as information for action by government' and 'a means of encouraging "saints" and shaming "sinners"'. All three could be perceived, in NPM terms, as means of improving 'performance'. In the context of quasi-markets, rankings could inform 'consumer choice' exerting pressure on those 'lower' in the ranking. Rankings could inform 'government action' such as the imposition of changes in unit management in the context of consistently low-rated and hence 'failing' units. There is a perceived motivational effect of being at the top or bottom. The third major form is the use of 'target systems' which 'measure actual performance against one or more specified … standards' (Hood 2007: 95). The operation of this form in the UK will be discussed in detail below. In the case of the National Health Service (NHS), for example, maximum waiting times for admission to NHS hospitals were specified and functioned as norms by which 'performance' could be judged.

With reference to the first two forms of public sector 'managing by numbers' identified by Hood there are problems in conceptualizing them as 'Taylorist'. As he notes (Hood 2007: 95), 'intelligence systems' involve 'no fixed interpretation of the data'. However, Taylor clearly intended that output targets should have a 'fixed interpretation' as they represented realizable output levels on a sustainable basis. Taylor's approach also does not sit easily with the 'rankings system' approach. Taylor *does* compare the output of individual workers. Thus, for example, in the pig iron handling example he states that in a gang of 75 pig iron handlers 'only one in eight was physically capable' of handling the recommended production target (Taylor 1913: 61).

For Taylor this did not show that the target was unrealistic, rather that it was essential to select workmen with the 'appropriate' characteristics. However, there is no rationale for *publishing* comparative data on output of individual workers. One argument for this practice in public sector 'managing by numbers' is to facilitate consumer choice of, for example, schools and hospitals. There is no parallel in Taylor. Data on the output of individual workers gives useful information to enterprise management but it has no direct role in purchasing decisions. There is also no parallel with the rationale of encouraging 'saints' and shaming 'sinners'. As was indicated above, the workers who cannot meet the production target are seen as 'unable' to do so; this is not a question of motivation.

It is therefore the use of 'target systems' which provides the closest parallel between Taylor and NPM 'managing by numbers'. Taylor's production norms are designed to compare performance 'against … specified standards' (Hood, 2007: 95). If, however, 'target systems' are an apparently 'Taylorist' aspect of public sector 'managing by numbers' it is necessary to explore how production targets were designed to function in the context of 'scientific management' and this issue is considered in the next section.

## Output Targets and 'Scientific Management'

To understand the role of output targets in 'scientific management' it is necessary to begin by considering the approach to management which Taylor was seeking to criticize. One of the concepts for which Taylor is famous is that of 'soldiering' (Kelly 1982: 7). This, he claims, takes two distinct forms, 'natural' and 'systematic'. 'Natural' soldiering derives from 'the natural instinct and tendency … to take it easy' (Taylor 1913: 19). However, it is 'systematic' soldiering which is much more central to Taylor's approach to management reform (Kelly 1982: 7–8). It is undertaken 'with the deliberate object of keeping … employers ignorant of how fast work can be done' (Taylor 1913: 20). One element in the causation of systematic soldiering was that 'employers determine upon a maximum sum which they feel it is right for each of their classes of employee to earn each day' (Taylor 1913: 21–2). Systematic soldiering is thus linked to the workers' view that 'when his employer is convinced' that output can be increased the employer 'will find sooner or later some way of compelling him to do it with little or no increase in pay' (Taylor 1913: 22).

Output restriction must then be 'systematic' and collective to preclude the employer raising production norms with no (remotely) proportionate increase in pay (Kelly 1982: 5). However, such output restriction rests on the fundamental foundation of management ignorance of the appropriate production norms (Kelly 1982: 8). Systematic soldiering can thus only be eliminated if management ignorance is tackled. Even if the putative 'best' 'pre-scientific' approach of basing norms on production records is used, such records are contaminated by the effects of systematic soldiering. The basis of the 'scientific' approach lies in the identification of the 'best' method of undertaking the work being studied. Taylor argues: 'among the various methods and implements used in each element of each trade there is always *one method* and *one implement* which is better than the rest' (Taylor 1913: 25, my emphasis). The analysis of these methods combined with 'motion and time study' creates a form of management which leads to 'the gradual substitution of science for rule of thumb throughout the mechanical arts' (Taylor 1913: 25).

What is therefore central to Taylor's approach is the link between the improved *method* and the production norm, and the link is continually emphasized in Taylor's examples. In the case of the very simple task of pig iron handling the basis for an improved production norm is claimed to be the identification of the appropriate distribution of working time between the worker being 'load-free' and 'load-bearing' (Taylor, 1913: 57 and 60–61). In this case Taylor attempts to set out a detailed derivation of his production norm seeking to show the compatibility between the norm, 'load-bearing' working time and the speeds at which ('first-class') workers could be expected to transport pig iron (Taylor 1913: 60–61). Other key examples do not have this level of detail. Nevertheless there is a consistent attempt to indicate the connection between improved production methods and higher output norms (see for example Taylor 1913: 79–80, 92 and 107–8, for the examples of bricklaying, quality control and speed of machine cutting equipment respectively).

It is, however, necessary to enter a caveat with respect to Taylor's account of his framework. Texts like *Principles of Scientific Management* give no independent sources allowing for 'audit' of the data presented. In addition when such 'audit' has been undertaken in the academic literature there is evidence that Taylor's accounts could be seriously misleading. An important paper by Wrege and Perroni (1974), for example, both compares accounts of the pig iron handling experiments given by Taylor at various points in time and contrasts Taylor's version of events with a report by Gillespie and Wolle who were directly involved in the pig iron experiments. They show that Taylor gave markedly contrasting accounts of the causes of the claimed productivity improvements (Wrege and Perroni 1974: 8–10); that the production norm set appeared to involve an arbitrary adjustment of an output figure regarded as unsustainable (Wrege and Perroni 1974: 14); and that Taylor failed to discuss high levels of labour turnover connected to the speed of work (Wrege and Perroni 1974: 16–18; on these issues see also Kanigel 1997: 320–22). Taylor's ideal framework (and one which arguably he did not live up to in his own work) was premised on the view that management should be able to combat 'systematic soldiering' by being able to *demonstrate* the feasibility of a production norm by reference to improved methods. In the next section the argument turns to the use of service improvement targets in the UK and how these differ from Taylor's approach outlined in this section.

## Managing by Numbers: Public Service Targets

The aim of this section is to discuss a major exercise in 'managing by numbers' in the public sector, the use of public service targets. Recently this policy has been most actively pursued in the UK by (New) Labour. It might appear to have been rejected by the current Coalition government. In its 2011 White Paper *Open Public Services* the use of targets is criticized as part of an 'old centralised approach to public service delivery' which is 'broken' (HM Government 2011: 7). Nevertheless, the practice of the Coalition diverges from this apparent repudiation of targets. For example, a key health service target used by Labour on maximum waiting times for hospital admission has been retained (Department of Health 2011: 36) and there is evidence that treatment priorities of 'providers' are still driven by such 'top-down' forces (Williams 2011: 14). There is thus considerable evidence that managing by numbers continues to flourish in the UK public sector.

It is also important to note that the scope of managing by numbers was limited by another important Labour policy – devolution. The core approach adopted in England was to attach powerful incentives (to some extent positive but mainly negative) to targets. This approach was not taken in Scotland and Wales (see for example Reynolds 2008 for education in Wales and Propper et al. 2008 for health policy in Scotland). Naturally, of course, given that England accounts for 85 per cent of the UK population this still means that a 'tough' managing by numbers approach has operated in the bulk of the UK. This section initially considers the broad background to the use of targets by Labour administrations; it goes on to examine targets set for the NHS and education; and the section concludes with a consideration of how the treatment of targets in key New Labour policy documents *differs* from Taylor's treatment of production norms considered in the last section.

The use of targets as a means of achieving 'improvements' in the performance of public services was a significant feature of Tony Blair's first administration. The White Paper *Public Services for the Future*, published in December 1998 (HM Treasury 1998), was important for linking departmental funding to 'public service agreements' (PSAs). In the White Paper Tony Blair claimed that PSAs outlined in the document 'set out what we shall deliver for the ... resources provided' (HM Treasury 1998: foreword). It was also made clear that 'targets are at the heart of the PSA' (HM Treasury 1998: 5) and the second section of the White Paper outlined the PSAs for specific government departments. Health and education were perceived as particularly significant. Hood and Dixon (2010: i284) point, for example, to UK poll evidence, covering the period 1996–2005 which suggests that health and education were the two most important issues which voters identified as determining their voting behaviour.

The 1997 White Paper *Excellence in Education* included two major education targets. By 2002, 80 per cent of 11-year-olds were to have reached the 'expected standard' in English and 75 per cent in mathematics (Department for Education and Employment 1997: 19). The 'expected standard' was the achievement of 'level 4' in key stage 2 tests under the National Curriculum introduced following the 1988 Education Reform Act. With respect to health a crucial document was the 2000 *NHS Plan*. *Public Services for the Future* had included the target of reducing the waiting list for inpatient treatment in the NHS over the lifetime of the parliament (HM Treasury 1998: 20). These included the commitment that by the end of 2005 the maximum waiting period for inpatient hospital treatment was to be reduced from 18 to 6 months (Department of Health 2000: 105).

There might appear to be certain similarities between New Labour education and health targets and Taylor's production targets. For example, a consistent failure by a worker to meet the production target was taken by Taylor as an indication of their lack of suitability for the particular job. In the same way failures to meet targets suggested that provider units were 'failing' and that a change of management was required. For example the NHS regulatory body Monitor has the power to remove any or all of the directors of a Foundation Trust board on grounds which can include performance 'failures' (National Health Service Act 2006: sections 26 and 52). However, an examination of the key policy documents in which targets were set indicate crucial differences between the approach taken and that of Taylor.

As was indicated in the last section, integral to Taylor's approach was the relationship between putative improved methods and the production norm. Furthermore, as he sought to suggest in the pig iron handling example, it ought to be possible to justify production norms by reference to scope for productivity improvement allowed by the improved methods. However, if the section of the *NHS Plan* on the key NHS targets is examined it is clear that at no point is there any attempt to justify the target by reference to improved methods. For example, in the discussion of the length of waiting times which the revised waiting time targets were designed to reduce, various criticisms were advanced of then current practices in the NHS. These included the claim that longer waiting times resulted from a failure to coordinate clinical tests and diagnosis (Department of Health 2000: 104). However, these examples are brief and insubstantial and no reference is made to evidence to justify the claims either that current practices are causing the problem indicated or that changes in working practices will improve the area of performance specified. (For the similar superficial treatment of accident and emergency targets see Department of Health 2000: 105.) Reflecting these limitations, Harrison and Appleby (2005: 23) argue that as the Plan did not indicate 'how targets were to be reached' it was not a plan but rather a 'set of aspirations'.

Parallel difficulties can be found in education. *Excellence in Schools* did propose that each school was to be 'advised to devote a structured hour a day to literacy for all pupils' (from September 1998) (Department for Education and Employment 1997: 20). However, there was no attempt to discuss why this *standard* time allocation was deemed necessary given that schools would have wide variations in the literacy standards of their students (Institute of Education 1997: 6). The discussion of mathematics was also paradoxical. The White Paper announced the creation of a 'Numeracy Task Force' but this was to publish its preliminary report (Department for Education and Employment 1997: 21) at the end of 1997; that is, *after* the mathematics target had been set in the White Paper in July 1997. The lack of any attempt to link method and target means that it is also never clear why the *particular* target has been selected. The lack of an evidence base for such targets was frequently raised in evidence given to the House of Commons Public Administration Select Committee in its investigation of 'government by measurement' published in 2003. The Committee referred to a tendency for government departments to 'pluck targets out of the air' and that targets were defined in an 'arbitrary' way (House of Commons Public Administration Select Committee 2003: 16–17).

Thus the lack of an attempt to justify targets by reference to methods defining 'the best way' is a crucial difference between Taylor's approach to 'managing by numbers' and public service targets. In the next section the focus is on the relationship between the management of responses to production targets in Taylor's work and under public service targets.

## The Responses of the 'Managed': 'Gaming' and 'Systematic Soldiering'

'Systematic soldiering' was identified by Taylor as a response by production workers to the 'pre-scientific' approach to management. In this section this concept is revisited and contrasted with a parallel response to public service targets, 'gaming'. The section begins by defining 'gaming' and examining its effect of complicating any assessment of the efficacy of 'tough' targets regimes. It goes on to consider some of the forms taken by gaming and then discusses similarities and differences between gaming and systematic soldiering. The section finally considers why Taylor's prescriptions for responding to 'systematic soldiering' could *not* be applied in a 'targets' regime such as that applied in the UK.

'Gaming' is defined by Bevan and Hood (2006: 521) as 'reactive subversion' and it includes 'hitting the target and missing the point' or 'reducing performance where targets do not apply'. Some key forms of gaming will be examined below but the concept has two principal elements. 'Reactive subversion' involves an active attempt by a group being 'managed' to create the appearance of having achieved the target when this is not the case. In this context achievement of the target means not just 'hitting' the specified target but adopting means which do not mean that there are negative effects on unmeasured parts of the organization's work.

Instances of such gaming have been identified by regulatory bodies in the UK and discussed in the academic literature. Such discussions have led to qualifications in assessments of the effectiveness of the use of 'tough' targets and this can be illustrated by reference to the NHS. (For some of the difficulties of presenting the *education* targets as a 'success' see Tymms 2004.) The NHS targets regime could be seen as successful in two broad ways. Firstly, following the introduction of the key targets there have been major improvements in measured performance with respect to key indicators. For example, in 2000 49.5 per cent of those waiting for inpatient treatment in England had been waiting for more than 13 weeks; by 2007 this had fallen to 8.8 per cent (Harrison and Appleby 2009: 169). Secondly, the fact that a much tougher target regime was introduced in England has allowed for comparisons with devolved administrations in the UK. Such comparisons have shown that performance with respect to key health targets was much superior in England when contrasted with devolved administrations (Bevan and Hood 2006: 527–8, Propper et al. 2008: 11).

However, the phenomenon of gaming naturally raises potential issues regarding the interpretation of the targets regime as a 'success'. This can be illustrated by considering two forms of gaming. The first can be classified as 'inappropriate adjustment of data'. An important example concerns the practice of 'suspending' patients from the waiting list for inpatient treatment. This can be an appropriate practice. If, for example, a patient is regarded as not sufficiently fit to undergo the clinical procedure concerned it is appropriate that they be suspended from the list until they are reach the required fitness level. The corresponding appropriate treatment of the data regarding such a patient is that the waiting time 'clock' is 'stopped'; for example, if the patient has already been waiting three months this is recorded as their waiting time while suspended. An inappropriate adjustment is, for example, to 'reset' the waiting time clock to zero. This understates the time the individual has been unnecessarily waiting for clinical treatment (see National Audit Office 2001: 2).

A second important form of gaming refers to the relationship between measured and unmeasured unit performance. 'Tough' target regimes operate with a relatively small number of 'key' targets. Naturally, such a limited range cannot encompass the scope of the organization's work; thus there is a substantial degree of 'unmeasured' activity. The relationship between the measured and the unmeasured thus invites a strategy of 'reactive subversion', the concentration on measured activity at the expense of unmeasured. Thus the Clinical Director of the Bristol Eye Hospital claimed that the waiting time targets at the hospital were achieved because follow-up appointments (not key targets) were cancelled or postponed (House of Commons Public Administration Select Committee 2003: 18).

There are parallels in education. Because education targets often refer to a particular range of performance (such as the percentage of pupils achieving grades A–C in national educational tests) they generate an incentive to concentrate resources on pupils who are just below the required 'threshold' level but are perceived as capable of achieving that level with sufficient support (Gillborn and Youdell 2000, Booher-Jennings 2005). This means, for example, that students who are perceived as highly unlikely to be able to achieve the threshold target will receive significantly less attention; the performance of such students is measured but effectively does not 'count' in the organization's performance strategy. This form of gaming could be conceived as 'hitting the target and missing the point'.

There are both important similarities and differences between systematic soldiering and the gaming of public service targets. Both are collective processes. Thus Taylor stresses the crucial role of production workers acting as a group to prevent 'pre-scientific' management appreciating the output level which is possible. Similarly, gaming involves groups (including, see below, managers) in manipulating data and distributing resources from unmeasured to measured areas with the object of 'hitting' targets. They also both involve distortion so that groups 'lower' in the organizational hierarchy are presenting a false picture of organizational performance (actual or potential) to groups 'further up' the organizational hierarchy.

There are some differences between the practices. Systematic soldiering operates on the process of setting an output norm; in other words it is designed to preclude management knowledge of potential output levels. In contrast, gaming generally operates with targets which are given and the distortion relates to the appearance of the achievement of targets. There is also a difference in the dramatis personae. In the case of systematic soldiering the 'reactive subversion' is by production workers who are seeking to deceive various levels of enterprise management. In the case of the gaming of public service targets the 'reactive subversion' is undertaken by provider unit staff including managers (for examples of management participation in such practices see National Audit Office 2001: 12, 19, 23) to effectively deceive groups such as senior departmental officials and Ministers.

Nevertheless, whatever the differences, both practices present a 'management' problem. For Taylor the distortions involved in systematic soldiering should be approached via 'scientific management' where through method study and timing of work an appropriate production norm can be set. However, as was indicated in the last section, this option was not available in the management of 'gaming' in UK 'tough' target regimes. Taylor claims that 'scientific management' gives industrial managers the cognitive tools to demonstrate the feasibility of the production norm by showing how it can be consistently achieved if the 'best' method is applied. However, public service targets like those in the *NHS Plan* or *Excellence in Schools* do not have a complementary prescribed 'best method'. This issue will be revisited in the conclusion which, in addition to bringing the elements of the argument together, examines some suggestions as to how the gaming of public service targets might be 'managed'.

## Conclusion

Certain aspects of NPM have been viewed as 'Taylorist'. In particular, parallels have been traced between Taylor's advocacy of prescriptive output norms in manufacturing and the adoption of 'managing by numbers' in jurisdictions where NPM has driven a 'public management reform' agenda. Examining the variants of 'managing by numbers' the argument sought to show that the use of public service 'targets' appear to most closely parallel Taylor's production norms. This is particularly so under a 'tough' targets regime where performance against targets has clear positive and negative consequences. Thus, for example, Taylor's view that consistent failure to meet production targets should lead to a worker being replaced has echoes in the tough targets approach that failure of a provider unit to meet targets should lead to a change of management.

However, there are also salient differences. Most significantly, Taylor's discussion of production norms is consistently linked to the identification of a 'best' method which is seen as a condition of higher output. However, such links are absent in key policy documents setting out public service targets under 'New Labour'. While managerial prescriptions are included in such documents there is no attempt to demonstrate that the adoption of such prescriptions will allow a target to be achieved. A corollary is that it is not clear why the *particular* target was adopted.

A further issue where there is an apparent 'Taylorist' component of NPM 'managing by numbers' concerns parallels between gaming and systematic soldiering. While systematic soldiering is designed to understate the appropriate production norm in contrast to gaming which is designed to give the false impression that the target has been achieved, there are also important similarities. Both are forms of 'reactive subversion' where groups lower in the organizational hierarchy cooperate to deceive those further up the hierarchy. However, there is an important difference in the tools available to manage such 'subversion'. Scientific management is designed to demonstrate the feasibility of the proposed production norm whereas the 'arbitrary' character of public service targets precludes this option.

This takes the argument on to the possible practical consequences of the analysis. In the academic literature on gaming there have been attempts to explore how it might be minimized while retaining the use of targets. Such approaches have suggested, for example, that greater use of independent audit of performance should operate (Bevan and Hood 2006: 534). It has also been argued that random inspection could be used to possibly uncover evidence of deceptive practices from manager, professionals and front-line workers (Bevan and Hood 2006: 535). Such methods could be seen as designed to strengthen the hand of those at the top of the public service management hierarchy both by revealing gaming and hence creating incentives not to engage in it. This strategy might seem reasonable given the problematic character of gaming. Self-evidently it reduces the transparency of information regarding the performance of organizations providing public services. Furthermore it can also have a negative impact on the quality of services provided and on equity of service provision between service users.

However, there is another dimension of this issue which seems not to have been considered in the discussion of the management of gaming. As the argument has sought to show, the 'arbitrariness' of public service targets rests on the absence of a demonstrated link between targets and methods. If, therefore, the management of gaming contains prescriptions to ensure that it is minimized, ought there not to be a parallel obligation on those seeking to 'manage change' at a senior level in public services to demonstrate the feasibility of targets and their links to 'improved methods'? This could be seen as mirroring Taylor's criticism of 'pre-scientific' management on the grounds that it failed in its implicit obligation to manage in a systematic way. As indicated above, evaluation of Taylor's practice by reference to independent data sources throws doubt on the claimed precision of his demonstrations. This should also caution against a search for a single 'best way' in public service provision. Nevertheless, arguably the idea that those who propose 'targets' should be able to defend them by reference to evidence is perhaps a lesson from 'Taylor' for public service management.

## References

Aucoin, P. 1990. Administrative reform in public management: paradigms, principles, paradoxes and pendulums. *Governance*, 3(2), 115–37.

Bevan, G. and Hood, C. 2006. What's measured is what matters: targets and gaming in the English public health care system. *Public Administration*, 84(3), 517–38.

Booher-Jennings, J. 2005. Below the bubble, 'educational triage' and the Texas accountability system. *American Educational Research Journal*, 42(2), 231–68.

Cutler, T. 2011. Performance management in public services 'before' new public management: the case of NHS acute hospitals 1948–1962. *Public Policy and Administration*, 26(1), 129–47.

Department for Education and Employment. 1997. *Excellence in Schools*, Cm. 3681. London: HMSO.

Department of Health. 2000. *The NHS Plan: A Plan for Investment: A Plan for Reform*, Cm. 4818-I. London: HMSO.

Department of Health. 2011. *The Operating Framework for the NHS in England 2011/12* [Online: Department of Health]. Available at: http://www.dh.gov.uk/en/Publicationsandstatistics/Publications/PublicationsPolicyAndGuidance/DH_122738 [accessed 7 November 2011].

Gillborn, D. and Youdell, D. 2000. *Rationing Education: Policy, Practice, Reform and Equity*. Buckingham: Open University Press.

Harrison, A. and Appleby, J. 2005. *The War on Waiting for Hospital Treatment: What has Labour Achieved and Which Challenges Remain?* London: King's Fund.

Harrison, A. and Appleby, J. 2009. Reducing waiting times for hospital treatment: lessons from the English NHS. *Journal of Health Services Research and Policy*, 14(3), 168–73.

HM Government. 2011. *Open Public Services White Paper*. London: Stationery Office.

HM Treasury. 1998. *Public Services for the Future: Modernisation, Reform. Accountability: Comprehensive Spending Review Public Service Agreements 1999–2002*. London: HMSO.

Hood, C. 1991. A public management for all seasons. *Public Administration*, 69(1), 3–19.

Hood, C. 2007. Public service management by numbers: why does it vary? Where has it come from? What are the gaps and the puzzles? *Public Money and Management*, 27(2), 95–102.

Hood, C. and Dixon, R. 2010. The political payoff from performance target systems: no-brainer or no-gainer? *Journal of Public Administration Research and Theory*, 20(supp 2), i281–98.

Hood, C. and Peters, B. Guy. 2004. The middle aging of new public management: into the age of paradox? *Journal of Public Administration Research and Theory*, 14(3), 267–82.

House of Commons Public Administration Select Committee. 2003. *On Target? Government by Measurement*, vol. 1, HC 62-I. London: Stationery Office.

Hughes, O. 2003. *Public Management and Administration*. 3rd edn. Basingstoke: Macmillan.

Institute of Education. 1997. *White Paper, 'Excellence in Schools': A Response from the Institute of Education*. London: Institute of Education.

Kanigel, R. 1997. *The One Best Way: Frederick Winslow Taylor and the Enigma of Efficiency*. London: Little, Brown.

Kelly, J. 1982. *Scientific Management, Job Redesign and Work Performance*. London: Academic Press.

National Audit Office. 2001. *Inappropriate Adjustments to NHS Waiting Lists*, HC 452, Session 2001–2. London: Stationery Office.

National Health Service Act 2006, Chapter 41 [Online]. Available at http://www.legislation.gov.uk/ukpga/2006/41/contents [accessed: 7 November 2011].

Pollitt, C. 1993. *Managerialism and the Public Services*. 2nd edn. Oxford: Blackwell.

Pollitt, C. and Bouckaert, G. 2004. *Public Management Reform: A Comparative Analysis*. 2nd edn. Oxford: Oxford University Press.

Propper, C., Sutton, M., Whitnall, C. and Windmeijer, F. 2008. Did 'targets and terror' reduce waiting times in England for hospital care? *B.E. Journal of Economic Analysis and Policy*, 8(2), 1–27.

Reynolds, D. 2008. New Labour, education and Wales: the devolution decade. *Oxford Review of Education*, 34(6), 753–65.

Taylor, F.W. 1913. *The Principles of Scientific Management*. New York and London: Harper & Brothers.

Tymms, P. 2004. Are standards rising in English primary schools? *British Educational Research Journal*, 30(4), 477–94.

Williams, D. 2011. Low-priority patients rejected. *Health Service Journal*, 27 October, 14.

Wrege, C. and Perroni, A. 1974. Taylor's pig-tale: A historical analysis of Frederick W. Taylor's pig-iron experiments. *Academy of Management Journal*, 17(1), 6–27.

# 8

# If It Moves, Measure It: Taylor's Impact on UK Higher Education

*Christopher Bond and Darren O'Byrne*

## Introduction

If a collection dedicated to interrogating the long-term impact of Frederick Taylor and his principles of 'scientific management' upon contemporary society is timely and apt, it is because – despite claims to the contrary from policymakers and business leaders and the like, who find any association with Taylor embarrassing since many of his suggestions have been long-since discredited – those principles have continued to permeate almost all areas of organizational life into the twenty-first century. While few would openly endorse those principles and profess to being unapologetic Taylorists in their approach to management, such has been the negative reaction to the Taylorist programme over the years, nonetheless those principles, whether or not clothed in a different language, have continued to exert influence on managerial styles and government policies, and in many areas of organizational life, managers and policymakers have responded to this in a disturbingly uncritical way. Nowhere is this uncritical acceptance of a thinly disguised scientific management more evident than in the field of higher education in the UK. Yet it is precisely in this field – which is so familiar, of course, to the contributors to this collection, and no doubt many of its readers – that the inherent *contradictions* of the Taylorist project become most apparent.

This chapter will focus on two of Taylor's key principles, specifically: the application of scientific methods to task specification ('Principle One') and the division of labour between the workers and management ('Principle Four'). The chapter presents an argument that following the *massification* of UK higher education in the early 1990s and the application of Taylorist approaches to management and quality assurance, UK higher education has experienced a number of problems commonly associated with the application of scientific management. In particular the authors contend that there has been an over-rationalization of academic processes and systems and that the role of the academic as a key stakeholder in the university has been minimalized, marginalized and de-professionalized. In presenting this case, the authors sit unapologetically within the tradition of Critical Management Studies, an approach concerned with treating organizations as sites of power struggles, and committed to challenging the politics of domination within organizations in its multiple forms which championing the social and political importance of new, critical, forms of knowledge (Alvesson 1987, Alvesson and Willmott 1992, 2003).

The authors contend that such developments are leading to an impoverished model of higher education in the UK and that the over-rationalization of approaches to quality assurance coupled with the loss of an academic voice (the worker) needs to be addressed if the UK wants to maintain a world-class university sector. The chapter draws on Taylor's original monograph, other writers in the intellectual tradition of bureaucracy and rationalization and current literature on the impact of change in UK higher education.

First, we locate Taylor's work within the wider intellectual debates relating to bureaucracy and rationalization that were taking place at the time he wrote his seminal monograph. This is followed by an examination and critical appraisal of how models of quality assurance in the sector have essentially been predicated on Taylor's advocacy of task specification. We then move on to consider how Taylorist notions of division of labour, manifested in approaches based on 'New Public Management' (thus building on the previous chapter by Tony Cutler), have impacted on the role of the academic. The chapter concludes by offering an alternative approach to quality and management in UK higher education that is based on the notion of the academic as a professional and ideas of universities as *communities of practice*.

## Taylorism in Context: The Bureaucratic Tradition

While it is not entirely clear how much, if at all, Taylor had Max Weber in mind when he first developed the paradigm that would come to be known as 'scientific management', subsequent commentators are generally in agreement that Taylor sits within the broader Weberian tradition in organization studies;

the tradition concerned with the organization as a machinery of *bureaucracy*. Weber initiated this tradition as part of his more general social theory, most famously articulated in *The Theory of Social and Economic Organization* (Weber 1997) and in his most famous work, *The Protestant Ethic and the Spirit of Capitalism* (Weber 1992). It was here that Weber presented the idea that the dominant force within society is *rationalization*. It is often forgotten, though, that rationalization in this sense has two meanings, a general and a specific one. The general theory of rationalization incorporates a plurality of distinctive ways of seeing, understanding, and being in the world. In this respect, *zweckrational* or instrumentally rational action is contrasted with other strategies employed to 'rationalize' a situation, not only those 'non-rational' actions which appeal instead to custom and tradition, or charismatic authority, but also, significantly, to *wertrational* action driven by an appreciation of inherent value.

In its more specific usage, though, rationalization refers directly to the triumph of *zweckrational*, or 'rational action', over these other forms. While 'affective action' appeals to emotion, and 'traditional action' to custom, 'rational action' is action directed by the strategic, instrumental, calculated pursuit of a specific goal. Weber claimed that modern societies are increasingly characterized by the dominance of rational action; it becomes the single defining form of social organization. Weber's broad depiction of modernity as instrumental rationality still conjures up bleak images of an impersonal, even dehumanizing, world, and Weber himself bemoaned the decline of appeals to emotion or tradition as evidence of an increasing and inevitable *disenchantment* with the world, as individuals become more and more detached from the systems and processes that order their lives. For Weber, the modern nation-state with its centralized power structures and its formal machinery of administration represents the definitive form of this. Of course, it was left to Weber's disciple, Robert Michels, to demonstrate the inevitability of such systems and processes, which we call *bureaucracy*, within modern mass society, in his 'iron law of oligarchy' (Michels 1962).

Resigned as they apparently are to this grey imagery, the inevitability of bureaucracy which renders modern society an 'iron cage', Weber and Michels are considered representatives of the conservative 'elite theory' tradition within political and organizational sociology. In the inter-war years of the twentieth century, it was left to the scholars of the Frankfurt Institute for Social Research to somewhat rescue Weber from this abyss, by blending his insights with a progressive, revolutionary neo-Marxist philosophy. For Max

Horkheimer and Theodor Adorno (1969) in their *Dialectic of Enlightenment*, and more recently Jürgen Habermas (1987) in his treatise on the 'colonization of the life-world', the process identified by Weber and Michels becomes once again only a *form* of rationalization – the dominant form, for sure, but not the only one. Horkheimer and Adorno posited this instrumental rationality against a 'true' rationality grounded in the pursuit of human freedom. Habermas extended this analysis by showing how the application of instrumental rationality has migrated beyond its natural home in economics and science – where the pursuit of explanatory facts is paramount – and become prevalent in other areas, such as art and social interaction. Thus, the 'colonization of the life-world' is the negation of the project of human emancipation, the transformation of the critical and creative imagination into a means-end calculation.

The significance of this for the study of contemporary higher education is obvious. The increasing application of Taylorist principles, operating within a broadly Weberian framework of bureaucracy and a triumphant instrumental rationality, are clearly part of a broader process in which education itself is transformed into an industry driven by means-end calculability, its purpose being the production of what Habermas calls 'technically useful knowledge'. The shifting emphasis from knowledge to skills, the changing identity of the student from free-floating intellectual to fee-paying consumer, and the physical relocation of the administration of higher education in the UK from the Department of Education to the Department of Business, Innovation and Skills provide further evidence of this. As a result, commentators have found themselves re-opening the classic debate: what is the *idea of a university*?

It is not the purpose of this chapter to venture too far into that particular debate. Suffice to say, the humanist ideals of the university as espoused by such diverse commentators as Newman, Fichte and Habermas seem to have little place in an organization increasingly characterized by an emphasis on employability. Regulatory procedures dressed up as 'quality assurance' and standardized processes of teaching and learning championed as 'best practice' beg the very question that Habermas implies in his account of the colonization of the life-world: best *for whom*? How does one 'measure' the 'quality' that is being 'assured'? The very construction of 'objective' centralized criteria is demonstrative of the Weberian 'iron cage', while the application of Taylorist strategies to the administration of the university provide the ideal framework for its implementation. In what follows, we will interrogate these strategies in greater depth.

## Taylor's 'Principle One': Quality Assurance based on a Technical-Rational Paradigm

> *The managers assume, for instance, the burden of gathering together all of the traditional knowledge which in the past has been possessed by the workmen and then of classifying, tabulating, and reducing this knowledge to rules, laws and formulae which are immensely helpful to the workmen in doing their daily work. (Taylor 1911: 27)*

These words of Taylor's seem to resonate more than ever with contemporary relevance. Over the last twenty-five years the UK higher education system has undergone a major transformation in moving from a model of *elite* to *mass* participation in education. Commensurate with this large increase in students has been a declining unit of resource per student, increased staff–student ratios and the introduction of management styles and approaches largely informed by New Public Management. Anderson (2006) and Parker and Gould (1999) note that this change in management style has been characterized by policy development and management which has a key focus on efficiency and effectiveness, quality assurance, performance evaluations and rankings within an overall desire to effect cost savings.

During the course of these changes to UK higher education the sector has been subjected to a plethora of externally driven initiatives related to quality assurance. At the heart of these policies has been a desire by government and many of the educational quangos it establishes to increase accountability within the sector and to gain more control of the curriculum, pedagogic approaches and the very function of a university education.

In recent times the sector has been subjected to increased external scrutiny through bodies such as the Quality Assurance Agency, the Higher Education Funding Councils and exercises such as the Research Excellence Framework. All of these processes have sought to standardize and regulate a sector that was to a large extent quite autonomous. Although the 'New Right' has pursued this agenda under the banner of ensuring value for money and promoting excellence the sub-text has clearly been a desire to harness more control over the practice and operation of academic activity. This has been a priority for the 'New Right' in its pursuit of promoting a neo-liberal capitalist ideology. Such an ideology requires universities to becoming the training grounds for its instrumentalist economic agenda rather than the champions of new knowledge and critical perspectives on society and the very governance that they exercise.

The authors contend that the dominant approaches to and models of quality assurance which have been imposed on academics in the UK are based on a technical-rational perspective. In this respect they not are not only illustrative of the broader social processes identified by Weber, but, more specifically, embrace the notions of task specification and differentiation promulgated by Taylor. Quality driven from a technical-rational perspective assumes that professional activity needs to follow standard procedures and is largely a matter of technical performance and follows a logical sequence as part of an efficient system. Gore et al. (2000: 77) note that 'such an approach to quality places paramount performance on instrumental variables that are easily defined, observed and monitored; it appeals to the bureaucratic mind and sits easily with notions of quality drawn from the industrial sectors in which Taylor was operating.'

Models of quality operating from this paradigm adopt a nomothetic approach. They view systems as being of paramount importance and assume that these can be made efficient through the application of logic and strategy. This technical-rational approach relies heavily on laws, rules, prescriptions, schedules and routines to standardize and control the system. Since the introduction of modularization into the UK higher education sector, learning and intellectual enquiry has essentially been packaged, compartmentalized and measured as units or modules of learning determined and driven by university academic regulations rather than the legitimate needs of a discipline or field. Indeed the introduction of UK- and Europe-wide schemes for credit accumulation and transfer have themselves significantly contributed to such notions of standardization and a belief that 'one size fits all'.

Meanwhile the flexibility of the academic to engage in a lived and dynamic learning experience where knowledge and assessment are co-shaped and co-created by the academic and their students is lost in a mass of overly rigid regulation that stifles innovation and professional activity. This is precisely the scenario that, taken to its extreme, results in the development of what Ritzer (1996) calls the 'McUniversity'. Within a quality system predicated on technical-rationality, 'innovation' and 'best practice' become reframed as those activities which conform to the rules and regulations, which do not disturb or challenge the quality framework and which are easily quantified and measured. Innovation thus has to 'fit' within the rational framework or, if it challenges it, be managed and rationalized so that the needs of the system can be met. Innovation and best practice also become externally driven, thus initiatives such as personal development planning (PDP), employability and key skills are all determined nationally and imposed on institutions and disciplines through systems of regulation, accreditation and monitoring.

The technical-rational paradigm of quality assurance values standardization of procedures. In this context it adheres to the values articulated in Taylor's principles. Quality in this respect requires that basic standards or benchmarks be clearly defined, usually in terms of regulation and quality indicators, in order to have a baseline from which the measurement of quality can proceed. The proliferation of codes of practice (precepts), the higher education framework (HEQF) for determining levels of learning and the generic subject benchmark statements all draw their ideological existence from Taylorist desires for task specification. The role of academics within such a framework of quality becomes to ensure that regulations and procedures are consistently met. Carr (1989) suggests that working within such a paradigm can lead to a system that is 'paternalistic' and 'morally impoverished', and as enshrining a view of education which is better called training.

The authors share with Carr this concern and believe that the current over-emphasis in higher education on regulation and control are leading to increased standardization and greater commodification of the UK higher education sector, resulting in homogenization and a lack of differentiation. Models of quality assurance, built on ideologies driven from the technical-rational paradigm, inevitably have to construct elaborate and rigid models of assessment, inspection, appraisal and validation. As Taylor himself stated, 'in the past the man has been first; in the future the system must be first' (1911: 2).

These ideologies have manifested themselves in most academic time now being spent on producing learning outcomes, module descriptors, programme specifications, programme annual reviews and other documentation required by the new quality bureaucrats to justify their often inflated levels of responsibility and commensurate salaries. Harvey (2005: 271) notes that the result of this onslaught of quality initiatives driven from externally imposed ideologies has been that 'quality monitoring in the UK has been beset by overlapping and burdensome processes, competing notions of quality, a failure to engage learning and transformation, and a focus on accountability and compliance.' Table 8.1 on the following page, developed by Gore et al. (2000), effectively summarizes the ideologies upon which the technical-rational paradigm of quality is predicated. These are contrasted with notions of seeing quality as being vested in the role of the professional academic and being driven by values that underpin notions of professional rather than technical accountability.

Table 8.1    Contrasting paradigms of quality assurance
            (adapted from Gore et al. 2000)

| Quality as a technical-rational activity | Quality as professional (intellectual) activity |
| --- | --- |
| Rules, laws and schedules | Starts where rules fade |
| Routines, prescriptions | Prepared to abandon routine |
| Efficient systems | Creativity, room to be wrong and exploration |
| Permanent knowledge | Knowledge is temporary, problematic and contested |
| Visible performance, technical skills | Professional expertise more than a technical skill |
| Standards 'to be raised' | Quality through deepened insight |
| Pre-determined goals | Not all can be pre-determined |
| Technical accountability | Professional and moral answerability |
| Appraisal, control and inspection | Reflection and investigation of practice |
| The processes are all that matter (instrumental view) | The ends are what matter (pluralist view) |

## Taylor's 'Principle Four': De-Professionalization of the Academic through the Application of New Public Management in UK Education

In parallel, and many believe in collusion with, the assault on the academic through the rationalization of her or his professional responsibilities and the over-regulation of their professional activity, the UK higher education has found itself increasingly in the thrall of the management ideology known as New Public Management (NPM).

Successive reforms to UK higher education from the 1980s to the present day have been driven by this ideology of NPM. Underpinning this has been a shift in funding models that are market- and consumer-driven, increased use of private sector management techniques to manage academics and a general desire to move from a model of professional responsibility to employee accountability.

NPM is essentially a management philosophy that developed in the 1980s embracing the ideologies of the 'New Right'. NPM was applied to the reform of public services such as health, education and local government. Its fundamental ideology is that marketization of public services should be coupled with the introduction of management initiatives and styles drawn from the private sector. Advocates of NPM claim that this results in greater efficiency and value for money in the delivery of public services. It reifies the economy as the only thing in society that is 'real' and classes (apparently without irony) all other structures and ideologies as mere rationalization. NPM has often resulted in a proliferation of general management and finds a comfortable home in Taylor's advocacy of a division of labour by separating professional activity from managerial responsibility.

In our contemporary universities there has been a proliferation of specialist non-academic departments (such as marketing, international development, employability, enterprise and external relations, learning and teaching), coupled with a growth in specialist advisers (most of whom seem to be directors) and an increase in the number of quasi-academic managerial roles. Many of these specialist departments have become, in effect, self-regulating and ultimately self-justifying systems, setting priorities, imposing deadlines, and placing increasing demands upon academics with little or no broader systemic or strategic thinking. Even more traditional support departments whose services are directly linked to the idea of the university as a place of learning, such as the university library, have not escaped from this process of bureaucratization, thanks in no small part to the increasingly self-rationalizing manipulation of new technologies and the associated regulations and new systems of practice they generate. This has all occurred as a result of the application of practices associated with role specification and division of labour. In some institutions and departments, academics themselves have not escaped this as they become 'programme managers' who report to Directors who are ultimately accountable to Chief Executives. A review of the composition of most university senates at the current time highlights that academics now exercise very little control over the strategic or operational direction that their university is taking. Role specification and division of labour have been a major contributing factor to what Gombrich (2000) bluntly terms, in the sub-title of his volume on the subject, 'the murder of a profession'.

Whilst Taylor promotes his ideas as being based on principles of scientific enquiry his outright rejection of approaches based on what he terms 'initiative and incentive' and his insistence on a clear division of labour between workers and management share many of the values and practices currently embodied in NPM. Deem and Brehony (2005: 220) identify these characteristics as 'emphasizing the primacy of management above all other activities; monitoring employee performance (and encouraging self-monitoring too); the attainment of financial and other targets, devising means of publicly auditing quality of service delivery and the development of quasi-markets for services.'

Ferlie et al. (1996), drawing on research into service reforms in the UK's National Health Service, identified four models of 'new managerialism'. These are: (i) the efficiency model (based on doing more with less and the use of league tables); (ii) downsizing and decentralization (removal of layers of middle management and developing units as cost and profit centres); (iii) the learning organization (an emphasis on culture change, teamwork and empowerment of employees); (iv) consumer-led services (greater engagement with and influence of service users in shaping service provision). Research conducted by an ERSC-funded project in 1998–2000 and reported by Deem and Brehony (2000) indicates that the main approach to new managerialism in the UK higher education sector was closely aligned to the efficiency model. They note that this has led to, amongst other things: an increase in academic staff workloads; the introduction of cost centres to university departments and faculties; greater internal and external scrutiny and measurement of all academic output; and an increase in the number of managers in the sector. Deem and Johnson (2003) also note that this increased number of managers had led to a stronger divide between what they term manager-academics and academics.

We contend that the introduction of NPM into UK higher education has led to a fundamental challenge to the values, beliefs and culture of the sector. The result of this has been to essentially further de-professionalize the role of the academic and to increase the power and influence of two other stakeholder groups in universities, namely that of management and students. Traditionally academic culture has centred on developing communities of enquiry where knowledge is generated, shared, explored and further developed through processes of teaching and research. Within such communities the power of knowledge and thought and the freedom to explore complex, contradictory and problematic conceptions of truth have been privileged as the *raison d'être* of university sectors. Within this type of approach a technocratic or academic culture in which academics and students share conversations has been at the forefront of operating practices. NPM has challenged this approach and privileged discourses from a management perspective and the commodification of students into consumers over this notion of a community of practice engaged in academic enquiry. Stiles (2004) supports this notion in identifying three forms of management practice commonly used in university contexts. He labels these as separatist, integrationist and hegemonist. The separatist style is seen as cohesive and collegial and represents many of the traditional academic values that have underpinned the management and organization of universities as communities of enquiry. The hegemonist style is more akin to NPM and focuses on administrative effectiveness and customer orientation. This is the model which now imbibes the management and organization of our higher educator sector.

## Conclusion

Despite the claims by Taylor that task and role specification (Principles One and Four) will ultimately lead to satisfied managers and contented workers, this has not been the case in UK higher education. Numerous studies have found that the increasing pressure for excellent performance across all key areas of academic work (that is, learning and teaching, research and administration) have resulted in declining levels of employee satisfaction (Bellamy et al. 2003, Anderson et al. 2002, Coaldrake and Stedman 1999). A study conducted by Pop-Vasileva et al. (2010) on Australian academics across 37 institutions found that academics' job satisfaction was moderately low, with workloads and a lack of communication being major contributing factors. Moses (1996: 14) states that as a result of high levels of managerialism in universities 'academics experience impingement on their autonomy and creative space through performance reviews, student evaluations, accreditation … and pressure to publish, plan, predict and perform according to negotiated standards.'

There is a risk that those reading this chapter, particularly those in management in UK higher education or those that occupy one of the many non-academic bureaucratic roles, will dismiss this analysis as little more than a polemic rant and nostalgic yearning for an era of elite participation. In order to counter this it is important to consider how the impact of Taylorist working practices has affected the student experience in higher education. In effect, a convenient comparison can be made between one type of student experience, and the experience of a solitary diner enjoying breakfast in an exclusive resort hotel, served by a tiny garrison of seven waiters, three managers, two chefs and a maitre d' all busily carrying out their allotted roles. Whilst the attention to detail in serving and clearing the breakfast tables may have been perfected to standards that Taylor himself would have been proud of, the overall quality of the experience, for the diner, is likely to feel disjointed, over-regulated and somewhat over-managed.

Compare this experience with that of students who now enrol on degrees and can have up to 30 different lecturers during the course of their modular degree, have to engage with learning support staff, e-learning advisers, academic liaison officers, welfare support staff, departmental administrators, registry staff in their hundreds, examination officers, disciplinary officers, special needs advisers, and many more besides. A casual observer cannot help but feel that the contemporary experience of engaging with higher education in the UK is akin to the overly managed breakfast in the resort hotel, except of course for the obvious fact that, for the solitary diner, the experience of breakfast seems over-regulated because it is disproportionate. The student, who since massification may find herself or himself increasingly lost in a vast crowd of equally nameless, faceless students, weaving their respective ways through the labyrinth of systems and regulations, does not even have the luxury of feeling so privileged within this machinery of bureaucracy.

As academics have been disempowered and higher education has been regulated to a fine art, students themselves unwittingly now become part of the great machine that drives for efficiency at the expense of delivering a personal education. Students now have to download their own teaching materials from impersonal virtual learning environments, communicate largely with academics via e-mail or online discussion forums, participate in mass lectures where there is little room or space (physically or intellectually) for discussion, debate and enquiry, work to assessment specifications that leave little or no room for creativity and innovation and be assessed on such a regular basis that both students and academics start to suffer from assessment fatigue.

At the beginning of this chapter, we spoke of the 'contradictions' within the Taylorist project that are laid bare in the example of the higher education sector today. Throughout this discussion we have sought to highlight these contradictions. Chief among them, of course, is the seemingly inescapable contradiction between the *idea* of a university as a space for self-discovery and the pursuit of knowledge for its own sake, and the *reality* of a university within a market-driven economy, forced to operate purely and simply as a business. While we are not naïve enough to believe that the university has not always been to some extent, a business of sorts, the problem lies in the extent to which the business function of the university impacts upon, and ultimately comes to dictate, the intellectual function. From a Weberian perspective, this contradiction derives from the apparent incompatibility of *zweckrational* and *wertrational* as organizing principles. The traditional organizing principle of the 'front-line' role of the university is that of *wertrational*, in this case, the pursuit of knowledge as an inherent value in its own right. However, as with all institutions within a capitalist economy, albeit more obviously so within a neo-liberal ultra-capitalist one, the university has throughout history resorted to *zweckrational* as an organizing principle when engaging with market-driven demands. This has rarely been seen as problematic so long as academics, as well as students, exercised the power that comes from cooperative management via such bodies as the university senate or the independent students' union.

The dominance of New Public Management and its associated systems and strategies upon the university has radically transformed that traditional model. Academic representation on many university senates, as previously stated, has been seriously cut, and in any case has become identified with the presence of heads of department or deans of school who, though in most cases still academics, are nonetheless managerial appointments and hardly representative of the views of the academic community. As a result, such decision-making bodies have increasingly lost their critical capacities and become akin to executive boardrooms, comprising managers blindly committed to crude instrumental rationality, agreeing on strategic objectives which are wholly divorced from the intellectual project of the university and the value of knowledge for its own sake. These objectives then become packaged as 'best practice', a term that is presented in the guise of scientific objectivity, or else as a self-defining force for good with which one would have to be a fool to disagree, but in truth 'best practice' is a heavily ideological concept. It begs the question posited earlier: best for whom? As each government body, funding council or university non-academic support service implements its own strategies for developing 'best practice', and sets its own deadlines and priorities in order to further its own (perceived) productivity, the university front line, the classroom as a space in which knowledge is pursued, becomes the battleground in which these competing rationalities, these ideologies, are contested. Suddenly, this very front-line activity of the deliberation of knowledge, which is at the core of the role of the university, becomes subjected to systems and regulations resulting from the 'best practice' of, and thus ideologically in the interests of, administrators and managers, and the academic voice is rendered irrelevant.

The danger of all this, though, is more than the damage it no doubt does to the academic's already inflated sense of her or his own self-importance as a 'free-floating intellectual'. The broader impact goes beyond even the transformation of the student experience, beyond even the changes to the curriculum which may result in the prioritization of what Habermas (1970) calls 'technically-useful' knowledge and the possible closure of 'unprofitable' courses in the arts or humanities. The broader impact is at the societal level itself. Habermas (1987) introduced the concept of the 'colonization of the lifeworld' as an apt description of the most fundamentally dangerous and challenging process of modern society. The logic of instrumental rationality, of the system, he warned, has increasingly entered into and become dominant within other spheres of social life which need not and should not be reducible to such a logic. It is akin to a form of commodification, so correctly defined by Marx, in which the value of something is increasingly determined by the market, rather than by its inherent beauty, by taste or by its subjectively meaningful worth. This has severe political implications. When Marcuse (1964), whose work inspires Habermas, described 'one-dimensional society' he was referring to the 'closing down of the alternatives', a world in which a single logic dictates what we know and how we think. One-dimensional society will not tolerate opposition, so the university, traditionally a breeding ground for independent thinking, must instead become a factory for the production of 'technically-useful knowledge'. How is that best achieved? It is achieved by imposing regulations and systems, and standardizing practices, which render the experience of the university indistinguishable except at a superficial level from any other institution of the system. That is the point, and the practice, of Taylor's scientific management.

## References

Alvesson, M. 1987. *Organization Theory and Technocratic Consciousness: Rationality, Ideology and the Quality of Work*. Berlin: De Gruyter.

Alvesson, M. and Willmott, H. (eds). 1992. *Critical Management Studies*. London: Sage.

Alvesson, M. and Willmott, H. (eds). 2003. *Studying Management Critically*. London: Sage.

Anderson, D., Johnson, R. and Saha, L. 2002. *Changes in Academic Work: Implications for Universities of the Changing Age Distribution and Work Roles of Academic Staff* [Online: Department of Education, Science and Training, Australia]. Available at: http://www.dest.gov.au/NR/rdonlyres/57E92071-C591-4E15-879C-468A9CDE80A1/910/academic_work.pdf [accessed: 9 January 2012].

Anderson, G. 2006. Carving out time and space in the managerial university, *Journal of Organisational Change*, 19(5), 578–92.

Bellamy, S., Morley, C. and Watty, K. 2003. Why business academics remain in Australian universities despite deteriorating working conditions and reduced job satisfaction: an intellectual puzzle. *Journal of Higher Education and Policy Management*, 25(1), 13–28.

Carr, W. (ed.). 1989. *Quality in Teaching: Arguments for a Reflective Profession*. London: Falmer Press.

Coaldrake, P. and Stedman, L. 1999. *Academic Work in the Twenty-First Century: Changing Roles and Policies* [Online: Higher Education Division, Department of Education, Training and Youth Affairs, Occasional Paper Series No. 99H]. Available at: http://www.dest.gov.au/sectors/higher_education/ publications_resources/profiles/archives/academic_work_in_the_twenty_ first_century.htm [accessed: 9 January 2012].

Deem, R. and Brehony, K.J. 2005. Management as ideology: the case of 'new managerialism' in higher education. *Oxford Review of Education*, 31(2), 217–35.

Deem, R. and Johnson, R.J. 2000. Managerialism and university managers: building new academic communities or disrupting old ones? *Higher Education and Its Communities*, edited by I. Mckay. Buckingham: Open University Press, 65–84.

Ferlie, E., Ashburner, L., Fitzgerald, L. and Pettigrew, A. 1996. *The New Public Management in Action*. Oxford: Oxford University Press.

Gombrich, R. 2000 *British Higher Education Policy in the Last Twenty Years: The Murder of a Profession*. Available at: http://www.atm.damtp.cam.ac.uk/ mcintyre/papers/LHCE/uk-higher-education.html [accessed: 9 January 2012].

Gore, C., Bond, C. and Steven, V. 2000. Organisational self-assessment: measuring educational quality in two paradigms. *Quality Assurance in Education*, 8(2), 76–84.

Habermas, J. 1970. *Toward a Rational Society*. London: Heinemann.

Habermas, J. 1987. *The Theory of Communicative Action*, vol. 2, *System and Lifeworld: The Critique of Functionalist Reason*. Cambridge: Polity Press.

Harvey, L. 2005. A history and critique of quality evaluation in the UK. *Quality Assurance in Education*, 12(4), 263–76.

Horkheimer, M. and Adorno, T. 1969. *Dialectic of Enlightenment*. New York: Continuum.

Marcuse, H. 1964. *One-Dimensional Man*. Boston: Beacon Press.

Michels, R. 1962. *Political Parties*. New York: Free Press.

Moses, I. 1996. Tensions and tendencies in the management of quality and autonomy in Australian higher education. *Australian Universities Review*, 38(1), 11–15.

Parker, L. 2002. It's been a pleasure doing business with you: a strategic analysis and critique of university management. *Critical Perspectives on Accounting*, 13(5–6), 603–19.

Parker, L. and Gould, G. 1999. Changing public sector accountability: critiquing new directions. *Accounting Forum*, 23(2), 109–35.

Pop-Vasileva, A., Baird, K. and Blair, B. 2010. University corporatization: the effect on academic work-related attitudes. *Accounting, Auditing and Accountability Journal*, 24(4), 408–39.

Ritzer, G. 1996. *The McDonaldization of Society*. Rev. edn. Thousand Oaks CA: Pine Forge.

Stiles, D.R. 2004. Narcissus revisited: the values of management academics and their role in business school strategies in the UK and Canada. *British Journal of Management*, 15(2), 157–75.

Taylor, F.W. 1911. *The Principles of Scientific Management*. New York: Harper & Row.

Weber, M. 1992. *The Protestant Ethic and the Spirit of Capitalism*. London: Routledge.

Weber, M. 1997. *The Theory of Social and Economic Organization*. New York: Free Press.

# PART III

# Management a Century On: Contradictions, Dilemmas and Prospects

# 9

# Modern-Day 'Schmidts': The Legacy of Taylorism in Elite 'Professional' Roles

*Yvonne Guerrier*

## Introduction

In Mohsin Hamid's (2007) novel *The Reluctant Fundamentalist*, Changez, a young Pakistani who has been educated at Princeton, is recruited into a management consultancy company in New York. He flourishes within a highly competitive environment where trainees are taught to value efficiency above all and where individual rankings determine bonuses and survival within the company, and where work is all-consuming even if the pay can fund a lavish lifestyle. After 9/11, Changez begins to question his identity and his allegiances. Eventually, Changez walks out of an assignment, is fired from his company and returns to Pakistan to become, perhaps, the instigator of terrorism against the West. The book is ambiguous about this.

At first sight, it may seem there is little similarity between the world of elite knowledge workers that Hamid's fictional Changez finally rejected and the world of F.W. Taylor's industrial workers. Changez was a grade A student at an elite university and it was these elite qualifications that 'fitted' him for work in an elite management consultancy. Taylor concerned himself with the management of pig iron handlers: he described the characteristics of a man suited to this occupation as 'that he shall be so stupid and so phlegmatic that he more nearly resembles in his mental make-up the ox than any other type' (Taylor 1911: 46).

But it is instructive to compare Taylor's description of the selection of Schmidt, his famous (and possibly fictional) champion pig iron handler, with

Hamid's description of how Changez was recruited into the elite consultancy. Taylor describes how Schmidt was selected as the most suitable pig iron handler for Taylor's experiments with scientific management after examination of his character, habits and ambition:

> *He was a little Pennsylvania Dutchman who had been observed to trot back home for a mile or so after work in the evening about as fresh as he was when he came trotting down to work in the morning ... He also had the reputation of being exceedingly 'close', that is of placing a very high value on the dollar. (Taylor 1911: 33)*

Changez is also a migrant and impresses his recruiter not so much through his academic credentials but because of his sporting credentials and his desire for and lack of money. Even though he is not being hired for manual labour, the recruiter for the management consultancy becomes interested in him on learning he can still run a six-minute mile, despite a knee injury, and that he needed financial support for college, as that made him 'hungry'.

Both Schmidt and Changez were hired, for very different jobs, because they were seen as being fit for work. Being fit for work is not just about having a strong body, but also a disciplined body and mind – to be prepared to control and manage one's body for the benefit of one's employer – so that one remains fit for work. This chapter will explore this aspect of Taylorism and demonstrate how it permeates even skilled elite roles.

## Taylor and Fitness for Work

As Bahnisch (2000) demonstrates, despite the veneer of rationality in scientific management, Taylor seems to have been obsessed by bodies and fitness. Workers, in Taylor's terms, were seen merely as bodies: his first-class man has enormous physical strength but is 'so stupid that the word "percentage" has no meaning to him' (Taylor 1911: 46). At the same time, the bodies of workers are seen as anarchic and dangerous to bourgeois society (Bendix 1974 in Bahnisch 2000). Taylor was concerned about breaking up informal groups who he believed systematically 'soldiered' (that is, collaborated to reduce their rate of work); by separating and individualizing workers he also thought that they would become less dangerous and easier to discipline. (Taylor's concern that workers collaborated to limit their labour might seem to contradict his view that they were stupid. As Wagner-Tsukamoto (2008) also points out, his description of Schmidt as a man who was building his own house also seems to contradict Taylor's view that he was as stupid as an ox.) At the same time Taylor seems to have admired 'fit bodies' and indeed been somewhat jealous of those with them. Rose (1978 in Bahnisch 2000) claimed that Taylor longed to be 'a muscular six-footer' and admired those managers who maintained control of their workers because of their physical prowess and control.

A number of themes, therefore, emerge from Taylor's original works in relation to fitness at work. First, Taylorism is not just about the planning and management of work: it is also about the scientific selection of a person who is 'fit' for work. That fitness is not just about physical prowess and strength but also about the willingness to be disciplined so that physical prowess is harnessed for the benefit of the company, rather than potentially posing a threat to the company.

Wagner-Tsukamoto (2008) argues that it is too simplistic to claim that Taylor's only saw human nature in terms of 'economic man'. Taylor certainly thought that his ideal workers, who were prepared to discipline themselves at and outside of work, would benefit from an improved income, which, according to this extract, they will use in a sensible and disciplined way, for example through saving up for a house. Taylor viewed his workers as 'heartily cooperative' (see Wagner-Tsukamoto 2008) – good men who, by working with scientifically informed managers and keeping themselves fit for work, could be helped to achieve a good income and a better lifestyle for themselves and their families.

Despite Taylor's claims that his scientific system is of mutual benefit, both to the company and the worker, a major criticism of Taylor is of the physical and psychological damage done to the worker of a system of intensified work and tight control. Whilst the worker is expected to keep himself (*sic*) 'fit for work', Taylor's critics argue that his body and soul are destroyed through doing this work.

## The Work of the New 'Professionals'

The discussion so far has focused on the way Taylorism requires workers who are prepared to discipline their minds and their bodies in order to be and remain fit for their work. I shall now consider how this is relevant to the work of those who are normally considered to be elite knowledge workers, such as management consultants. Since such work is commonly characterized as professional work, I shall first consider the way in which professional work is changing.

Whilst the nature and characteristics of professional work have been much debated by sociologists, professionals have normally been thought of as people with a high level of skill and knowledge (including knowledge of abstract concepts), whose work requires a high degree of discretionary judgement, who operate within a collegiate and cooperative work environment and whose primary allegiance is to their professional institutions and to their occupation rather than to the organization in which they are currently working (Evetts 2011). Professionalism has been characterized as a 'third logic' (Freidson 2001) in terms of organizing work, a logic which is in opposition to the Taylorist mode of organizing. However, this traditional model of professionalism is under threat. Professionals increasingly work with large corporate organizations and, it has been argued, are increasingly managed by more normal bureaucratic methods (Evetts 2011, Kipping 2011).

Whilst these changes are affecting the established professions, they are even more apparent in what have been termed 'new professions' such as management consultancy. Kipping (2011) characterizes management consultancy as 'hollow' or 'image consultancy'. He argues that it is useful for management consultancies to project the image of professionalism to their clients in order to enhance their status and prestige, but at the same time it is important for them to retain 'close control over their employees' (Kipping 2011: 544). They maintain this control through methods of selection, training, rewards and management of staff which, as I will show, have parallels with 'scientific management'.

## RECRUITMENT AND SELECTION

According to research, the fictional description of Changez's recruitment into an elite management consultancy (Hamid 2007) represents typical practice in this sector. Up until the 1950s it was typical practice to hire experienced business people. Then McKinsey pioneered the approach of recruiting graduates directly from elite business schools (initially Harvard), a practice which the rest of the industry quickly adopted (Kipping 2011, Armbrüster 2004). One of the arguments in favour of this practice was that younger and less experienced graduates which would be easier to mould (Kipping 2011).

Armbrüster (2004) provides a detailed account of the recruitment practices used by these consultancies. Whilst most industry sectors that recruit graduates systematically make use of assessment centres, management consultancy firms typically rely on a case study interview conducted not by a trained HR professional but by one of the consultants who may have received little or no training in selection methods. Armbrüster (2004) argues the business cases used are decontextualized: the 'correct' answer for the case is one where the candidate treats the data provided as neutral facts and provides neutral and quantifiable solutions. In effect the focus of this method of selection is on identifying people who are prepared to conform to the culture and expectations of the company and 'accept … the limitations of what is acceptable' (ibid.: 1262). He highlights one aspect that successful candidates must accept as 'the worldview of positivist sciences … and [a] marginalizing [of] socio-political issues' (ibid.: 1266). The successful candidate is, therefore, someone who is supremely skilled at analysing and calculating in a particular type of way but who does not, or does not allow themselves to, question or think more broadly.

## TRAINING

Given that the emphasis of the selection process is to identify 'talent' rather than performance, a rigorous selection procedure needs to be followed by a rigorous and systematic training process. Kipping (2011) argues that one of the aims of the training is to ensure uniformity across different operations: to promote, in effect and in Taylorist terms, one best way of working. In *The Reluctant Fundamentalist* Changez describes his initial training as a consultant as follows:

> *I see you are impressed by the thoroughness of our training. I was as well. It was a testament to the systematic pragmatism – call it professionalism – that underpins your country's success in so many fields. At Princeton, learning was imbued with an aura of creativity; at Underwood Samson, creativity was not excised – it was still present and valued – but it ceded its primacy to efficiency. Maximum return was the maxim to which we returned, time and again. We learned to prioritize … and then to apply ourselves single-mindedly to the achievement of that objective. (Hamid 2007: 41)*

## REWARDS AND MANAGEMENT CONTROL

In the *Reluctant Fundamentalist*, Changez also describes the training process in the consultancy as a period when the new recruits were encouraged to think of themselves as part of a special elite. One of the ways in which this was done was to be generous in terms of financial rewards. He comments:

*Do you know exhilarating it is to be issued a credit card and told that*
*your company will pick up the tab for any ostensibly work-related meal*
*or entertainment ... [F]or me, at the age of twenty-two, this experience*
*was a revelation. I could, if I desired, take my colleague out for an*
*after-work drink – an activity classified as 'new hire cultivation' – and*
*with impunity spend in an hour more than my father earned in a day!*
*(Hamid 2007: 42)*

As Alvesson and Robertson (2006) point out, giving access to scarce resources, like funds for development, access to lavish company events and, as discussed here, lavish expense accounts, are ways in which organizations symbolically reinforce an elite identity. But rewards are, of course, primarily about pay and about the system of rewards. Changez was told by a vice-president of the consultancy company at the beginning of the training: 'We're a meritocracy ... We'll rank you every six months. You'll know your rankings. Your bonuses and staffing will depend on them. If you do well you'll be rewarded. If you don't, you'll be out the door. It's that simple' (Hamid 2007: 39). Rewards, then, are individualized: they encourage staff to compete against each other; they are based on performance; they contain a threat of sanctions for poor performance as well as rewards for high performance; and the general level of rewards with monetary and symbolic values are higher than the individual might expect to earn in similar work in other sectors.

Taylor, of course, is famous for using financial rewards to incentivize his workers: by giving his 'chosen' workers higher rates of basic pay, for example, paying the two 'first-class workers', selected to participate in his experiments to develop a 'best' way of doing manual work, double wages, as well as linking earnings to work. Taylor, as I have discussed above, also focused on individual rewards because individualizing workers and breaking up groups made them easier to manage.

The 'meritocratic' rewards and management system used in Changez's management consultancy may be argued as being not just about motivating staff to work hard but also about keeping them in line and under control (in the same way as Taylor used individual rewards to discipline workers). Luyendijk (2011a), who has been conducting a set of interviews with people working in finance in the City of London, comments on how high pay levels in this sector make people less likely to 'rock the boat', especially when they know that there are periodic 'cullings of the herd' and when there is little chance of getting work at a similar pay level elsewhere.

In conclusion, the way in which new professionals within elite management consultancies are managed seems designed to take people who are malleable, because they are young and do not bring 'baggage' with them, train them in 'one best way' to conduct a set of operations whilst at the same time not encouraging them to think too broadly, and then manage them through individualized rewards and sanctions which lock them in to the system (or move them out of it quickly if they do not conform).

## Keeping Oneself Fit for Work

Taylor, of course, professed that his objective was to design work which could be sustained over long periods: 'the best day's work that a man could do, year in year out, and still thrive under' (Taylor 1911: 42). His critics argue that the reality was very different. Taylor's calculations about what was a sustainable rate of work had not been as carefully researched as he claimed and, in practice, no one could achieve these rates for more than short bursts (Lepore 2009). 'Speeding up production meant that workers came home knackered. Some Bethlehem ironworkers were so wrecked after a Taylor-size day's work that they couldn't get out of bed the next morning' (Lepore 2009: 4).

There is a similar debate about work within 'new professions' such as management consultancy. Hewlett and Luce (2006) use the term 'extreme jobs' to describe high-earning work which requires long and unpredictable hours, fast-paced work with tight deadlines and usually extensive travel. Such work inevitably has an impact on family and social life and potentially on health. But Hewitt and Luce argue that people doing these roles do not see themselves (and are not seen by broader society) as victims. 'Today's overachieving professionals are recast as road warriors and masters of the universe,' they argue (ibid.: 50). 'Our most intense jobs are seen not as exploitative but, rather, as glamorous, desirable and virtuous' (ibid.: 53). It is instructive to compare these comments with those of Bahnisch (2000) who (drawing on Collinson 1992 and Knights and Willmott 1989) argues that manual workers consented to Taylorized, heavy manual work, which was alienating and physically damaging, by constructing it as masculine work. Thus it too became work which enhanced the identity of the 'man' who did it, and its toughness was also part of its glamour.

Both Taylor's manual workers and the new professionals doing 'extreme jobs', therefore, can be motivated to take on physically and psychologically demanding work not only through the offer of superior financial rewards but also because of the way the work is symbolically portrayed. People who can 'hack it' in tough environments that others cannot cope with are glamorized in the popular media: for example in programmes such as *The Apprentice* which depicts success in business as being about surviving in a tough 'work hard, play hard' environment, and programmes such as *Masterchef* with its 'cooking doesn't come tougher than this' mantra. But staying 'fit' for such jobs affects people's lives outside work and not just because of the long hours at work. It requires additional work to keep oneself 'fit' for work.

Taylor's ideal workers needed to be disciplined outside work as well as at work. Taylor comments in relation to wider experiment with manual workers at Bethlehem Steel:

> *A careful inquiry into the condition of these men developed the fact that out of 140 workmen only two were said to be drinking men. This does not of course imply that many of them did not take an occasional drink. The fact is that a steady drinker would find it almost impossible to keep up with the pace which was set, so that they were practically all sober. Many, if not most of them, were saving money and they all lived better than they had before. (Taylor 1911: 55)*

In the same way, research has shown how new professionals have recognized the need to keep themselves healthy and physically fit in order to cope with the rigours of work. Waring and Waring (2009) in a study of city workers in London and Manchester comment that their participants 'sought to create a "professional body"... from following diets, such as "low-carb" diets, to abstaining from certain drugs or substances' (ibid.: 357). Further, they comment that 'physical activities themselves were work orientated, and for many respondents, the health club was thought to be an extension of the working day and thus was considered to be an integral part of professional life' (ibid.: 358).

Yet, in practice, the work cultures of the new professionals, similar to the work cultures of manual workers, often also involve less healthy activities, such as drinking heavily with work colleagues after work. Waring and Waring (2009) comment on the contradictions in the lifestyles of their participants: 'a number of participants reportedly drank and smoked heavily, despite engaging in health-related activities' (ibid.: 359). They conclude that the organizational discourse encourages individuals to "look" fit and healthy, without necessarily "being" fit and healthy' (ibid.: 359).

So there are two opposing narratives about the way in which people in 'elite' professional roles respond to their roles. On the one hand, there is an 'ideal' narrative which argues that these are demanding roles for which people are, appropriately, well paid but which are sustainable and do-able providing people are disciplined to adopt a healthy and physically active lifestyle outside work: such practices are encouraged by well-being policies within their organization. On the other hand, there is a critical narrative which argues that people in 'elite' professional roles need to present an image of themselves as being 'fit' for work in order to demonstrate that they are disciplined and in order to continue to work in these roles. Ironically, the need to keep 'fit' becomes another demand in an already exhausting role. In practice, the mechanisms that these people use to manage their stress may be less healthy, for example smoking and drinking heavily. This is acceptable and even encouraged within the culture, provided that the appearance of 'fitness' for work is sustained. If it is not, they will be 'out'. For Changez, the Reluctant Fundamentalist, the first sign of his resistance against the discipline of working for a management consultancy was a minor infringement against the rules of how a professional should present himself: he grew a beard.

## Modern-Day Janissaries

At the beginning of this chapter, I commented that Taylor's Schmidt and Hamid's Changez shared the characteristic of being migrants. Taylor describes having selected Schmidt not just because he was fit but also because he was known to be motivated by money. Whilst it is not specifically stated, it may be surmised that Schmidt was also a suitable candidate for Taylor's experiments because, perhaps because of the nature of his migrant status, he was not part of the gang of workers whom Taylor saw as deliberately limiting their effort. Schmidt would therefore be willing to submit himself to Taylor's regime.

In *The Reluctant Fundamentalist*, as he is beginning to question his lifestyle, Changez is sent on an assignment to Valparaiso in Chile where he encounters Juan-Bautista, the chief of a publishing company that he has been employed to value. Juan-Bautista asks Changez:

> *'Have you heard of the janissaries?' 'No,' I said. 'They were Christian boys,' he explained, 'captured by the Ottomans and trained to be soldiers in a Muslim army, at that time the greatest army in the world. They were ferocious and absolutely loyal: they had fought to erase their own civilisations, so they had nothing else to turn to.' (Hamid 2007: 172)*

The role of migrant workers in modern workplaces is a complex and contested issue. It has frequently been argued that a major motive for employing migrants is cost minimization: migrants, as they have less market power, will work for lower wages and are more flexible (that is, their hours can be reduced or they can be made redundant more easily) which also means they cost less. It is true that most migrants are found in low-skill, physically demanding work for which they are often over-qualified (MacKenzie and Forde 2009). But there is another rhetoric in relation to migrant workers which is more relevant here; the notion of the migrant worker as the 'good' worker with a strong work ethic, and who is prepared to work hard and follow management instructions (ibid.). These perceived characteristics may make migrant workers desirable employees even when they cost as much as a local and desirable in high-skill roles as well as in low-skills ones (Rodriguez 2004). Banerjee (2006), for example, shows how Indian IT professionals are widely used in the US but also how they are exploited by being kept on temporary contracts so they are what Banerjee describes as 'a ready-to-use, docile workforce'. They are also tied to employment as their visas to remain are linked to it. Changez was also affected by this. When he lost his job in the management consultancy he also lost his right to remain in the US.

There is an underlying but unstated principle in Taylor's *Scientific Management*, which is that the old 'elite' structures within a workforce must be destroyed. Elite manual workers, who recognized their own skills and who expected to manage their own work, are dangerous because their interests do not necessarily coincide with those of the managers. It is logical to upend the old hierarchies and favour those who have a more marginal status as they will be more docile. Migrant, especially new migrants who have not yet been tainted by the local work culture, are particularly 'fit for work'.

## Conclusions

Hamid (2007) called his novel *The Reluctant Fundamentalist*. The obvious interpretation of this title is that it is a story of a man, Changez, who, when he rejects America and the corporate lifestyle, reluctantly finds himself aligned to the fundamentalists of Pakistan. But there is another interpretation: that the life of the executive in corporate America itself represents a type of fundamentalism which Changez is reluctant to embrace in its entirety.

Taylorism and *Scientific Management*, of course, would normally be seen as a modernist movement. Indeed, its emphasis on rationality and the application of science to re-examine and overturn traditional work practices could be said to make it a perfect example of modernism at work. 'Fundamentalism', in all its manifestations, is usually defined in opposition to modernism: it is about the rejection of modern ways of life and an adoption of a set of clear principles which hark back to the supposed values of pre-modern society.

In practice, however, Taylorism is about much more than a rational, limited transaction of labour for money: it is about more than saying, 'In exchange for a wage, I will give you my time and effort and follow your rules'. For the ideal worker, in Taylor's terms, is expected to exchange more: they are supposed to lead healthy lives to keep themselves fit for work. And they are supposed to be docile, disciplined workers who do not question what they are supposed to do. In this sense, Taylorism can be seen as closer to a 'fundamentalist' project than a modernist one.

I have argued here that it is these aspects of Taylorism that we are in danger of reproducing not just in unskilled jobs but also in supposedly elite, highly skilled roles. What we may ask people to do in those roles may be complex and demanding but that we ask them to do it in a particular way is not up for question.

'This job involves in some part selling my soul for a good salary. I am very troubled by that. A lot of people aren't. I am.' This is a quote from a woman working in the finance sector interviewed by Luyendijk (2011a). The troubling aspect of Taylorism is not so much that it asks for you for your time or effort but that it also asks for your soul.

## References

Alvesson, M. and Robertson, M. 2006. The best and the brightest: the construction, significance and effects of elite identities in consulting firms. *Organization*, 13(2), 195–224.

Armbrüster, T. 2004. Rationality and its symbols: signalling effects and subjectification in management consulting. *Journal of Management Studies*, 14(8), 1247–69.

Bahnisch, M. 2000. Embodied work, divided labour: subjectivity and the scientific management of the body in Frederick W. Taylor's 1907 'Lecture on Management'. *Body and Society*, 6(5), 51–68.

Banerjee, P. 2006. Indian information technology workers in the United States: the H-1B visa, flexible production, and the racialization of labor. *Critical Sociology*, 32(2–3), 425–45.

Bendix, R. 1974. *Work and Authority in Industry: Ideologies of Management in the Course of Industrialisation*. Berkeley: University of California Press.

Collinson, D. 1992. *Managing the Shopfloor: Subjectivity, Masculinity, and Workplace Culture*. New York: De Gruyter.

Evetts, J. 2011. A new professionalism? Challenges and opportunities. *Current Sociology*, 59(4), 406–22.

Freidson, E. 2001. *Professionalism: The Third Logic*. Cambridge: Polity.

Hamid, M. 2007. *The Reluctant Fundamentalist*. London: Penguin.

Hewlett, S. and Luce, C. 2006. Extreme jobs: the dangerous allure of the 70-hour workweek. *Harvard Business Review*, December, 49–59.

Kipping, M. 2011. Hollow from the start? Image professionalism in management consulting. *Current Sociology*, 59(4), 530–40.

Knights, D. and Willmott, H. 1989. Power and subjectivity at work: from degradation to subjugation in social relations. *Sociology*, 23(4), 535–58.

Lepore, J. 2009. Not so fast. *The New Yorker* [Online], 12 October. Available at: http://www.newyorker.com/arts/critics/atlarge/2009/10/12/091012crat_atlarge_lepore [accessed: 1 July 2011].

Luyendijk, K. 2011a. Voices of finance: risk and compliance consultant at a major bank. *The Guardian* [Online], 3 November. Available at: http://www.guardian.co.uk/commentisfree/2011/nov/03/voices-of-finance-risk-and-compliance?INTCMP=SRCH [accessed: 16 March 2012].

Luyendijk, K. 2011b. Where are the financial whistle-blowers? *The Guardian* [Online], 27 December. Available at: http://www.guardian.co.uk/commentisfree/2011/ dec/27/financial-whistleblowers-silence [accessed 15 March 2012].

MacKenzie, R. and Forde, C. 2009. The rhetoric of the 'good worker' versus the realities of employers' use and experience of migrant workers. *Work, Employment and Society*, 23(1), 142–59.

Rodriguez, N. 2004. 'Workers wanted': employer recruitment of immigrant labor. *Work and Occupations*, 31(4): 453–73.

Rose, M. 1978. *Industrial Behaviour: Theoretical Development since Taylor*. London: Pelican.

Taylor, F.W. 1911. *The Principles of Scientific Management*. Reprinted by Forgottenbooks.org, 2010. Available at: http://www.forgottenbooks.org/ info/ 9781606801123 [accessed 14 March 2012].

Wagner-Tsukamoto, S. 2008. Scientific management revisited. *Journal of Management History*, 14(4), 318–72.

Waring, A. and Waring, J. 2009. Looking the part: embodying the discourse of organizational professionalism in the City. *Current Sociology*, 57(3), 344–64.

# 10

# Job Design: From Top-Down Managerial Control to Bottom-Up 'Job Crafting'

*Christina Evans*

## Introduction

> *Under the old type of management success depends almost entirely upon getting 'initiative' of the workmen, and it is indeed a rare case in which this initiative is really attained. Under scientific management the 'initiative' of the workmen (that is their hard work, their good-will and their ingenuity) is obtained with absolute uniformity and to a greater extent than is possible under the old system; and in addition to improvement on the part of the men, the managers assume new burdens new duties and responsibilities never dreamed off in the past. (Taylor 1911: 26–9)*

Despite widespread criticism, Taylor's principles of scientific management have played an influential role in the way that managers think about organizational and job design. Brewster et al. (2011) suggest that Taylor's views on organization and job design provide a benchmark (albeit in an extreme form) with which other approaches to job design are compared and contrasted. As we can see from the opening quote at the beginning of this chapter, Taylor's philosophy on management involved removing the scope for worker initiative by increasing managerial control: this, Taylor argued, was critical for enhanced organizational performance. A key assumption was that not only would this lead to greater cost efficiency for the employer, but it would be beneficial for workers too: doing a simple and tightly defined task, and doing it well, would result in Taylor's notion of 'a high class man', that is, someone who could earn consistently more than his peers (Taylor 1911: 34).

Yet as already discussed in the introductory chapter, in many parts of the global economy the nature of work has changed significantly since Taylor's original work: information and knowledge are now considered the primary source of economic value (Castells 1989). Yet despite the growing importance of knowledge and service work, questions have been raised as to what extent the theory of job design has kept up with the realities and expectations of twenty-first century workplaces (Parker et al. 2001), particularly in relation to the notion and scope for discretionary behaviour. The discussion later in this chapter around the concept of employee engagement highlights this tension. In post-bureaucratic organizations with the free flow of information, supported by intelligent information systems, in principle it should be easier for employees to exert more discretionary behaviour. Yet despite the rhetoric of employee engagement, organizations still want to exert tighter controls for a variety of reasons (for example, economic or operational factors). In the contemporary workplace, Taylor's equivalent of the 'high class man', in theory, is someone who valued for her/his brains (not brawn), with a repertoire of 'soft' behavioural skills that can be drawn on to 'delight the customer': standardized discretionary behaviour, as in Taylor's era, one would assume, has no place in the contemporary workplace. However, as we will see in the discussion below, the rhetoric and the reality of discretionary behaviour is distinctly different.

This chapter begins by mapping out key historical developments in the theory and practice of job design over the past century: scientific management; flexible firm; lean manufacturing; high-performance work systems (HPWS) and the contemporary preoccupation with employee engagement. These developments have been accompanied by the changing organizational rhetoric of 'people are our most importance asset' particularly given the growing importance of human resource management (HRM) as a discrete area of managerial specialism (Gratton et al. 1999). However, despite the unitarist nature of Beer et al.'s (1985) 'soft' model of HRM, the reality of the working lives of many employees falls more within the 'hard' model of HRM which '… stresses the "quantitative, calculative, and business-strategic aspects" of managing the "headcount resource" in as "rational" a way as for any other factor of production' (see Gratton et al. 1999: 41): there are clear parallels here with Taylor's rationalistic form of management.

The chapter then moves on to discuss some of the key issues of job design in knowledge- and service-intensive businesses, specifically relating to difficulties with balancing organizational needs for quality, consistency in customer service and professional standards with employees' need for meaningful, or good, work (Duchon and Plowman 2005, CIPD 2006b, Work Foundation 2011).

The chapter concludes by considering whether a focus on 'job crafting', as opposed to the current managerial preoccupation with employee engagement, could help redress this imbalance.

## The Evolution of Job Design (from Scientific Management to Employee Engagement)

Although there have been major changes in the nature and scope of businesses over the past century, with the shifting emphasis from manufacturing to knowledge- and service-intensive work, several commentators argue that the thinking and practice of job design has not radically changed (Parker et al. 2001, Brewster et al. 2011). This is despite a plethora of managerial approaches, particularly since the 1970s, aimed at improving employee performance through various forms of employee participation and engagement techniques.

### JOB DESIGN – SCIENTIFIC MANAGEMENT ERA

Taylor's view on work design was influenced by his preoccupation with what he perceived as a generic management problem, that of consistently obtaining the best initiative of every workman. But unlike contemporary views on management, Taylor's solution to the problem was to organize work such that all scope for initiative was removed: 'To summarise: Under the management of "initiative and incentive" practically the whole problem is "up to the workman" while under scientific management fully one-half of the problem is up to the management' (Taylor 1911: 26–9).

By breaking jobs into discrete tasks, careful selection of workers for each task, and rewarding workers for completing tasks exactly as prescribed, Taylor argued that worker output could be increased. The trade-off for the workers, and to earn the label 'high class man', was relinquishing all rights to independent thought and action. This, according to Taylor, could be left to someone more suitably qualified (that is, a foreman or manager):

> *Schmidt started to work, and all day long, and at regular intervals, was told by the man who stood over him with a watch. 'Now pick up a pig iron and walk. Now sit down and rest. Now walk – now rest'. He worked when he was told to work and rested when he was told to rest and at half past five in the afternoon had his 47 and half tons loaded on the car. And he practically never failed to work at this pace and to do the task that was set him. (Taylor 1911: 36)*

Despite the limitations of this regulated form of work design, perhaps contemporary workplaces could benefit from Taylor's logic that an inappropriate pace of work is likely to be detrimental to workers' health:

> *These tasks are carefully planned so that both good and careful work is*
> *called for in their performance, but it should be distinctly understood*
> *that in no case is the workman called upon to work at a pace which*
> *would be injurious to his health. The task is always so regulated that*
> *the man who is well suited to his job will thrive while working at his*
> *rate during a long term of years and grow happier and more prosperous*
> *instead of being overworked. (Taylor 1911: 29–30)*

Nonetheless this approach to work design was in stark contrast to the earlier work regime of craft workers where managers were dependent '... almost entirely upon getting "initiative" of the workmen' (Taylor 1911: 26), as it was they who were in control of the knowledge and expertise to resolve problems. Fast forward seventy years and a similar type of reductionist thinking about job design seems prevalent in the car manufacturing sector:

> *What they [management] didn't understand at that time was that in*
> *doing so they restricted themselves to an additative and reductionist*
> *way of thinking. Although this approach is also valid, it is not conducive*
> *to the creation of something new and more efficient than the existing*
> *systems. There are alternative approaches and I suggested another way*
> *to think and act from a holistic model which focuses on content and*
> *context from the workers' point of view. (Sandberg 2007: 76)*

Whilst some organizations, for example Volvo, have experimented with more 'humane and democratic work practices' (Adler and Cole 2007: 158), sadly the short-term economics of these approaches were short-lived. Nonetheless the experiments conducted at two of Volvo's manufacturing plants in Sweden did generate key learning from an organizational and job design perspective according to Adler and Cole (2007). First, to ensure organizational flexibility all employees need to develop an understanding of why things are done in a particular way and, equally importantly, have an understanding of the interrelationships between jobs – what Adler and Cole (2007: 169) refer to as 'understanding a broader range of jobs'. Second, the quality of work-life can be greatly improved through 'democratising the work design process and business governance' (Adler and Cole 2007: 168). Third, to encourage people to contribute new ideas requires a reward system that reflects this aim.

## JOB DESIGN – THE LEAN ERA

Despite key learning that emerged from innovations in job design in organizations such as Volvo, 'lean production' techniques are still advocated by major consultancies as a way of eliminating waste and improving quality. This is not just the case in low-skilled manufacturing environments but also to high-skilled knowledge- and service-intensive work contexts. Lean production techniques (though not necessarily labelled as such) have been introduced in public sector services, for example in healthcare, aged care services, the UK Civil Service, UK local authorities, the UK police service and retail and retail distribution (see Bolton 2004, Kim et al. 2006, Wright and Lund 2006, Seddon 2008, Harley et al. 2010, Carter et al. 2011).

## Adoption of Lean Production Techniques in the Healthcare Sector

In the healthcare sector, for example, changes in organizational practices (inevitably affecting individuals' jobs) have been introduced under the banner of quality improvements, aimed at improving the patient experience, whilst at the same time driving down costs through eradicating waste. Bolton (2004: 326) points out that 'consumer rhetoric has acted as a powerful transformative device. By redefining "patients as customers", quality has become a new form of managerial control, that can have both positive and negative effects on employees.' Bolton's (2004) study of quality control initiatives introduced in one particular NHS trust highlights the tensions with managerial approaches that on the one hand seeks to build a 'one best way' approach (quality agenda) with that of building a 'patient as customer' culture, arguing that these two approaches are not mutually compatible. Yet as Bolton discovered, nurses often went along with managerial quality initiatives where there seemed to be mutual gains, in other words curtailing the power of doctors/consultants. In the short term at least there were some benefits for nurses from these new managerial control initiatives.

However, Fisher (2006) offers a less optimistic view of managerial change in the US healthcare setting, following the introduction of radio frequency identification (RFID) technology – a technology that has been extensively used in the retail/distribution sector to enhance managerial control (accuracy and flexibility). From a managerial perspective RFID technology enables better control over hospital assets, either costly equipment, or people (patients and staff). The managerial argument for tagging equipment is to avoid situations where time is wasted 'hunting down' equipment, time that could be directed at meeting patient needs. Nurses, however, as Fisher (2006) identified, had a different perspective on the introduction of this new technology – they saw it as another form of surveillance management. This was particularly the case in one hospital that used RFID technology to 'streamline hospital processes', especially the patient discharge process (Fisher 2006: 84). The thinking was that if RFID technology could be incorporated into patients' wristbands, then this would remove the additional burden of nursing staff having to inform central housekeeping that a bed had become free. Nurses, however, had a different perspective on this managerial change, given that it removed scope for 'discretionary behaviour'; that is, allocating time for rest breaks in the time period between discharging one patient and the arrival of the next patient. The collective response by nurses to change of this nature has parallels with the practice of 'systematic soldiering' in Taylor's era: skilled professionals (in this case nurses), recognizing that their discretionary behaviour was being eroded, found ways of getting round the system.

## Case Study: Adoption of Lean Transformation Techniques in the Biotechnology Sector

The following case study, drawn from previous work by the author, highlights tensions between employees' needs for more meaningful/less repetitive work and the organization's need to meet growing drug production targets, combined with achieving the stringent quality control standards demanded by regulators.

BioPharma is a key European operational site for one of the global pharmaceutical companies, established in the late 1990s. As a greenfield operation, the initial entrepreneurial management team appeared to have a lot of autonomy over how the work organization and job design. The managerial practices and routines in the company were based on what might be considered a more enlightened employee relations philosophy; that is, high performance achieved through employee engagement, as opposed to a more traditional confrontational employee relations approach. A spirit of involvement and participation was encouraged though the promotion of a managerial philosophy of 'Be your own leader'. This linked with the then organizational values of high trust, high involvement and participation, and minimal rules and policies. This philosophy seemed a better fit with the management team's aim to ensure a balance between structured and unstructured ways of working.

However, as the business grew in size, the senior management team struggled with reconciling how to grow the business in a cost-effective way but at the same time pursuing a high employee engagement approach to people management. Flexibility was seen as key to organizational survival. Flexibility in this context meant greater flexibility over the day-to-day operational working, thus enabling resources to be reallocated to different drug testing/ quality assurance processes to match changing demand from customers. To achieve this goal, the organization embarked on a number of transformation projects based on lean six-sigma techniques. Managers then were thus faced with trying to reconcile tensions between the structures inherent with the adoption of lean six-sigma technologies in an environment that consisted of a high-skill workforce: a large percentage of the workforce (66 per cent) in the company were graduates, who joined with the expectation of having access to challenging and interesting work. However, the reality for many employees in this type of environment was different from their expectations. One issue from the employees' perspective was gaining recognition for their individual contribution in a job that had essentially become more routine as a result of the transformation processes: adhering to stringent quality metrics left little scope for discretionary behaviour. Yet one way that individuals were able to differentiate their performance arose through their contribution to achieving key metrics. Individual actions that contributed to safety targets being met through something known as 'good saves' were looked on favourably in performance reviews.

Some respite from the routine nature of work did arise when employees were taken 'off line' to work on 'short-term' transformation projects: these were projects set up to explore how other operational efficiencies could be identified and implemented. In essence then, employees were being sold short-term developmental opportunities (that is, through getting involved in transforming existing work processes) which inevitably would lead to more routine work in the future. So whilst perhaps initially appealing/liberating, the benefits were short-lived.

As this short case study illustrates, scope for discretionary behaviour is limited in this type of work environment, despite the high dependency on skilled knowledge workers. Other writers point to similar observations about the experience of knowledge workers in the pharmaceutical industry. Kelly et al. (2010) identified that despite the importance of job design amongst knowledge workers in the pharmaceutical sector much of the work is very repetitive and routinized. They suggest that this is due to the highly regulated (in terms of quality standards) nature of the industry. From an HRM perspective, one solution to this tension would be to adopt more innovative development opportunities, consistent with Nonaka and Takeuchi's (1998) notion of 'redundancy' (see Kelly et al. 2010), where knowledge workers are allowed some space to engage in work that is meaningful for them, even if this work may not appear connected to their current role. Whilst an attractive proposition from an individual's perspective, one of the tensions will be convincing managers that this is a cost-effective use of resources.

One potential way for knowledge workers in the pharmaceutical industry to escape routine work is to develop more of a 'hybrid career'; one where they pursue a more generalist career role, for example through more project-based work (Kelly et al. 2011). This type of career change, in the short term at least, can provide an escape route from the monotony and frustration with routine work, due in part to more opportunities for 'exploratory type learning' (Kelly et al. 2011: 609). As will be discussed later, roles that involve more interaction with different stakeholders (as is likely to be the case with project-based work) can provide greater scope for 'job crafting'. However, there may well be longer-term career implications of such roles, as we saw in the case of hybrid workers in the ICT sector in an earlier chapter.

## Employee Engagement Era – Managerial Initiatives aimed at getting Workers to go the 'Extra Mile'

With the growing economic importance of the service sector, the concept of employee engagement crept into managerial discourse in the late 1990s; a managerial approach initially pushed by US-based consultancies, such as the Gallup Organization (Shuck and Wollard 2010), but then one quickly promoted by other consultancies in the UK and then the UK government. The discourse surrounding employee engagement is positioned as positive – employee engagement is good for business 'Business and organisations function best when they make their employees' commitment, potential, creativity and capability central to their operation', was how MacLeod and Clarke (2009: 7) positioned engagement in their review of employee engagement commissioned by the UK Secretary of State for Business, Innovation and Skills. Despite numerous studies, often with contradictory results, the business case for employee engagement persists. 'Levels of engagement matter because employee engagement can correlate with performance … and this is at the heart of our argument why employee engagement matters to the UK' (MacLeod and Clarke 2009: 11).

It is plausible that concerns over organizational performance due to 'burnout' (linked to work intensification) or 'boreout' (effects of lean production) created fruitful ground for consultancies to sell the concept of employee engagement to business executives. Maslach et al. (2001) suggest that employee engagement is the positive antithesis to burnout, defining employee engagement as 'a persistent positive affective state … characterized by high levels of activation and pleasure' (in Shuck and Wollard 2010: 99). Later definitions of employee engagement refer to an 'individual's involvement and satisfaction with, as well as enthusiasm for work' (Harter et al. 2002, in Shuck and Wollard 2010: 99). The concept is developed further by Saks (2006) who suggests that as employee engagement develops through a social exchange, different aspects of employee engagement – job engagement and organizational engagement – need to be considered (Saks 2006, in Shuck and Wollard 2010). Yet the approach adopted by most organizations is typically directed at organizational engagement, hence the use of organizational-wide employee surveys aimed at identifying the state of employee engagement, with a view to then taking some form of action to improve it.

But the validity and reliability of employee engagement surveys has been questioned, given the lack of clarity around what employee engagement is and also whether engagement is something that can be mandated for, or forced (Shuck and Wollard 2010). Some engagement surveys are based on an assumption that engagement consists of three interrelated subcomponents: cognitive engagement, emotional engagement and physical engagement (CIPD 2006a). The expected outcome from such surveys is to get a measure of employees' individual performance (that is, the physical effort that employees put into their work and their assessment of how this affects their performance). The issue, though, is that the data is based on self-reported responses to statements that include: I stay until the job is done, I take work home to do, I exert a lot of energy performing my job, I avoid extra overtime where possible: these are not observed behaviours. Moreover, the data is gathered without any supporting contextual information; so in what contexts do employees report that they adopt these behaviours?

Despite some of these limitations, the appeal of employee engagement surveys for management is perhaps understandable: employee responses can be categorized, quantified and an overall engagement index derived, which can then be benchmarked internally and externally. Where organizations adopt a consultancy-provided engagement tool not only are they able to benchmark their engagement index with other comparable businesses, but a script can be provided too for how to improve their overall engagement index. So although engagement is an individual characteristic (Shuck and Wollard 2010), most engagement surveys (including the widely used Gallup Q12 survey) result in change initiatives directed at increasing engagement scores at the team/departmental level. Managers, armed with (scientific) data, then involve their team(s) in drawing up action plans to address areas that seem to get in the way of engagement. Whilst this perhaps acts as an important employee voice mechanism (an assumed antecedent of engagement) the individual's voice in this process appears missing. Commenting on the CIPD's (2006a) *Working Life* research, Marks (p7) suggests that not only should team leaders balance support and challenge at the team level, but they also need to support staff to 'identify their own personal strengths, interests and skills, and seek to enhance their opportunities to use them at work. This will promote a virtuous cycle of positive emotions that broaden and build their capabilities.' Other research highlights tensions for individuals where their skills are under-utilized and thus working below potential (Kersley et al. 2006, Grant et al. 2006). Despite the positive discourse surrounding employee engagement, as Purcell points out, organizations need to pay more attention to job design – 'creating more "elbow room" for people to do their jobs' (CIPD 2006a: 4).

This next section discusses a more contemporary view of job design – the concept of 'job crafting' – where individuals appear more in control of shaping their job role on a day-to-day basis in order to meet their affective needs; for example, a desire for work to be more interesting, or meaningful (Shuck and Wollard 2010).

## Contemporary Perspective on Job Design – 'Job Crafting'

More recently, certainly amongst the academic community, there has been a growing interest in the concept of 'job crafting' (Wrzesniewski and Dutton 2001, Arnold 2011), which Wrzesniewski and Dutton (2001: 179) define as 'the physical and cognitive changes individuals make in the task, or relational boundaries of their work'. Whereas job enlargement/enrichment is a top-down managerialist approach to job design (group-based), job crafting is perceived as a proactive, improvised, dynamic and bottom-up form of job design, initiated by individuals. Job crafting is not a formalized management process, but an individualized situated activity; situated in the sense that it is the individual who initiates changes, on a day-to-day basis, about how to carry out different aspects of their work in order to derive more meaning from the work that they do. Crafting then can take many forms: taking on additional tasks; changing the nature and, or scope, of day-to-day relationships with others, as well as creating new relationships, or reframing one's own perception of how meaningful/impactful a specific job role is (Wrzesniewski and Dutton 2001, Berg et al. 2010). Thus in contrast to traditional job design approaches, such as Hackman and Oldham's (1980), where managers try to elicit the meaning that employees derive from pre-defined tasks, job crafting is assumed to work on reverse causality; that is, 'the opportunity and motivation to craft elicit job crafting', even in jobs that might be low in autonomy (Wrzesniewski and Dutton 2001: 181).

Arguably the concept of job crafting is not new, as this exert from *The Signalwoman*, dating back to the 1920s, illustrates. In this quote we can see how the signalwomen, free from direct observation by management, crafts her day-to-day work to make her work-life more bearable:

> *Of course I grumble at times. How often have I cursed the job to all eternity on arriving at my cabin on a bitterly cold Monday morning to find everything frozen solid ... signals pulled off on a Saturday night now frozen in that position, requiring a walk down the line, and after climbing up them, a good stiff clout with the coal hammer ... [but when] the kettle is boiling, and the platelayers have arrived to salt the points, you settle down with a mug of tea and the morning paper, not really wishing to be anywhere else. (Thomas 1999: 140)*

A combination of factors might help contextualize the contemporary interest in job crafting. First, there is the current preoccupation with well-being in the workplace, including a focus on fun and happiness, linked to assumptions about positive emotions and 'good functioning' (Fredrickson 2005, in CIPD 2006b). Here, then, the emphasis is on individuals building meaningful lives through utilizing (and building) their own strengths, interests and competences. Second, there is an increased use of flexible work arrangements (such as location-independent working), particularly in knowledge-intensive firms, that potentially offer greater scope for autonomous working and job crafting. Third, financial constraints due to the current economic situation make alternative reward strategies (such as promoting employee engagement and well-being) more appealing. Fourth, changing customer expectations in the service economy require a more individualized and personalized service. It is in this context, as discussed above, that employers have become preoccupied with building an engaged workforce. However, the approach adopted is arguably more prescriptive than the improvised and dynamic crafting behaviours associated with job crafting. Berg et al. (2010) suggest that job crafting can take one of three main forms:

*(1) **Task crafting**: where individuals alter the scope of their work in order to make their job content more interesting, or to develop a new interest.*

*(2) **Relational crafting**: where individuals engineer opportunities to build/shape relationships with others (inside or outside) the organization. This form of crafting may be initiated where individuals want to work with others with whom they perhaps enjoy a better affiliation, or to reinforce their sense of professional identity, or to build new knowledge that they can then take back and apply in their day-to-day work.*

*(3) **Cognitive crafting**: redefining, or reframing, one's own perceptions about a particular job, so that it appears to be of greater value (either to oneself or others), or to derive more meaning from the work that an individual is engaged in. This type of crafting, Berg et al. (2010) suggest, is more likely to arise where individuals have less scope for task crafting.*

Although in theory any individual can adopt job crafting behaviours (as we saw above in the exert from the *Signalwoman*), Clegg and Spencer (2007) argue that in reality there are a number of factors that are likely to influence the context and scope for individual crafting: level of competence; performance level/rating and degree of trust afforded by others. As job crafting is a dynamic-situated process, so changes in one individual's job crafting behaviours will invariably have implications for others with whom they interact, and the degree to which individuals are trusted by others (manager, peers, clients) is likely to affect opportunities and scope for job crafting. Given these factors it has been suggested that the types of jobs where it is potentially easier for individuals to craft occur in professional service environments, such as caring or educational roles (such as childcare educators, specialist education teachers) and specialist nursing roles, such as midwives (see Berg et al. 2010). The nature of this form of professional service work, which invariably involves a more individualized way of working with clients, reinforces an individual's sense of identity, including what it means to be a professional. This then affects how others (clients) experience the service that these professionals provide.

Even in caring environments the scope for job crafting (both task and relational) can be severely restricted with wider workforce redesign initiatives, especially those aimed at re-shaping the boundaries between professionals' roles. A study by Prowse and Prowse (2008) that investigated the impact of work redesign on the role of midwives identified how the scope for job crafting was diminished in contexts where the midwifery service was located in hospital settings, as opposed to in a community setting. In the hospital setting, midwives felt constrained by the new technologies and processes they were expected to utilize in their work, introduced under the changing NHS HRM agenda. Under this change agenda, midwives experienced tensions with the management requirement to 'get them [women] in, get them delivered, and ship them out (referred to by the midwives as the production-line model) and their professional identity as care providers' (Prowse and Prowse 2008: 702). In contrast, where the midwifery service was located in the community, midwives appeared to have more scope for job crafting since this was then mediated through the unique relationships that they developed with their clients.

A further example of the tensions with changing structures and professional identity was identified by Pritchard and Symon (2011) in their investigation into the effect on professional identity amongst HR professionals working in an HR shared service centre. The HR profession is one that is in constant state of flux and transition, as it strives to demonstrate the value that it contributes to business: a hierarchy of roles is currently observable within the profession, ranging from the prestigious strategic business partner to the operational role located in a shared-service centre environment. HR professionals working in the shared service environment observed by Pritchard and Symon (2011) appeared to engage in cognitive job crafting in an attempt to protect their professional identity in relation to other HR professionals. They described the service provided to employees as complex (providing knowledgeable advice to employee queries, not scripted solutions), adding value to service users (through providing personalized, professional advice) and unique (they are the only group of HR representing employees). Pritchard and Symon (2001: 445) suggest that the way that this group of HR professionals construct their role indicates that 'CSRs [call centre representatives] stake a claim for a unique role within the new HR organization: that of understanding and being on the side of the employees'. By differentiating their role from that of other HR professionals this particular group of HR professionals appear to be crafting their own boundaries, thus protecting their professional identity.

Thompson and McHugh (1990: 315) point out that 'identity becomes not only the basis of individual involvement in organizations, but also the basis of manipulation by them': manipulation, though, can occur from both sides. Managers can manipulate workers through their adoption of practices that give the illusion of supporting employee involvement and/or increasing the scope for discretionary behaviour (as pointed out above, in the discussion on employee engagement). Yet these practices arguably amount to no more than a type of 'Super Taylorism', as they draw on similar tools – specifying, measuring and timing (Thompson and McHugh 1990: 219).

Individuals too can manipulate formal, rational, work systems, particularly where they feel that their identity is under threat. Depending on the nature of an individual's job, and the scope for managerial surveillance, individuals may adopt 'distancing' behaviour (that is, finding ways to escape the mundane aspects of a particular job), or job crafting behaviour, even if this involves taking on extra work. In the absence of any effective organizational job design approach, resourceful individuals find ways to craft their own job in order to maintain a positive work identity. Organizations may, or may not, profit from this proactive behaviour; this will depend on the managerial response.

However, the introduction of monitoring techniques under the guise of quality assurance, as we saw above and in earlier chapters, can restrict the scope for certain forms of job crafting. Conti et al. (2002), though, suggest that it is possible to adopt a 'hybrid process and job design' approach that ensures optimum quality in the areas where it is essential to do so, yet at the same time provides scope for discretionary job crafting. They illustrate this point with reference to a case example from a hand-crafted acoustic guitar company. To meet customers' needs for consistently reliable outstanding sound, this particular guitar company automated the process for producing the guitar neck (the part that affects sound), but then combined this with opportunities for their highly skilled craft workers to demonstrate job crafting behaviours when producing the other parts of the guitar. The overall outcome – 'the zero discretion neck routing, combined with high discretion body construction' (Conti et al. 2002: 10).

It might be assumed that senior employees will find it easier to craft their job, given that they are likely to have more power, or authority, to do so. Yet Berg et al.'s (2010: 179) research suggests otherwise: 'high-rank employees are more likely to simply "settle" with the opportunities to job craft that they perceive as possible at work, as reflected in their strategy to sometimes take work home.' Thus the scope of an individual's job responsibilities, combined with their perception of the amount of time needed to complete various tasks to meet the expectations of others, can act as an enabling, or restraining factor when it comes to job crafting, particularly amongst high-rank employees (such as managers and professionals). A further contextual factor is trust, the degree to which managers and co-workers trust individuals to perform effectively when given scope to exercise discretionary behaviour.

We have seen above how professionals engage in job crafting behaviours as a way of protecting their professional identity, yet job crafting could also act as a form of 'career defence' mechanism for others. Jackson et al. (1996, in Kramar and Syed 2012) suggest that a combination of increased job insecurity and fewer promotion opportunities (linked to objective career success) could plausibly result in more 'career defence' behaviours amongst lower and middle managers. Within the contemporary careers literature there has been an increasing interest in the notion of individuals' 'subjective' career experience. In a global study of careers, encompassing 11 countries, Briscoe et al. (2012) discuss the critical relationship between job/task characteristics and career success. Job/task characteristics occurred in the top three rank items of the perceived meaning of career success. Individuals who participated in Briscoe et al.'s study referred to how 'engaging in the types of work one desires' affects their sense of career success (ibid.: 66). They suggest that this reflects a more actor-centred perspective on career success. Other writers suggest that a critical role for managers is helping employees identify their 'deeply embedded life interests' (Butler and Waldroop 1999: 149). In contrast to blue-collar workers, Briscoe et al. also identified that businesspeople are more likely to attribute career success with 'making a difference' and 'the balance they can attain between the demands of their professional lives and their personal and family lives' (Briscoe et al. 2012: 71–2).

In an increasingly uncertain world, where objective career success becomes more difficult to achieve, are we likely to see more job crafting behaviours in the future as individuals exercise their personal agency in order to build careers that balance their objective and subjective careers success criteria? Where career success is derived from interesting, challenging and personally satisfying work, then in the absence of any organization interventions to design jobs in such a way that subjective careers success is considered alongside more objective success criteria then it is highly likely that job crafting behaviour will continue. But as discussed earlier in this chapter, individual agency can often be constrained by contextual factors, such as changing structures and the quality of leadership, especially amongst line managers.

Despite optimistic views, then, about the changing role of line managers, a tension still exists between their role as controller and that of coach and facilitator (Kramar and Syed 2012): it is the latter roles that need greater emphasis if managers are to guide and support individuals 'to identify their own personal strengths, interests and skills and seek to enhance their opportunities to use them at work' (Marks, in CIPD 2006b: 5). From their international careers research, Briscoe et al. (2012: 193) identified variability in the extent to which line managers demonstrated the supportive behaviours needed to help individuals make successful career transitions: first-line leaders in mastery-driven countries seemed to prioritize career development discussion in one-to-one dialogue with individuals, however there was less evidence of this in other contexts.

## Conclusions: The Future of Job Design

As this chapter has discussed, tensions between managerial control and employee autonomy/discretionary behaviour have remained a common feature of organizational life over the past century. Despite isolated examples of organizations that are attempting to address the mundane/isolated nature of work, as in the example of the Brazilian ship component firm Semco (see Kramar and Syed 2012), the reality of working life for many workers is not a positive and engaging experience. Taylor argued that removing discretionary behaviour was crucial for organizational performance, and was helpful to individual workers:

> *The managers assume, for instance, the burden of gathering together all of the traditional knowledge which in the past has been possessed by the workmen and then of classifying, tabulating and reducing this knowledge to rules, laws and formulae which are immensely helpful to the workmen in doing their daily work. (Taylor 1911: 26–9)*

A hundred years on, and organizations seem to think the opposite, that discretionary behaviour is fundamental to improving organizational performance, hence the preoccupation with employee engagement. Yet a closer inspection of organizational employee engagement approaches (introduced with the aim of extracting more discretionary behaviour from employees) indicates an equally controlled and prescriptive approach. Data from employee engagement surveys, the start point for most engagement approaches, enables managers to categorize (and quantify) employee responses to aspects of their daily working lives and thus derive an overall engagement index. Thereafter a top-down process for raising the organization's overall engagement index, or within specific teams and/or departments, then follows – a process which is typically highly scripted.

In theory, organizational and job design should be a fundamental building block of HRM; however, in practice this topic has not featured extensively in the HRM literature (see Brewster et al. 2011). What is perhaps even more surprising is that it is only recently that organizational design has featured as a key area of professional competence in the CIPD's HR Profession Map (CIPD 2012). Boxall and Purcell (2011: 113) argue that the design of work systems is a strategic choice factor, pointing out the symbiotic relationship between strategy and HRM. Yet despite the strategic importance of work design, they suggest that HR professionals should not assume total responsibility for this area. This raises the question as to who should be in control. As we have seen above, in the absence of any effective organizational approach to job design that reflects individuals' subjective career success criteria, resourceful individuals utilize their individual agency to craft their own jobs. Yet as also discussed, the scope for job crafting is affected by situational (for example, types of work tasks) and relational factors (for example, customers/clients, managers and co-workers). Furthermore, organizational restructuring and widespread workforce changes can restrict opportunities for job crafting. In this context more relational and cognitive forms of job crafting are likely to be observed, particularly amongst professionals, as they strive to protect their professional identity (Bolton 2004; Prowse and Prowse 2008).

In the future then, are we likely to see more evidence of individuals taking more control over how jobs are designed, thus ensuring a better fit with their identity, as well as their own measure of career success? Job crafting presents a paradox for managers. On the one hand individuals who craft demonstrate the creative behaviours that organizations claim that they want, yet on the other hand job crafting behaviours result in an erosion of managerial control. Job crafting invariably involves improvisation, something that does not fit well with a 'technical rational' managerial paradigm. As Sinha and Gabriel pointed out in Chapter 5, customers have become a key entity in the labour process within the service economy: managers can use customers as the means to legitimize tightly controlled work routines. Yet, as they also point out, skilful workers quickly learn that they too can use the customer card to help them disrupt management's power bases.

In a devolved HRM model, line managers invariably play a key role in creating the context for, as well as supporting, job crafting behaviours. Yet as Kramar and Syed (2012) point out in organizational contexts characterized by continuous change, managers often resist change where they fear it may affect their own power base: rather than supporting employees' job crafting behaviours, they may well adopt a more controlling style, possibly to protect their own identity. This point has been reinforced by several of our co-contributors: managers, fearful for their own future, are more likely to resort to micro management – the type of management that destroys all form of creativity and autonomy. Soldiering, in particular systematic soldiering, was the curse of management in Taylor's era: perhaps in the future, with the prominence of the service culture, job crafting, as long as this is not systematized by HR professionals, will be the future curse of management.

## References

Adler, P.S. and Cole, R.E. 2007. Designed for learning: a tale of two auto plants, in *Enriching Production. Perspectives on Volvo's Uddevalla Plant as an Alternative to Lean Production*, edited by A. Sandberg. Farnham: Avebury.

Arnold, J. 2011. Career concepts in the twenty-first century. *The Psychologist*, 24(2), 106–9.

Berg, J.M., Wrzesniewski, A. and Dutton, J.E. 2010. Perceiving and responding to challenges in job crafting at different ranks: when proactivity requires adaptivity. *Journal of Organizational Behaviour*, 31(2/3), 158–86.

Bolton, S. 2004. A simple matter of control? NHS hospital nurses and new management. *Journal of Management Studies*, 41(2), March, 317–33.

Boxall, P. and Purcell, J. 2011. *Strategy and Human Resource Management*. 3rd edn. Hampshire: Palgrave Macmillan.

Brewster, C., Sparrow, P., Vernon, G. and Houldsworth, E. 2011. *International Human Resource Management*. London: CIPD.

Briscoe, J., Hall, D.T. and Mayrhofer, W. 2012. *Careers Around the World. Individual and Contextual Perspectives*. New York: Routledge.

Butler, T. and Waldroop, J. 1999. Job sculpting. The art of retaining your best people. *Harvard Business Review*, September–October, 144–52.

Carter, B., Danford, A., Howcraft, D., Richardson, H., Smith, A. and Taylor, P. 2011. 'All they lack is a chain': lean and the new performance management in the British Civil Service. *New Technology, Work and Employment*, 26(2), 83–97.

Castells, E. 1989. *The Information Age: Economy, Society and Cultures*, vol. 1. London: Blackwell.

CIPD (Chartered Institute of Personnel and Development). 2012. *CIPD's HR Profession Map* [Online: Chartered Institute of Personnel and Development]. Available at: http://www.cipd.co.uk/cipd-hr-profession/hr-profession-map/ [accessed 4 March 2012].

CIPD. 2006a. *Working Life: Employee Attitudes and Engagement 2006. Research Report*. London: CIPD.

CIPD. 2006b. *Reflections on Employee Engagement. Change Agenda*. London: CIPD.

Clegg, C. and Spencer, C. 2007. A circular and dynamic model of the process of job design. *Journal of Occupational and Organizational Psychology,* 80(2), 321–39.

Conti, R.F. and Warner, M. 2002. A customer-driven model of job design: towards a general theory. *New Technology, Work and Employment,* 17(1), 2–19.

Duchon, D. and Plowman, D.A. 2005. Nurturing the spirit at work: impact on work unit performance. *The Leadership Quarterly,* 16(5), 807–33.

Fisher, J.A. 2006. Indoor positioning and digital management, in *Surveillance and Security: Technological Politics and Power in Everyday Life,* edited by T. Monahan. New York: Routledge.

Grant, L., Yeandle, S. and Buckner, L. 2006. *Working Below Potential: Women and Part-Time Work. Executive Summary. Gender and Employment in Local Labour Markets.* Sheffield: Sheffield Hallam University.

Gratton, L., Hope Hailey, V., Stiles, P. and Truss, C. 1999. *Strategic Human Resource Management.* Oxford: Oxford University Press.

Harley, B., Sargent, L. and Allen, B. 2010. Employee response to 'high performance work system' practices: an empirical test of the disciplined worker thesis. *Work, Employment and Society,* 24(4), 740–60.

Kelly, G., Mastroeni, M., Conway, E., Monks, K., Truss, K., Flood, P. and Hannon, E. 2011. Combining diverse knowledge: knowledge workers; experience of specialist and generalist roles. *Personnel Review,* 40(5), 607–24.

Kelly, G., Monks, K., Conway, E., Flood, P., Truss, K., Mastroeni, M. and Hannon, E. 2010. Job design, HR practices and policies in knowledge intensive firms in Ireland. Working Paper [Online: Irish Research Council for the Humanities and Social Sciences and the Economic and Social Research Council]. Available at: http://www.esrc.ac.uk/my-esrc/grants/RES-062-23-1183/read [accessed 7 February 2012].

Kersley, B., Alpin, C., Forth, J., Bryson, A., Bewley, H., Dix, G. and Oxenbridge, S. 2006. Inside the workplace. First findings from the 2004 Workplace Employment Relations Survey [Online: Department for Business, Innovation and Skills]. Available at: http://www.berr.gov.uk/files/file11423.pdf [accessed 4 March 2012].

Kim, C.S., Spahlinger, D.A. and Billi, J.E. 2006. Lean health care: what can hospitals learn from a world-class automaker. *Journal of Hospital Medicine,* 1(3), 191–9.

Kramar, R. and Syed, J. 2012. *Human Resource Management in a Global Context.* Basingstoke: Palgrave Macmillan.

Lawrence, P.R. 2010. The key job design problem is still Taylorism. *Journal of Organizational Behaviour,* 31(2–3), 412–21.

MacLeod, D. and Clarke, N. 2009. Engaging for success: enhancing performance through employee engagement [Online: Department for Business, Innovation and Skills]. Available at: http://www.bis.gov.uk/files/file52215.pdf [accessed 7 February 2012].

Parker, S.K., Wall, T.D. and Cordery, J.L. 2001. Future work design research and practice: towards an elaborated model of work design. *Journal of Occupational and Organizational Psychology*, 74(4), 413–40.

Pritchard, K. and Symon, G. 2011. Identity on the line: constructing professional identity in a HR call centre. *Work, Employment and Society*, 25(3), 434–50.

Prowse, J. and Prowse, P. 2008. Role design in the National Health Service: the effects on midwives' work and professional boundaries. *Work, Employment and Society*, 22(4), 695–712.

Purcell, J. 2006. Building better organizations, in *Reflections on Employee Engagement*, edited by G. Aitken, N. Marks, J. Purcell, C. Woodruffe and D. Worman. London: CIPD.

Sandberg, A. 2007. *Enriching Production. Perspectives on Volvo's Uddevalla Plant as an Alternative to Lean Production*. Available at: http://mpra.ub.uni-muenchen.de/10785/1/Enriching_Production_complete_book_Digital_edition_2007.pdf [accessed 7 February 2012].

Seddon, J. 2008. *Systems Thinking in the Public Sector: the Failure of the Reform Regime ... and a Manifesto for a Better Way*. Axminster: Triarchy Press.

Shuck, B. and Wollard, K. 2010. Employee engagement and HRD: a seminal review of the foundations. *Human Resource Development Review*, 9(1), 89–110.

Taylor, F.W. 1911. *The Principles of Scientific Management*. Reprinted by Forgottenbooks.org, 2010. Available at http://www.forgottenbooks.org/info/9781606801123.

Thomas, K. (ed.). 1999. *The Oxford Book of Work*. Oxford: Oxford University Press.

Thompson, P. and McHugh, D. 1990. *Work Organisations*. Basingstoke: Macmillan.

Work Foundation. 2011. *Good Work and Our Times. Report of the Good Work Commission* [Online: The Work Foundation]. Available at http://www.theworkfoundation.com/Assets/Docs/Publications/GWC%20Final.pdf [accessed 4 March 2012].

Wright, C. and Lund, J. 2006. Variations on a lean theme: work restructuring in retail distribution. *New Technology, Work and Employment*, 21(1), 59–74.

Wrzesniewski, A. and Dutton, J.E. 2001. Crafting a job: revisioning employees as active crafters of their work. *Academy of Management Review*, 26(2), 179–201.

# 11

# Continuities, Discontinuities and Prospects for the Future of Management

*Christina Evans and Leonard Holmes*

A century on from the publication of Taylor's *Principles of Scientific Management*, an approach to management that arguably has no place in the contemporary knowledge and service economy given the business critical imperative for flexible and agile systems and people, debates abound about the purpose, scope and the state of management. Indeed, some of the much revered contemporary US management gurus, such as Gary Hamel and Henry Mintzberg, have recently voiced the need for a different type of management suggesting that 'Management, like the combustion engine, is a mature technology that must be re-invented for a new age' (Hamel 2009: 91).

Yet there are certain parallels in the way that these contemporary authors envision and write about management with that of Taylor and his followers. First, in *Moon Shots for Management*, Hamel (2009) refers to how the impetus for gathering together a group of academics, CEOs and consultants, to debate the need to re-invent management so that it becomes fit for purpose in contemporary society, was influenced by the work of the US National Academy of Engineering: the powerful status of the engineering profession, and its association with rational scientific methods, was clearly prominent in Taylor's writing too. Second, just as Taylor sought to reduce management to a set of 'rationalistic' principles, based on a 'management knows best' approach, so too is the recipe for re-inventing management prescribed by Hamel and his co-inventors: a point that we come back to later in this chapter.

Throughout this edited collection we have exposed tensions and contradictions with the way that Taylor's prescriptions on management have been interpreted, adopted and deployed within organizations over the past century, together with the implications for the status of the managerial profession. In the next section of this chapter we draw together key strands of continuity and change in management thinking and practice, drawn from the contributions in the previous chapters, as well as other sources.

## Grand Discourse of Management as a Rational Process

The façade of management as a rational activity is one that persists, despite clear evidence of behaviours by both managers and workers that are far from rational, since they are designed to dupe the system. In Taylor's era this duping took the form of 'systematic soldiering', the collective action of workers aimed at keeping managers in the dark as to how quickly work could be performed. With the rise of 'new public management', a new form of 'systematic soldiering' can be observed in public sector organizations, that of 'gaming': a form of 'reactive subversion' deployed by staff (including managers) in service provider units, adopted with the aim of creating the appearance of targets having been met, even where this is not the case. This practice is one that can be observed within the NHS in the UK (see Chapter 7) and in the UK higher education sector (see Chapter 8) where the logic of 'instrumental rationality' has resulted in HE institutions becoming akin to 'a factory for the production of technically-useful knowledge'. Despite this target-setting regime, introduced under the auspice of quality and standards, there appears to be a distinct lack of any attempt by management in this sector to link method and targets: a distinct difference here then from Taylor's rational approach of 'managing by numbers' (see Tony Cutler in Chapter 7).

Workers in call centres, a work environment that has been criticized for its Tayloristic work routines, have also found ways round the managing-by-targets game, yet with some distinctive differences. The shifting power relations in call centre environments, specifically the power that customers exert, can have both a negative and positive impact on the experience of call centre operatives, as Shuchi Sinha and Yiannis Gabriel described in Chapter 5. In some contexts, customers can be used as allies by call centre workers, providing them with the excuse to depart from pre-determined scripts, thus undermining the power of first-line managers. In addition, as Sinha and

Gabriel discovered, playing the 'threat to quit' card is one of the key levers that educated call centre workers can pull to thwart this target-setting regime: a very different situation then from that of Taylor's era, where workers who did not make the grade were quickly replaced with other manual workers who, hungry for work, were prepared to 'fit in' to the system.

Professionals in the contemporary knowledge and service sector are equally likely to manipulate formal rational work systems, particularly in contexts where they feel that their professional identity is under threat (see Chapter 9). Through the adoption of distancing behaviours, or job crafting behaviours, resourceful individuals seek out opportunities to craft their job in order to maintain a positive work identity. Thus in a similar way to call centre workers who utilize the power of consumers to manipulate target-based work routines, professionals employed in caring roles where they are expected to provide a more individualized service to clients can utilize the power of clients to help shape their job role in a way which challenges fixed work routines and maintains their professional identity.

## Managers as 'Heroic Figures'

Shuchi Sinha and Yiannis Gabriel (Chapter 5) refer to the image of management that emerged during the mass industrialization era as that of 'heroic figures' exercising control and power over production operations through technical mastery. Others, too, suggest that assumptions about the nature of managerial work are changing and that the image of managers engaged in 'fire fighting', lurching from one emergency to another, is perhaps outmoded, particularly given the growing number of women in managerial roles (see Schein 2007). Yet as we saw in Chapter 7, this 'tough management' image persists within the contemporary public sector through the setting of tough targets, even if these are unobtainable, or indeed measurable, or desirable.

Yet with the decline in industrialization and the rise in the service sector employment, the role and skill-set of managers, and indeed of others within organizations, has been changing. Front-line customer service agents (contemporary shop floor workers), as Sinha and Gabriel argue in Chapter 5, are expected to demonstrate 'emotional labour' since they are the face representing the organization, and thus are in positions where they are able to influence customer satisfaction. Irrespective, then, of the conditions in which these front-line workers work, they are expected to act professionally; that is, behave rationally and objectively at all times. In such contexts it might be assumed that a different type of management is required, one that demonstrates more concern (empathy) for the emotional needs of workers, especially where they are operate in stressful environments.

## Sophisticated Selection Methods

As Yvonne Guerrier (Chapter 9) pointed out, the scientific selection of workers was a key function of management under Taylorism. In Taylor's era, this sophisticated selection involved selecting men who were physically capable of carrying out manual work in a prescriptive way, but also self-disciplined to keep themselves 'fit' for work: this required ensuring that life outside work did not interfere with life at work. Yet despite the emphasis on sophisticated methods, as Huw Morris (Chapter 3) points out, there was no evidence from Taylor's writings, or that of his contemporaries, of managers receiving training in how to conduct the scientific selection of workers. Indeed it seems that the methods used were rather basic, and lacked the degree of sophistication currently deployed in high-performing organizations (see Boxall and Purcell 2011). Yet behind the rhetoric of scientific selection methods, there are a number of parallels between the selection methods deployed under Taylorism and in contemporary professional knowledge-based firms. Yvonnne Guerrier (Chapter 9) drew out parallels between Taylor's selection methods and those of prestigious consultancy firms: in both contexts, the importance of keeping oneself physically fit for work was a quality sought by employers. In the contemporary workplace though, this requires keeping oneself both physically and psychologically fit for work. Of course, in the contemporary workplace organizations have introduced a raft of well-being policies designed to help employees keep themselves fit for work: these include on-site gyms, subsidized gym membership, and various other challenge activities. Workers are at liberty to avail themselves of these facilities in their own time, either at the start or the end of a flexible, but none the less extremely long, working day.

In addition to carefully selecting individuals who keep themselves fit for work, careful selection also involves the selection of employees who demonstrate the disposition that is malleable to corporate cultural values. Willmott (1993: 523) refers to this 'corporate culturism' as the contemporary form of control adopted by managers (of all levels) intended to 'shape and regulate the practical consciousness and, arguably, unconscious strivings of employees', who are powerless to resist. However, Sinha and Gabriel suggest that this is perhaps too bleak a view of workers' ability to demonstrate resistance behaviours. The adoption of 'job crafting' behaviours, as we saw in the preceding chapter, is arguably one form of resistance to managerial control: behaviours are adopted to protect an individual's identity.

Buried deep within *The Principles of Scientific Management*, a different perspective on fitness for work can be found, where Taylor refers to the skills required to become a high-class ball bearing inspector:

> *In the Physiological departments of our universities experiments are regularly conducted to determine what is known as the 'personal coefficient' of the man tested. This is done by suddenly bringing some object, the letter A or B for instance, within the range of the vision of the subject, who, the instant he recognises the letter, has to do some definite thing such as press a particular electric button ... This test shows conclusively that there is a great difference in the 'personal coefficient' of different men. Some individuals are born with unusually quick powers of perception, accompanied by quick response time ... Mr Thompson soon recognized that the quality most needed for bicycle ball bearing inspectors was a low personal coefficient. Of course the ordinary qualities of endurance and industry were also called for.* (Taylor 1911: 83)

So although the scientific methods deployed to identify the best qualities needed to perform this type of work were conducted with men, women it seems were deemed more suited to work 'that requires the closest attention and concentration, so the nervous tension of the inspector was considerable' (Taylor 1911: 68). Such a delicate type of work, it would seem, does not fit with the masculine identity of physically demanding heavy work. There are parallels to be drawn here with Elson and Pearson's concept of 'nimble fingers' – the natural skills that women possess which make them suitable for work that requires the use of keyboard skills, for example as with data entry (see Glover and Guerrier 2010).

## The Paradox of the Ideal Worker

Over the past decade or so, there has been a growing emphasis on the importance of managers, and indeed other professionals, demonstrating emotional intelligence, following the popularization of this concept by Daniel Goleman in the late 1990s. Goleman and others suggest that there significant performance enhancements of individuals demonstrating emotional intelligence: reduction in interpersonal and organizational conflicts, thus more effective social relations in the workplace; enhanced quality of leadership, and even enhanced sales (see Lindebaum and Cassell 2010). Managers with emotional intelligence are arguably, then, more likely to demonstrate some of the root qualities of management: treat with respect, handle well and unleash hidden potential (see Sinha and Gabriel in Chapter 5). Such behaviours, though, do not appear to fit well with the aggressive masculine management style typically associated with highly competitive environments, as glamorized in populist TV programmes such as *The Apprentice*, as Yvonne Guerrier argued in Chapter 9.

With the growing importance of more flexible organizational forms (the post-bureaucratic model) there has been a growing emphasis on the concept of hybridity, moving away from binary thinking (and/or) to more flexible (both/ and) thinking. Professionals working in the transforming IT sector, for example, are expected to demonstrate hybrid skills (a mix of technical and 'soft' skills, such as communicators and translators; an ability to oil the wheels) as referred to in Chapter 6. Hybrid workers could be conceived as the contemporary equivalent of Taylor's 'high class' man, except Taylor's 'high class' man has perhaps now become the 'high class' female, since it is females working in the IT sector who are assumed to best embody hybrid skills, so much so that these performance skills are not ones that organizations feel they need to specifically reward. It is the association of 'soft' skills with females which means that female project managers have become the means to fill current skills gaps (see Evans et al. 2007). As Lindebaum and Cassell (2012) identified in their research into perceptions of emotional intelligence amongst project managers in the UK construction sector, there are distinct contradictions in the adoption of the concept of emotional intelligence in traditional masculine environments. In contexts where managers typically work their way up from trade roles into managerial roles, use of the word 'emotional' can cause discomfort amongst male managers; hence any attempts to teach emotional intelligence (assuming that this is something that is teachable) are often resisted.

## The Unchallenged Adoption of Prescriptive 'Best Practice' Approaches

In reflecting on the practice of management over the past century one of the key themes has been that of the search for the one 'best way' of managing, irrespective of the different contexts within which managers operate. But as Boxall and Purcell (2011) argue, typically accounts of 'best practice' become de-contextualized, thus making it difficult to assess the outcomes.

The adoption of prescriptive approaches to address the perceived issue of employee engagement is one of the more recent management fads, as discussed in the preceding chapter.

Yet despite the rhetoric of employee empowerment and, more recently, employee engagement, the main management preoccupation is that of maintaining discipline and control of the workers. This remains the case even though the nature and structure of businesses today, particularly in the West, is vastly different from that in Taylor's era. New organizational forms and new business models, supported by new and emerging technologies, have opened up the field of management, and different specialisms have emerged: human resource management, project management, diversity management, marketing management, financial management, customer service management, to name but a few. But the extent to which the key purpose of these more specialized forms of management concurs with the traditional notion of management is debatable; as Grey (1999: 572) argues, such change 'recasts the role of managers and the meaning of management'. The promotion of the notion of empowerment, where responsibilities for certain management activities are dispersed throughout the organization, has resulted in the claim of 'we are all managers now' (ibid.: 572). Whilst appealing on one level, the reality of this shifting discourse of management, as we saw in earlier chapters, is that front-line workers often face situations where their sense of self (identity) is threatened. Some writers even go so far as to suggest that management in the contemporary workplace colonizes employees' identity: the requirement for executing tasks in a prescriptive way to ensure maximum efficiency (thus having little scope for exercising discretion) results in stress and burnout of workers.

Control then remains a key part of the function of management, despite the shifting discourse that some aspects of control have been delegated to others. As other contributors pointed out in earlier chapters, managers in UK public sector organizations have equally become constrained by the adoption of instrumental rationalistic systems and the preoccupation with 'managing by numbers', despite the fact that little attention is paid to whether in fact such numbers are verifiable, or are merely a result of improved methods. As Tony Cutler (see Chapter 7) points out, in Taylor's era there was at least some attempt to associate increased production targets with a prescriptive 'best method' of working. Taylor's prescriptions on management, as Colin Hales concludes in his chapter, have become the 'fatal remedy' of management: 'the rationalizers are themselves being rationalized', as middle managers become the target of organizational rationalization.

As we bring this edited collection to a close, there is a further tension with traditional notions of management that we wish to consider. The collapse of the global financial markets in 2009/10 and the loss of faith in perhaps once-admired institutions have generated much discourse about the extent to which contemporary leaders can be trusted to make decisions that are in the best interest of diverse stakeholders. This shifting discourse could possibly explain why the renewed interest in the 'how' of management more so than the 'what'. In other words, what types of behaviours might employees and other stakeholders reasonably expect from those in leadership positions?

Rather than focusing on short-term goals that serve the interests of the few, increasingly there is an expectation that organizational leaders will demonstrate more ethical, sustainable and people-centred leadership: these are behaviours consistent with the concept of servant-leadership first coined in the 1970s by Greenleaf (van de Bunt-Kokhuis 2010, van Dierendonck 2011). Despite the contested nature of the concept of servant-leadership given then (for example, lack of clarity around definition, as well as evidence of application in practice), the concept appears to be gaining increasing visibility in both the academic and practitioner literature. Some of the characteristics of servant-leadership that appear to be of particular relevance in the current climate are those of conceptualization (thinking beyond day-to-day realities); foresight (understanding and relating lessons of the past with current realities); stewardship (taking responsibility for the wider institution); and sense of community (so a focus on creating strong ties/bonds through building strong interpersonal relationships).

The assumption is that servant-leaders prioritize the needs and well-being of followers above their own needs and goals (van Dierendonck 2011); the expectation is that leaders will put the development and growth needs of others (that is, followers) above those of self and the organization. In doing so, it is assumed that these values then become the organizational norm: followers are assumed to be self-regulating, in so far as they can then be trusted to behave in ways that meet the mutual needs of the organization. Servant-leaders, then, are assumed to combine the motivation to lead with that of serving others (Pekerti and Sendjaya 2010, van Dierendonck 2011). The outcomes of servant-leadership seem similar to that of employee engagement, in that it encourages employee commitment and engagement, although van Dierendonck (2011) suggests that there are other outcomes too. Whilst he includes dimensions of performance in his conceptual model of servant-leadership, the terminology used is similar to that associated with the 'soft' model of HRM, for example performance achievement through organizational citizenship behaviour and team effectiveness, as well as organizational outcomes of sustainability and corporate social responsibility.

Whilst servant-leadership may take us a step closer towards Grey's (1999: 579) notion of a post-managerial future in which coordination and control are underpinned by a moral communitarian approach (that is, a non-instrumental means-ends philosophy), this shifting focus may be more difficult to achieve in different contexts. If, as Holmes (Chapter 4) argues, the normative perception of situated managerial performance implicates processes of construal as such, individual managers must engage in identity work, seeking to present themselves and their actions as being in accord with the ascriptions by significant others. Dominant understandings of what constitutes managerial behaviour, and particularly *effective* managerial behaviour, affect and are also affected by the attempts by managers to present their behaviour as matching such understandings. We may see change in those dominant understandings, such as a shift to this servant-leadership model, or any change in managers, or we may see managers themselves attempt to adopt such a model. Either way, there will be a shift in the interplay between identity and practices, and so a problematic disruption to the construal process.

So, whilst appealing at one level, no doubt leaders from cultures where domination and control are the cultural norm will find the concept of servant-leadership challenging. How easy will it be for leaders in private sector companies in particular to relinquish their tough macho image in favour of what appears on the surface to be a softer people-centric focus? This comment is from the founder of Matsushita: 'For us the core of management is the art of pulling together the intellectual resources of all employees in the *service* of the firm. Only by drawing on the combined brain power of all its employees can a firm face up to the constraints of today's environment.' Boxall and Purcell (2003: 100) suggest that the notion of leaders as servants is not one that will easily resonate with business leaders, even though contemporary management gurus prescribe this as the solution: 'Fully embed the ideas of community and citizenship in management systems … depoliticize decision making through seeking the advice of rank and file employees' (Hamel 2009: 91–8).

What role might business schools and other management educators play in this transition? As we saw in Chapter 3, business schools can play a key role in the creation and diffusion of new thinking; however, the growing focus on new public management techniques in higher education institutions means that they, too, are not immune to the command and control ideology of management which can limit the scope for exploring new concepts and curricula. If servant-leadership is the way forward, then how will the leaders of tomorrow learn of such concepts? How will they 'rehearse' the modes of behaviour that are consonant with such concepts, and how will they translate them into their own identity work as managers? Perhaps only when ethics and sustainability become core subjects on MBA and other management programmes, or where business schools teach the skill of '*savoir-relier*' (the capabilities to connect people, generations, cultures and ideas) (see Judith Glover in Chapter 6), will we start to see this new leadership paradigm become more mainstream.

## References

Boxall, P. and Purcell, J. 2003. *Strategy and Human Resource Management*. 1st edn. Basingstoke: Palgrave Macmillan.

Boxall, P. and Purcell, J. 2011. *Strategy and Human Resource Management*. 3rd edn. Basingstoke: Palgrave Macmillan.

Evans, C., Glover, J., Guerrier, Y. and Wilson, C. 2007. *Effective Recruitment Strategies and Practices: Addressing Skills Needs and Gender Diversity in the ITEC and Related Sector*. London: DTI.

Glover, J. and Guerrier, Y. 2010. Women in hybrid roles in IT employment: a return to 'nimble fingers'? *Journal of Technology Management and Innovation*, 5(1), 85–94.

Grey, C. 1999. 'We are all managers now'; 'We always were': on the development and demise of management. *Journal of Management Studies*, 36(5), 561–85.

Hamel, G. 2009. Moon shots for management. *Harvard Business Review*, February, 91–8.

Lindebaum, D. and Cassell, C. 2012. A contradiction in terms? Making sense of emotional intelligence in a construction management environment. *British Journal of Management*, 23(1), 65–79.

Mintzberg, H. 2009. Rebuilding companies as communities. *Harvard Business Review*, July–August, 140–43.

Pekerti, A.A. and Sendjaya, S. 2010. Exploring servant leadership across cultures: comparative study of Australia and Indonesia. *International Journal of Human Resource Management*, 21(5), 752–80.

Schein, V.E. 2007. Women in management: reflections and projections. *Women in Management Review*, 22(1), 6–18.

Taylor, F.W. 1911. *The Principles of Scientific Management*. Reprinted by Forgottenbooks.org, 2010, http://www.forgottenbooks.org/info/9781606801123 [accessed 15 March 2011].

van de Bunt-Kokhuis, S. 2010. Servant-leadership and talent diversity – a China case study where East meets West. *Lifelong Learning in Europe*, 15(4), 229–41.

van Dierendonck, D. 2011. Servant leadership: a review and synthesis. *Journal of Management*, 37(4), 1228–61.

Willmott, H. 1993. Strength is ignorance; slavery is freedom: managing culture in modern organizations. *Journal of Management Studies*, 30(4), 515–52.

# Index

Page numbers in *italics* refer to tables.

For Product Safety Concerns and Information please contact our EU
representative  GPSR@taylorandfrancis.com
Taylor & Francis Verlag GmbH, Kaufingerstraße 24, 80331 München, Germany

www.ingramcontent.com/pod-product-compliance
Ingram Content Group UK Ltd.
Pitfield, Milton Keynes, MK11 3LW, UK
UKHW051832180425
457613UK00022B/1212